"Devin's series presents us with a new kind of witch: one who does not merely learn spells, but lives them....Even if witchcraft is not your path, there is a treasure trove of information here useful to those who work with spirits, with psychic ability, and with any inborn power they're seeking to harness. Highly recommended."

—Michelle Belanger, author of *Walking the Twilight Path*

"This book does not disappoint! The final installment of the Witch Power series delivers even more essential techniques to help you build your repertoire of witchy tools. It's exactly what this series calls for with additional ritual technology, insight, and stories to lead you on your path to personal mastery. So, what are you waiting for? Break your chains, tread the mill, and fly!"

—Christopher Orapello, podcaster, artist, and coauthor of *Besom, Stang & Sword*

"For the reader willing to dive deep, to invest the time to gain the hands-on experience, and who has built (or is willing to build) a solid groundwork in the basics of meditation, energy practices, ritual, and psychic development, this is pure gold. To use a term that is too often used, it is truly a grimoire of modern witchcraft. 'Grimoire' is a word that gets tossed about a lot these days and usually means a hodgepodge of old and new material wrapped in a fancy dress of pseudo-archaic language. This, however, is the actual item. Top-notch and highly recommended."

—Aidan Wachter, author of *Six Ways*

"In *The Witch's Book of Mysteries*, Devin Hunter takes readers on an incredible journey into the deepest depths of Witchcraft. Masterfully combining elements of art, science, and magic, Hunter illuminates long-hidden components of the Craft which add a felt sense of primordial connection within oneself and along one's individual path."

—Kelden, author of the blog *By Athame and Stang*

The
WITCH'S
Book of
MYSTERIES

About the Author

Devin Hunter (Antioch, CA) holds third-degree initiations in both the Northern Star Tradition of Wicca as well as the Dianic Tradition of Witchcraft (the Cult of Diana) and is the founder of his own tradition, Sacred Fires. His podcast, *The Modern Witch*, has helped thousands of people from all over the world discover and develop their magical abilities. Devin is currently teaching with the Black Rose School of Witchcraft and is the reigning Master of Ceremonies at the New Orleans Witches' Ball.

DEVIN HUNTER

FOREWORD BY JASON MILLER

The
WITCH'S
Book of
MYSTERIES

Llewellyn Publications
WOODBURY, MINNESOTA

FIRST EDITION
First Printing, 2019

Cover design by Kevin R. Brown
Interior sigils and vapor image by Llewellyn Art Department

Llewellyn Publications is a registered trademark of Llewellyn Worldwide Ltd.

The publisher and the author assume no liability for any injuries caused to the reader that may result from the reader's use of content contained in this publication and recommend common sense when contemplating the practices described in the work. Please consult a standard reference source or an expert herbalist to learn more about the possible effects of certain herbs.

Library of Congress Cataloging-in-Publication Data
Names: Hunter, Devin, author. | Miller, Jason, author of foreword.
Title: The witch's book of mysteries / Devin Hunter ; foreword by Jason
    Miller.
Description: First edition. | Woodbury, Minnesota : Llewellyn Publications,
    2019. | Includes bibliographical references and index.
Identifiers: LCCN 2019000121 (print) | LCCN 2019008541 (ebook) | ISBN
    9780738757742 (ebook) | ISBN 9780738756561 (alk. paper)
Subjects: LCSH: Witchcraft. | Magic.
Classification: LCC BF1566 (ebook) | LCC BF1566 .H849 2019 (print) | DDC
    133.4/3—dc23
LC record available at https://lccn.loc.gov/2019000121

Llewellyn Worldwide Ltd. does not participate in, endorse, or have any authority or responsibility concerning private business transactions between our authors and the public.

All mail addressed to the author is forwarded, but the publisher cannot, unless specifically instructed by the author, give out an address or phone number.

Any internet references contained in this work are current at publication time, but the publisher cannot guarantee that a specific location will continue to be maintained. Please refer to the publisher's website for links to authors' websites and other sources.

Llewellyn Publications
A Division of Llewellyn Worldwide Ltd.
2143 Wooddale Drive
Woodbury, MN 55125-2989
www.llewellyn.com

Printed in the United States of America

We are led to Believe a Lie
When we see not Thro the Eye
Which was Born in a Night to perish in a Night
When the Soul Slept in Beams of Light
God Appears & God is Light
To those poor Souls who dwell in Night
But does a Human Form Display
To those who Dwell in Realms of day

———

William Blake, *Auguries of Innocence*

Do not imagine that art or anything else is other than high magic!—is a system of holy hieroglyph. The artist, the initiate, thus frames his mysteries. The rest of the world scoff, or seek to understand, or pretend to understand; some few obtain the truth.

Aleister Crowley

Wisdom, newly acquired in this way, feels right because it by-passes the everyday ego and resonates powerfully with something already present, deep inside: the true, spiritual self. It feels like a reminder and confirmation of something already known but forgotten.

Larry Culliford

The generation of atmosphere, the aura of the uncanny, is one of the most important secrets of magic. It contributes to the willing suspension of disbelief, the feeling that, within the circle, or in the presence of the magical shrine, anything may happen.

Doreen Valiente

Contents

DEDICATION
and
ACKNOWLEDGMENTS

As with each book in this series, I would like to first and foremost dedicate this to the Goddess of Witches. She is my constant companion and my truest friend. Following her led me to explore the greatest mysteries of my life and I have no doubt she has many more for me. I also need to thank the God of Witches. Though he doesn't make as large of a footprint in these pages as she, none of this would have been possible without his intercession. It is by he that I was able to bring this final work to life. I lift this entire series to them as an offering of my devotion. May they always reign!

To my beloved Sacred Fires and Black Rose communities. It is for them that I strive to be better and grow, and by their light I am able to do so. Though I share some of our mysteries here, know that those we personally share shall last forever. I will see you where the Magister awaits, somewhere in the circle betwixt the stones.

To my partners in life and magic, Storm and Chas. Without your support through good and bad, I never would have been able to pull this book stuff off. When I was weak, you were my strength. When I was sad, you were my joy. When I was lost, it was you who found me. Our love is a forever love, and no matter what comes tomorrow or in the years to come, I will be there always by your sides.

I would also like to thank my editor Elysia for taking a chance on my work and for always demanding the very best from me. She encouraged me to write about difficult topics and to remain authentic as I explored territory that usually remains untouched. It was with her and a host of other editors and staff at Llewellyn Worldwide that this series came to life, and for that I will be forever grateful.

To Jason Miller for writing the foreword and for being a constant source of inspiration as an occultist. His books are hands-down some of the most important books being written in modern magic, and it is an honor to have him be part of this project.

Lastly, I would like to thank a few departed teachers and writers for their contribution to the craft and their influence on me personally. It is by their spark that the fires of gnosis within me were ignited. To Andrew Chumbley, Michael Howard, Victor and Cora Anderson, and Scott Cunningham. What is remembered lives!

FOREWORD

What is a witch? It's a tricky label. For some people, witchcraft is a religion. If you worship the old gods and follow a religion like Wicca, then for these people you are a witch. Other people focus on the *craft* part of witchcraft and consider the use of folk magic as the defining characteristic of a witch. If you know the magical properties of herbs, the words of spells, and the use of oils and candles and stones, then you are a witch.

Folklore tells us that witches are supernatural monsters, people who are born with magical powers or have gained them through a pact with spirits, usually the devil. They may possess a book or a familiar, but it is the witches themselves that are magical. Of course, other than in the movies, this is a vision of the witch that we usually don't talk about. But maybe we should.

When you cut past the paranoid fear-mongering about stealing babies and fornication with the devil, we are left with a vision of witches as beings of power. They don't just believe in old gods and local spirits, they know them personally. They don't just have magical knowledge in their heads, they possess magical powers. If you are this kind of witch, you are not just doing something different than the rest; you *are* something different.

Assuming you were not lucky enough to be the seventh son of a seventh son, born with a caul on Walpurgisnacht, possess a magic third nipple, or any of the other circumstances that are alleged to hand you magic powers from birth, we are left to wonder: how do we transform ourselves into this kind of witch? The answer is training. Not the kind of training where you memorize a ritual to perform, but a kind of training that is more like a martial art. In this kind of training, knowing how to do something is only the entry point of a journey that you will continue your whole life. You keep getting better and better at it until you are dead. This is what it takes.

There are very few people who teach magic this way. It is not easy to tell students and readers that they have to develop a skill before they do something, and not just understand it in theory, but be competent in practice. It is demanding work, and those who cannot stop entertaining themselves by consuming book after book long enough to actually practice anything in them will not like it. In this type of witchcraft, you can't just have the right candle, oils, and words—you need to be able to stand in the path of power and direct it through your body, breath, and mind. It's not enough to call the Goddess; you need to be able to hear what she says and make sure that it is not just your own wishful thinking. There are few who teach this way, but Devin Hunter is one of them.

This book is divided into two parts. The first is where the witch develops their skills. You will learn the secrets of dreaming true, how to extract the magical quintessence of plants and places, how to channel the witch power through the body, and how to communicate effectively with the unseen. The second part is all about what you can do with these abilities. Without the skills developed in the first part, the second part is just words. If you want to soar through the night to the sabbat, first you need to learn to fly.

Everything in this book is placed in context. Apart from the numerous stories from Devin's own adventures, several strands of Witchcraft come together in this work. I don't think you will find many people who can invoke Wiccans like Scott Cunningham and Gerald Gardner alongside traditional witches like Paul Huson and Andrew Chumbley, but Devin does this with skill and respect. Here the mysteries of traditional witchcraft are laid bare, with none of the obfuscations or pretense that can occasionally plague such writings. You will know what to do and how to do it, with no confusion or guesswork.

Even John Jones, another traditional witch whose line of work is threaded into this book, was asked by the ceremonial magician William Gray to define what a witch is. His answer was:

> If one who claims to be a Witch can perform the tasks of Witchcraft, i.e. summon the spirits and they come, can divine with rod, fingers and birds. If they can also claim the right to the omens and have them; have the power to call heal and curse and above all, can tell the maze and cross the Lethe, then you have a Witch.

If you follow the instructions and undertake the explorations in *The Witch's Book of Mysteries*, you will be this kind of witch. The sabbat will not only be a coven meeting or open circle you attend after dinner, but a world-shifting event where the Black Goat leads you into the darkness to behold the Magister and the Sabbat Queen.

—Jason Miller, author of
Elements of Spellcrafting,
Protection and Reversal Magic,
and *Strategic Sorcery*

INTRODUCTION

*Authentic inspiration endows individuals with mental or
spiritual energy which they are then able to transform into
positive action. It can make the difference between a man,
woman, or child allowing despair to permanently paralyze
any dreams they may have for their lives or exercising
sufficient strength of will to make those dreams a reality.*

———

Aberjani, *Journey Through the Power of the Rainbow:
Quotations from a Life Made Out of Poetry*

In *The Witch's Book of Power*, we explored the various aspects that
construct and inform your power and how to tap into that preternatural ability we call the witch power. We looked at your soul and
studied its various parts to trace the flow of spiritual power within,
and we mapped the influences of other forces of power that affect
your own. In my second book, *The Witch's Book of Spirits*, we developed the witch power as we worked with spirits and the practices of
mediumship, soul flight, and conjuration that compose what we call
the familiar craft.

With this, the last book in the series, we are going to take one final look at the witch power, this time as a key to the Divine. We are going to push our boundaries once again and question what we think we know of our own power and its limitations. We will need to take back power from previous religious and spiritual programming, break the chains that bind us from creating our own connection with the Divine, and redirect the flow of that energy so that we can build the life we choose to live. We are going to explore extensions of the witch power, like the witch eye and the witch's dream, and use them to tame the landscape that surrounds lucid dreaming and the witch's sabbat. We will tread the mill as we cross the hedge and examine energy and ritual like never before, working with the Witch Queen and Witch King as they guide us through the mysteries of quintessence and the mind.

Lastly, I am going to introduce you to a set of spirits that come from my spiritual tradition, Sacred Fires. These spirits are known to us as the Cosmic Grigori, the guardians of the universal powers and influence of space, time, matter, energy, and quintessence. You will also meet the Terrestrial Grigori, those you are likely more familiar with and who govern the powers of earth, air, fire, water, and spirit. Through our work with all the Grigori, we will investigate the nature of our witch power one final time as we explore its connection to the divine forces of creation.

This is a book written with the experienced practitioner in mind, and it builds on the work from the first two books in this series. Many of the themes and subjects will feel out of place for those who have had limited exposure to occultism and folk magic. You will find themes from traditional witchcraft, a style of witchcraft that developed simultaneously but independently of Gerald Gardner's Wicca. You will find concepts from Spiritualism and shamanism. You will also find a healthy dose of language and definition that come from my work as a psychic medium, aspects of metaphysics that are not usually used to help frame witchcraft. For us to take this particular journey, we will need to draw from each of these.

You don't need to agree with me and my own gnosis as it is laid out in these pages. My hope instead is that you will follow along and allow yourself to be challenged, draw upon your own experience, and then build a religious practice of your own—one that places you and your connection to the Divine (however and whatever that is to you) at the center of all focus.

Part One

Introduction

*Incredible change happens in your life when you
decide to take control of what you do have power over
instead of craving control over what you don't.*

———

Steve Maraboli

As free thinkers, we are faced with the responsibility of seeking our own answers and finding a way through life that brings meaning and value to it. For those who are spiritual, this often means being able to sense and feel real power—power that they can rely on and trust, power that, even if it only ever shows itself for a moment, gives them faith enough to go on. As witches we do not need to wait for this power to be revealed; our witch power gives us the ability to sense and find it no matter where we are.

The most difficult part of this is looking back at what we think we know of the road so far and having the courage to review our connection to the fundamental aspects of our craft. As a serious practitioner, you now have the wisdom to see and feel things you did not when you were introduced to them. In this section we are going to strengthen our witch power and take back the power that was taken from us, revisit parts of our craft and prime them for working with the witch power, and then we are going to use our new upgrades to travel to the witch's sabbat.

Be sure to have a journal or sketch pad handy while you read. Part of what we will be doing is constructing ways for your mind to engage the witch power so that you can better access it. To do this we will need to think creatively and stretch our imagination as well as create pathways for that power to flow. Journaling, sketching, and documenting your experiences as you are prompted will help you establish the right kind of connection to the work of becoming a flourishing occultist.

Chapter One

Mysteries, Gnosis, and Power

*Witchcraft ... is a spiritual path. You walk it for
nourishment of the soul, to commune with the life force of
the universe, and to thereby better know your own life.*

—

Christopher Penczak, *The Inner Temple of Witchcraft*

We will be asked to do many things in the name of our craft that might look silly to others. We will be asked to remove all doubt, suspend disbelief, adopt superstitions, and welcome imaginary friends into our lives. At some point there is a line that the majority of witches draw: the one that separates those of us who have gone "too far" with how serious we take this business of spells and ancient gods from those of us who remain just on the edge of reasonable doubt.

Doubt is good. It is essential for every one of us to possess suspicion. It keeps us from making bad choices and is the result of a healthy mind. Doubt can also be darkness and death for some—doubting your worth, your ability to change and empower your life, the ability to find your own way. Doubt can keep us safe, but it can also put us in danger. Like a lotus sending shoots into the dark water, our goal is to reach into the unknown and try our very best to find light, to follow our senses and thrive. This can only happen if the lotus has the conviction to explore that darkness to begin with. If triumphant, from the murk of the substrate and watery unknown will emerge a fragrant and powerful flower capable of intoxicating the world.

That line we draw that keeps us holding on to our comfort and removed from the power that lies deep within is a line that must be crossed. Before it can cast its spell upon the night, the lotus must first send its shoots into the unknown. Your power and your ability to sculpt the universe to your will are somewhere in that murky water, and only you can find them.

The work of the student is to find the tools necessary to become the architect of their own lives. The work of the master is to be that architect, knowing that every block, every trial faced, is a lesson from the very medium they sculpt, and that every triumph is a testament to the degree of intimacy they have with it. In witchcraft the tools we use—meditation, ritual, breath work, ecstatic practices, creative visualization, altar and devotional work, spells, hexes, etc.—are all here to help us become the master. How we put the pieces together as the architects is entirely up to us, but that is, after all, the privilege of being a master.

What master should you model yourself after? Who should you study to unlock the mysteries that will lead you to greatness? **YOU.** The answer is you. I don't believe one can master witchcraft—it is an untamable beast—but you don't need to master witchcraft, you only need to master yourself. For me, witchcraft is all about crossing the line, and if you're like me, you want to cross the line so that you can be the one in control of your life and spirituality.

The Lonely Road

What is essential at this stage of the game is that you become intimately aware that you are alone in this process. No one is ever going to understand precisely what it is that you find on your search for light; those are your mysteries. No one can trade places with you and do the work of studying and exploring them.

In Sacred Fires we refer to this as "the lonely road." It is a path that all people who embark toward the priesthood of our order must understand and follow. Even though they have the support of our entire community behind them, they know that to be sovereign, they must experience the realm they govern alone because while we all may be visitors there, it is not our kingdom and we have no right to rule there. To be truly powerful in their own right, initiates must forge their personal relationships to the spirits and allies of the tradition and use those mysteries with the tools we share so they can build a better kingdom for ourselves and ultimately for all of humanity.

These are themes that we find all over the occult world. To truly cross the threshold of initiation, it is imperative to intimately understand the full depth of power we have as the masters of the world we live in. Our "kingdoms" are all that we see as we travel the lonely road.

Witches are lucky. Our craft gives us a set of skills, tools, and allies that help us along the lonely road. It provides us with the ability to alter and adjust the flow and frequency of our lives on our terms. This comes in handy when navigating the ocean that is spiritual awareness and occult mystery.

Witchcraft and Personal Gnosis

At the end of the day, when the journey is done, what will matter most is that we have used our time on the lonely road to building personal gnosis. This can only be gained through a lot of introspection, awareness, and respect for the spark of divinity inside yourself and others, and most importantly it can only be experienced firsthand. Why is this important? By the time you picked up this book, you already had loads of gnosis. You have opinions and ideas about the Divine, but over the years—especially if you come from a dogmatic religious background—there are likely aspects of your gnosis that were forced upon you. You accepted them because you either had to at one point or you rejected someone else's gnosis and have built aspects of yours solely on the idea of it being the opposite of whatever it was that left a bad taste. This pseudo-gnosis and the illusion it paints actually keeps us from being able to thrive magically and spiritually and limits our ability to psychically access incredibly valuable frequencies.

Any mystery worth precious value pertains to and informs your personal gnosis. Throughout this book, we will be challenging aspects of your gnosis and mapping out those parts where the terrain can get a little confusing. I want to remind you that your job isn't to mirror me or my values but to develop your own with a bit of inspiration. I believe that we are all created whole, with no missing pieces; the real work is in figuring out how they fit together. Whatever shape your personal gnosis and witch power take is entirely up to you.

Egregores and the Ghosts of Religion Past

The autumn after I performed my self-initiation, I had my first big crisis of faith as a witch. My psychic experiences were getting very intense and confusing—I suspect as a result of actively working with my witch power—and all of my friends were part of the local Pentecostal church. I had convinced myself that I was only attending because I wanted to hang out with my friends, with whom I was also practicing witchcraft in secret, but the truth was that I was hungry for spiritual community and fellowship of any kind. I didn't know it at the time, but they were rebelling; I, on the other hand, was on a serious spiritual quest.

Being a psychic, I could sense the power writhing in the air and would hang on every word as the church elders would let slip about how the Holy Spirit would manifest as a thin fog when the congregation would go particularly hard with their worship. Mysticism was something openly talked about, explored, and experienced by all, and even though it was within the confines of a particular paradigm, it was nevertheless a particularly potent aspect of life in the church.

After two months of attending the church and youth services twice a week, I had begun to slip away from my pagan faith. Paganism was proving to be lonely, and most of the people I found who were pagan were honestly just as scary and intense with their beliefs as any member of the church. I felt stuck between the parts of paganism that I definitely believed in and identified with and the components of Christianity that opened me up to something bigger. I would wear my pentacle necklace throughout the week and politely take it off when stepping into the church.

One Wednesday while the youth group was working on the church float for a local county parade, I realized that I had forgotten to take my pentacle necklace off. I remember it feeling unusually heavy, and I quickly took it off and threw it in my pocket. I still don't quite understand what happened next.

The friends whom I was circling with and I were hanging out on our end coloring in a banner when the lead minister came in to check on the lot of us. As he doted on us, the door to the chapel opened and a woman whom I had never seen before walked in. She wore big sunglasses and had short hair that went just past her ears. I couldn't take my eyes off of her while she waited quietly in the back for him to finish. It was a small congregation, and I knew that I had met all of the regulars, but I had no clue who she was.

The minister walked over to her as we all went back to work. "Who is that?" I asked one of my friends.

"I have never seen her," he said, "but she just pointed at us."

I looked up to see the minister now looking in our direction as the women spoke quietly but waved her hands while doing so. My heart sank; I could feel something bad coming, and as she left the minister exited the chapel in the opposite direction.

"What do you think that was about?" I asked nervously.

"Who knows?" another friend said. "Let's just get through the next hour and get out of here."

When eight thirty came around and the youth minister completed the closing prayer, the lead minister came back into the chapel with a stern look on his face. "Good night everybody, see you on Sunday!" he declared before adjusting his glance to us. "Boys, I need to see the three of you before you go. Can you spare a few minutes to talk?" Whatever had happened, something wasn't right.

As everyone else filtered past us and out of the chapel, I felt Diana, Goddess of Witches, come up behind me. As I took my seat next to the other guys, I suddenly realized that I had no way out and that I didn't feel safe. I had gotten a ride from the guys, had no cell phone, and all my mother knew was that I was at church.

Everything is going to be okay. Stay strong, you can handle this; you're my son, Diana said to me.

"We had a visitor tonight. She said she saw you boys practicing witchcraft," the minister said with firm accusatory tension while he stared us down. My heart sank, and for the next twenty minutes, I watched the other two guys aggressively repeat all of the basic pagan stuff that is said to refute Christianity as the minister looked on. "Christianity stole pagan holidays." "Christianity is responsible for war and racism." "Christianity is full of followers who are just fake, fake, fake." It went on and on until one of them finally confessed that he had only been dabbling and would stop immediately as long as the minister didn't bring his parents into it. The other cracked shortly after, upon the minister reminding him that this news would break his mother's heart, especially after him getting busted for drinking the summer before. Shortly after that, the minister announced that he would be giving me a ride home that night and that the other two could leave.

I hadn't said much during the arguing or the confessions the other two had made. I was still new enough to the community that I was hoping that playing dumb would be smart. As the other two left, I realized that they were also leaving me behind in what was a terrifying situation. There I was, alone in the chapel with the minister, who proceeded with his inquisition.

"How long have you been practicing witchcraft? My son (the youth minister) told me that you have dreams and prophecies. Do you understand that those gifts come from Satan?" he demanded, placing the words like bricks as he laid his case.

"I don't think they come from Satan. I don't think there is anything evil about what I see," I said in defense of myself. "I think they are from God."

"God only sends messages to true believers and the faithful like Moses. Why would he send them to you?" he asked, catching me off-guard.

"I don't know," I said.

"Well, Devin, you need to know that you are playing with the devil. Visions and spells are all ways that Satan works to steal your soul. There is an eternal war for the souls of mankind, and only those who accept Jesus Christ make it to the promised land."

"So, what about all the Buddhist, Hindu, Muslim, and Jewish people? God created them to just go to hell?" I shot back in anger.

"If they don't find Jesus and put him in their hearts, then yes, they are going to hell," he exclaimed.

I can't remember much of what happened next; I was upset by his response and got lost in my thoughts. Everything and anything I needed to know about Christianity and this particular church was being spelled out clearly, and it made me want to scream. *Talk about evil*, I thought. *What an evil thing to believe in and teach others. I don't even want to know what he would think if he knew I liked guys.*

To end the conversation, I played dumb again and told him what I thought he wanted to hear. "I'm scared by it all, and I don't want to be used by the devil. If it is the devil, then I will stop!" I declared, just wanting so desperately for it all to be over.

"It is, Devin. The devil is possessing you and using you. You must repent and accept Jesus Christ as your personal lord and savior." Suddenly I realized that as we were walking toward the chapel doors, the men's group was letting out. Before I knew it, the minister was beckoning them all to join us.

"Gentlemen, you all know Devin. He needs our prayers tonight. He is battling Satan and witchcraft for his soul. Satan has possessed this poor boy, and we have to save him in Christ's name!" the minister explained as the group of men huddled around me and formed a circle. They were all holding hands and bowing their heads as the minister began to lead everyone in prayer. Soon some of them were speaking in tongues, and I started to believe that there really was something wrong with me—that maybe Satan really had gotten to me and that the king of hell himself was after my soul. And then I started to laugh.

I couldn't stop laughing. It was more than a case of the nervous giggles, though I indeed used that as an excuse later on the car ride home; it was laughter that swirled from deep inside. The only way I can explain it is that I somehow suddenly knew that everything that was happening was entirely unethical, immoral, and an abuse of whatever power that minister thought he had over me. Somehow in my naive mind, an island of consciousness popped up in that instant that told me all of this was bullshit. *You don't belong with these people. These people will only confuse who you are,* a voice rang in my head.

The chain of linked hands broke in gasps as the minister prayed even louder and then himself began speaking in tongues. I caught hold of my outburst and settled myself as he finished. "Thank you, everyone. As you could tell, that was one strong demon! Please keep him in your prayers, and when we see him on Sunday, let's pray together again. Now, go home to your wives; it is getting late," the minister directed as he ushered me out of the building and into his shiny new town car.

The ride home was filled with mostly silence on my end while I looked out the passenger window and tried to come up with an excuse for why I was coming home at almost ten on a school night. When I got there, he dropped me off at the foot of the driveway and then sped off. My mother was still awake waiting for me.

"Are you all right? What happened? Something happened," she asked immediately upon seeing my face.

"Nothing, Mom. I'm fine, just tired," I lied.

She squinted and said, "Why did your friend drop you off so late? Did you just get out of church?"

"No, the lead minister gave me a ride. We were working on the float for the parade," I said as I swiftly made a beeline to my room.

"Hey, Devin. I don't think I have a good feeling about that church. I would like you to try out a few others before you get too involved. Something just feels off," she exclaimed as I opened my bedroom door.

"Yes, ma'am," I said, knowing that she somehow knew that something bad had happened to me.

Two days later I got a phone call from one of my friends explaining to me that we were no longer allowed to be friends. His parents, along with my other friend's mother, had been contacted by the minister. I was being excommunicated and was not welcome back in the church. He was also told to inform me that if I were seen on church property, the police would be called. The last thing he said to me was, "I'm sorry, man. The minister told everyone that you were possessed and were being used by Satan to infect the youth group. Everyone thinks you are an agent sent by the devil to destroy the work of the church. We can't be friends. I can't be anywhere around you."

That was the last time I spoke with him and the last time I put my spirituality in the hands of any institution. I have spent my life since then trying to squeeze every last bit of wisdom and gnosis that I can from the world around me. For me, this was an exhilarating freedom; my soul, my rules. Witchcraft became a personal revolution, and over the years it has helped me to find answers, discover true community, and most importantly to live a more powerful life.

My story is not the worst story out there, and chances are you or someone you know has suffered some form of neglect or abuse at the hands of an organized religion or spiritual group. As a professional psychic and spiritual counselor, I have worked with a lot of people who have stories that would shake you to your core. Stories from little boys who grew up within Christian sex cults like the Sons of God, stories from Catholics who were molested as children, and even stories from pagans who were mentally, sexually, and physically abused at the hands of their elders. No religion, religious order, or spiritual group that is run by people with unchecked and unfettered power and access is exempt from these types of atrocities. While these things go unchecked, many of us wear the scars, and we carry them with us into other aspects of our lives.

When I started teaching the craft, one of the first issues I ran into was that many practicing witches have these battle scars, and it was keeping them from experiencing a lot of what the craft has to offer practically, let alone what it could offer otherwise. When teaching Conjure and Hoodoo, witches would scoff at the mention of saints or Jesus. Calling upon anything related to Christianity was anathema to their idea of witchcraft, and that led to them wanting to replace spirits that had cultural and historical associations to that work with those who were more comfortable. Instead of working with St. Anthony in a St. Anthony spell for finding lost items, they wanted to work with Hermes. Instead of the Virgin Mary for peace, they wanted to work with Kwan Yin. They seemed to think that it was okay to take from a spiritual tradition, alter it to fit their comfort levels, replace the honored and elevated spirit associated with that work designated by that tradition, and still call it traditional and authentic. I had the same reaction, but I quickly learned that isn't authenticity, that is appropriation.

Yes, cultures mix, and that can be seen all throughout the history of witchcraft and the occult. However, spirits matter, and as witches we have to remember that. If we are going to live in a world where we say faeries are real, ancient gods are real, and the dead are capable of communicating with the living, then we cannot divorce ourselves from the intrinsic realness of all other spirits. When a cultural community who is devoted to working with a spirit develops a series of practices around that spirit, it is being done so through an intensely emotional and intimate psycho-spiritual connection. There is power there, intense power, that was explicitly designed as a method of achieving specific goals. I am all about mixing and developing magical techniques, but before we take from a culture, shouldn't we invest in it and develop a balanced relationship with it? Isn't it better for us to learn the intended lesson and do the planned work surrounding a magical technique before we alter it? Otherwise, we are just like scientists who throw away the procedure book and wing it based on what the guy in the lab next door is doing.

This indeed applies across the board with the vast majority of folk magic. I have yet to find an authentic folk magic practice in the Western world that doesn't include Christian mythos. In everything from California Conjure to Irish folk magic to trolldom in Iceland, Christ, the devil, heaven, hell, and all of the other Christian themes present themselves as integral parts of the practice. As modern witches seek to grow more knowledgeable about these practices and integrate them into their work, they are undoubtedly running into this issue.

Does this mean that we can just trade out some names and still be true to the traditions we are trying to keep alive? No, it means we have to adjust our worldview to include more of the magic and potential right before our eyes. For those of us with a pagan identity, this can create a bit of an existential crisis. Should you be forced to practice witchcraft with the very spirits and ideology that were used against you or someone you care for? No, it means we have two options. Option A is that we limit our practice to include those things that make us feel safe and sure. Option B is that we can grab the bull by the horns and figure out what exactly upsets us, then take our power back from it.

I am not in any way, shape, or form advocating that all witches suddenly let Jesus become their personal lord and savior. I am, however, saying that we need to widen our understanding of the aspects of magic in a spiritual universe.

For a psychic, everything is vibration, even spirits and theoretical places like heaven and hell or any other plane of existence. To us, anything that we encounter has its own vibration, and that vibration must come from somewhere. We also know that people are incredible psychic batteries who are capable of doing things like causing a poltergeist to manifest when psychic energy isn't focused. Imagine what millions of concentrated minds are capable of creating over thousands of years with the same shared beliefs.

In this, we know that heaven and hell are real, but they are likely not going to be anything close to what the loudest voices in the room are screaming. Instead, they take on the form of the collective consciousness. In witch terms, both heaven and hell are egregores. An egregore is a collective of psychic energy or thought forms that takes on a life of its own. We feed the egregore with psychic energy, and in return we can draw from the pool of collective energy it possesses. Anything that can collect psychic energy and provide it in this way would be considered an egregore, which in theory means that even if Merlin, Jesus, Aradia, and Buddha never existed, they are still quite real for those who work with them, at least as egregores. So even if we loathed and despised the way these egregores had been interpreted for us before, they still are parts of the spiritual landscape that we have to work within as people who live in a cultural paradigm ruled by Abrahamic faith.

This means a lot in the context of our conversation on personal gnosis. If every religion, culture, and society feeds these egregores, then that also means that there is a lot of room for interpretation and invitation. It means that there are plenty of paths we can take as we navigate the otherwise undesirable and forge our way to a better understanding of how we might master ourselves in relation to others.

In the Pentacle of Sovereignty,[1] an exercise from *The Witch's Book of Power*, we saw that in order to get to the point of Divinity, we had to move through the points of Balance, Power, Respect, and Awareness first. Part of the exercise included reflecting upon each of these points with the understanding that all sentient life is on the search for divinity. We are in a paradox of sorts. If we want a piece of chocolate cake, then we have to order an entire cake and share with everyone. The good news is that everyone will chip in to cover the cost; the bad news is that not everyone likes dark chocolate. So, you are still going to get your piece of cake, but it will likely have milk chocolate, white chocolate, and Mexican chocolate along with your original desired dark chocolate. If you say no to the cake, then you don't get any cake at all, and the worst part is that everyone else will be enjoying the cake.

Despite what some might have you believe, there is not one single shape an egregore takes on. It is at the whim of the psychic agent or believer as to how it manifests. This means that to some the cake will always taste like white chocolate, to others it will always taste like dark chocolate, and so on, and the only way to change the flavor profile is to approach it as if it were the flavor you wanted it to be. Regardless of what you want it to taste like, however, it will always be chocolate cake, and everyone will always be picking their own nuances in flavor.

What scares me the most about this is that for those people who believe hell is occupied by physical demons locked in a perpetual war for our souls, that is precisely how it will work out for them. This also means that all those people who complain about their lives being "pure

1 Hunter, *The Witch's Book of Power*, 97.

hell" are visiting that place every single day. They are both creating and being fed by their own eternal prison. Now that is a horror movie!

So what does all of this mean for us as witches who are exploring the occult mysteries related to personal gnosis? It implies that gnosis must outweigh exterior interpretation, and the value prescribed to any spiritual or etheric phenomena, be it spirit, plane, or phantasm, is done only *after* we have experienced it for ourselves. Otherwise, we are only capable of tuning in to someone else's version of the egregore. When we practice a tradition or any style of magic, we are tapping into specific egregores, and we are both informed by those egregores and led by them as we construct our gnosis. We should always be careful when choosing which egregores, group minds, and spiritual thoughts we follow and at the very least evaluate them from time to time.

For me, the witchiest thing you can do is seize your power from an oppressive force. Sometimes this means doing ritual work to help get someone wrongfully accused out of prison, and other times it means that you do ritual work to put the dirty cop behind bars. In the case of personal gnosis, this means that we have to identify and release specific patterns that do not authentically represent our own experience. After this is done, we then need to reintroduce ourselves to the egregore.

This can and should be done all across the board with any adverse experience related to religious or spiritual egregores. For our purposes, I want to address workings that can help people specifically take back their power from Judeo-Christian/Abrahamic abusive interpretation and practice. Abrahamic faiths have dominated most of the Middle East and West for over two thousand years and have had a significant influence on culture and cultural egregores. For us to be successful witches who remain in control of our energy and live without fear, we must be able to exist within these cultures and at times even work with their egregores to achieve our ends.

I will also remind you that energy follows the path of least resistance. Let's say your boss is Catholic and isn't treating you fairly. Would it be faster for you to get a result if you worked with Sekhmet or Archangel Michael? With your boss already being tapped in to a symbiotic relationship with an egregore that contains Michael, chances are Michael is the best route. But as a spirit, Michael isn't going to want to come and work with you if you hate him and despise the people he was made to protect. No, you would have to genuinely believe in him and his ability to protect even you. Your gnosis has to include this belief; however, before you can believe, you have to remove whatever part of your gnosis is keeping you from making personal contact.

I also think it is vital that we are capable of seeing witchcraft as a way of and response to living within an Abrahamic spiritual paradigm, at least within Western culture. If Christianity didn't exist and instead witchcraft and paganism were the dominant spiritual practices, they would be nearly unrecognizable compared to what we know of them today. The witch power is intrinsically connected to a queer current— *queer* as in "other" and "odd" or "strange." It is in this otherness that we find our attraction to the ways of wyrd, and it inspires us to follow our individuality even through the transcendental and religious. I believe that this otherness is a significant component of the witch power as well as what has made witchcraft so rebellious in the eyes of society throughout history.

Aside from the purely practical reasons for why this is a good idea, there lies the matter of baggage and how unhealthy it can be for us. If you have read my other work, you will have picked up that I am all about the self-improvement. Our gnosis will only grow as a result, and it removes the ability for others to hurt us by using our baggage against us, especially spirits! The baggage we carry from past religious and spiritual trauma is often some of the most toxic we can face, and I think every witch should rid themselves of it and heal as much as possible.

Some of this baggage and the healing that will need to happen will take a lifetime. Three practices can be done right now, however, that can help you take back your power and define the connection to the egregore on your own terms.

The Warlocking

Warlock is a term that is still used today in Scotland for a male witch. It is derived from the word *warloga*, which means "oath breaker." It was generally expected of women to fall for the forces of evil and give themselves to witchcraft and the devil, but it was another thing entirely for a man to do it. The oath broken was not to his coven, but to his church. There is a covenant between men and the church that was considered crucial for society to function. The man was to marry and then produce legitimate offspring that would be raised in the church. In the UK, the Church of England was, for all intents and purposes, the cultural head of the empire. When someone went against their patriarchal responsibility and contract with the church, it was considered to be quite the scandal. One of the strange interpretations in modern times has been that warlock is an internal derogatory term that is used to describe a witch who broke their initiation vows, when in reality that is a relatively modern interpretation specifically found in American paganism. Everywhere else in the world, it simply means male witch. Now, with all that being said, this particular working is named after the very act it describes: breaking oaths to churches (aka "wicked vows").

If you were baptized, christened, or became born again, you underwent a Christian initiation ceremony. The first step in breaking away from the egregore of your former church is to perform a Warlocking ritual so that you can free yourself from the shackles of oppressive spirituality. I have done this for my connection to evangelicalism as well as to a few occult communities I once circled with that became severely toxic. Paul Huson recommends doing a similar ritual as an act of rebellion against spiritual tyranny.[2]

The Warlocking ritual can be done to break the bonds of any wicked vow. A wicked vow is one that is taken without consent or made with-

2   Huson, *Mastering Witchcraft*.

out full knowledge of the community's intent. If it was forced upon you or you took the vow without being adequately informed as to what you were getting yourself into, this is the ritual that will break those spiritual ties.

To do this, all you need is to grab some white sage, or any other clearing smudge that you might like, and to go out into nature. You need the wildest and safest place you can find. If you are in a city, plan a day trip out. If you can make it to a beach, even better! Go to this deserted place and align your souls, ground your energy body, and tune in to the world around you with your witch power, then recite the Lord's Prayer backward. I know it may sound a little strange, but this is the prayer in which Jesus is asked to be your savior, and it is often considered to be the most famous prayer in the world. By saying it backward, you are unweaving it from your gnosis and disconnecting from the power its intention has over you. Once you have said the prayer backward, cleanse yourself with the smudge and realign your souls. Envision a white flame emerging from within and allow it to cover your entire being as an act of reclamation of your personal sovereignty. Take a few deep breaths and allow the energy from the white flame to settle before ending the ritual.

The following is a phonetic spelling of the prayer for easy use.

Nema! Livee morf suh reviled tub
Noishaytpmet ootnih suh deel
Suh tsnaiga sapsert taht yeth
Vigrawf eu za sesapsert rua suh vigrawf.
Derb ilaid rua yayd sit suh vig
Neveh ni si za thre ni
Nud eeb liw eyth
Muck mod-gneek eyth
Main eyth eeb dwohlah
Neveh ni tra owh
Retharf rua!

Rewrite the Script

Hindsight is 20/20. When confronted by experiences that disempower us, often we can look back and realize we should have said something or done something that we weren't capable of in the moment. Sometimes we experience something that we were utterly powerless in, and the only way it could have been stopped would have been through some sort of intervention. As we claim our power from these situations, it is often helpful to go back to that memory and rewrite the script.

Take out your journal and write the following questions in it with a few spaces between. Think about a moment in your former spiritual life when you felt disempowered, and then answer these to the best of your ability, taking time to consider each before responding.

1. Describe the moment and who was involved. List the names of those who were present and their affiliation to the organization.

2. What did each of these people do that contributed to your disempowerment?

3. What could they have done differently that would have kept you from becoming disempowered in that moment? (Should they have handled something differently? Should they have used different words? Should they have stood up for you? Etc.)

4. What could you have said or done in that moment that you feel would have made a difference (if anything)?

5. If you were able to relive this experience now, how would the present version of you respond at that moment?

6. What were the policies or doctrines (official or otherwise) that you feel allowed this to happen? Was this something

caused by a person or a person with the backing of an institution?

7. Do you think that person(s) or institution was personally practicing a version of the faith that was balanced and healthy? Were they hypocritical concerning the values of the faith?

8. If so, what would someone who is balanced and in alignment with the values of the faith have done or said at this moment?

9. Other than powerless and disempowered, how does all of this make you feel on an emotional level?

10. How long has this moment affected you? How many years or months have you felt this way about this experience?

After responding, invite your spirit allies to join you and spend a little more time with this moment meditatively. Now, walk away from it for a few hours to a day or two and do your best to disconnect as much as possible. Once you return, read through the questions once more, this time also reading through your original responses. If anything has changed, add that change to your journal. Hopefully, after answering all ten questions the first time and taking a break from focusing on it, you will have a little more clarity about things—I know I did—so when reading through the second time, it is perfectly reasonable for you to update the journal entries.

There will be things that don't change or realizations about the situation that rise to the surface and shed even more light on the matter. These are those things that we must attend to further, as they are most likely the roots of the continued disempowerment. To do this, we are going to begin the process of ritual lucid memory engagement. This means that we are going to revisit this memory ritually, but instead of just reliving it, we are going to take control and be active participants within it.

In my experience, this is best done three times and in accordance with the moon. The first time should be done on the full moon, the second on the quarter moon, and the last on the dark moon. Align yourself, invoke your spirit allies and any corresponding lunar allies, and sit before your altar. Visualize your aura turning into a violet flame that surrounds you completely, and know that this is a psychic shield that will help you through this task. Allow yourself to remember this experience, but while doing so know that even your memory is part of your imagination and helps you shape your will. Make the scene play out differently; this time, instead of you walking away disempowered, use your journal entries to help build an alternative ending, one that favors you. In this memory say whatever it is that you feel would have made a difference or visualize someone else interceding on your behalf if that is what would have truly helped. Visualize yourself walking away completely intact and in control.

When you are finished, empower yourself by drawing down the moon, in whatever form it is in, and using its power to clear away the emotional stress exposed or relieved surrounding the issue. Each time you do this, visualize a different alternate ending, one always with you as the victor, and allow the waning moon to take more and more of the pain and suffering away as it gives more and more of your power back.

Soul Retrieval

A key component in the philosophy of past lives is that one can suffer effects in a present life that are rooted in causes from previous lifetimes. This isn't precisely karma, but it is in the neighborhood. The idea is that you have lived possibly countless lives, and any number of those lives might have contained an experience that shook your soul to the core, and you are destined to be confronted with that same energy in every life until you can resolve any issues surrounding it. Karma, not the actual issues themselves, is what guides us in confronting these issues.

The practice of soul retrieval allows us to visit former lives and confront these issues so that we can retrieve the aspects of our power that remain trapped as a result. Basically, if we can develop baggage in this lifetime, imagine the sort of baggage we collect over multiple lifetimes! The good news is that usually it is just the big stuff that sticks with us in this way; the bad news is that it is often the big stuff that sticks with us.

How do you know which lifetime to visit or even how to get there? There is a trick to it, which is that you should enter into this with no preconceived notions of your past lives. This means that regardless of any past life experience you might have previously had, you cannot allow yourself to approach this experience with any assumptions as to the root of an issue. In our case, we are focusing on religious and spiritual traumas related to Abrahamic faiths, so we are only interested in discovering a past life where this was also an issue for us, and because of the likelihood of there being multiple lifetimes where this could occur, you must be open to witnessing them all. This will require a clean mental slate.

The most basic procedure for soul retrieval is done by entering a trance state and then performing the following meditation. It is often helpful to do this with a partner, when one person is in a trance while the other acts as a guide. You can do this solo, however.

Find yourself in a safe and objective mental place. As before, see your aura change into a brilliant violet flame that extends to encompass your entire body. Know that it will shield and protect you; in this instance, it will also help you process and connect to the appropriate lifetime. Connect with your issues and resistance surrounding past religious or spiritual trauma, and do your best to only be an observer. Instead of remembering this happening in the first person, try to view it objectively, as if you were watching it happen on television. You are there and can see everything, but you are no longer the star of the memory. That is being played by a younger version of you. You are here as the observer. Once you have connected to it in this way, envision yourself leaving this space and floating high up into the sky.

You will go through our atmosphere to a place among the stars, and then turn to face the planet. Take slow and steady breaths and then allow yourself to gently but quickly fall back to earth. This time, when you land in your body, it is not your current body but that of a previous incarnation. Allow yourself to wake up in this new body and then follow your mind as it travels in this body. Let it show you and guide you through the past life, and ask yourself three questions:

1. Who am I in this lifetime?

2. What did I experience that affected my soul so deeply?

3. What emotions accompany this experience?

Once you have these answers, return to your body and journal about as much of the experience as possible. The results vary and are subtle at first. For me, writing them out speeds up the process, and I find being able to revisit them in my journal to be quite helpful. Sometimes the act of merely going and experiencing these things makes all the difference, and whatever energy was there is released the instant we become aware of them. Sometimes, however, you will need to do more than just visit. You might need to visit multiple times, you may need to visit other lifetimes, and you may even need to ritually cut cords or break wicked vows made in a previous life.

For this, you will need Road Opener or Block Buster condition oil or a citrus essential oil such as lemon, sewing pins, and a violet or purple candle. Dress the candle with the oil, and as you do so charge it with the memory of the lifetime and the trauma you witnessed during your soul retrieval, and then place it on a firesafe dish. Take one sewing pin and apply saliva, either by safely running your tongue across it or by spitting on it and dressing it that way. As you do this, enchant the pin by charging it with violet flame and saying, "This pin is a dagger that cuts me free." And then plunge the pin into the side of the candle so that the tip goes deep enough to touch the wick. Do this as many times as you feel you need until you intuitively feel that the pins have provided enough interference between that life and this one. Then light the candle and say:

> My ancient right to claim my soul;
> My witch's might will make me whole.
> From this wretchedness I now ascend;
> In this lifetime I have a soul to mend.
> By the violet flame I cut the ties;
> By the violet flame I'm free of lies.
> What once was shall be no more;
> Return to me so I can soar!

Let the candle burn all the way out. Pay attention to energy shifts as the candle burns down to meet the pins. As it burns, the pins will fall to the bottom and should be cleansed before disposing of them. You alternatively may want to keep them and incorporate them into a charm bag or fetish for past life empowerment.

Witch Power Unchained

All of what we discussed in this chapter will become increasingly important in the following pages. As we explore the mysteries of the witch power and your connection to the Divine, being able to approach all spiritualities and religious egregores with confidence is vital. As I mentioned earlier, we are made whole, with no missing pieces; we just need to figure out how we fit together. A significant part of that is figuring out how the world fits together in relation to your otherness.

We often experience resistance to our otherness, and that resistance can be disturbing or violent in some situations. As we relinquish the chains wrought from the ghosts of religions past and move toward a more complete understanding of what we are capable of as witches, the battle scars need not be a constant reminder of that resistance once met; instead, they can be a reminder of what is and what had to be in order for you to become who you are today.

The lonely road is one full of choices that we must make for ourselves and experiences that only we can witness. We may not like what happened to us, but our sole responsibility is to love and appreciate the sovereignty of who we have become as a result of those happenings. As someone living in the present, you have to make a choice on how the past will affect your future.

JOURNAL TOPICS

In addition to the journal topics prompted within this chapter, answer the following questions in your journal:

1. Does the idea of the lonely road bring you comfort or discomfort? Why?

2. How do you feel your past religious and spiritual experiences have shaped the way you look at your own spirituality today? Do you feel that the power previously found in those traditions is no longer accessible to you? If so, why?

3. If you performed the warlocking ritual, describe your experience and what you are planning to do next time you are confronted with the group you have taken your power back from.

4. In this chapter we discussed otherness as an extension or part of the witch power. How do you feel your otherness separated you within previous spiritual or religious paradigms?

Chapter Two

Deepening the Witch Power

I have heard there are troubles of more than one kind.
Some come from ahead and some come from behind.
But I've bought a big bat. I'm all ready you see.
Now my troubles are going to have troubles with me!

———

Dr. Seuss, *I Had Trouble in Getting to Solla Sollew*

You are the ultimate piece of machinery in your arsenal as a witch. You don't need any ritual objects or other magical tools to master your craft; you merely need your own natural talents and a little discipline, and the world is at your fingertips. The truth is, your witch power came fully equipped with all the essential hardware; all you need to do is learn how to use it and apply its lessons in the right ways.

Regardless of the egregores you tap into, the spirits you summon, or the type of witchcraft that you practice, your witch power has already made you equipped to handle any mystery that might come your way.

This is especially true for those we will face along the lonely road that require us to be at the top of our game energetically.

Our mysteries are those of life and death, of renewal and decay, of manifestation and destruction. As we explore we learn to balance ourselves between the worlds like a daredevil on a tightrope. As our ability to find and bring balance grows, so too does our ability to touch the unreachable depths of our very being. Before we can dive into the depths or perform the workings that can take us over the hedges we seek to jump, we must first be sure that we master a few essential aspects to life with the witch power.

The Essential Practices of an Advanced Witch

Before any witch can take their craft to the next level, there must be specific mysteries that no longer remain in the shadows to them and individual practices that they must always strive to master. If you can't get formal training, these often stay out of the realm of perception, leaving you without vital information that can help you master your craft.

Self-Possession

Being sensitive is a beautiful thing, but not if you are so sensitive that you have no control over your energy and the effect it has on the environment and on other people. The more profound mysteries of the craft will reveal a need for personal discipline and focus, which starts with being aware of what your weaknesses are, especially those related to your witch power. Becoming inundated with psychic vibrations to the point of meltdown doesn't make you an excellent psychic; it makes you a weak one. Powerful, strong psychics understand how to shield themselves, ground their energy, and elicit supplemental help when needed, such as what can be gained by working with spirit allies and stones, all of which has been addressed in previous books in this series.

If you know you are sensitive, then you need to prepare for that sensitivity and stay clear of situations where you might lose control.

How do you prepare? By figuring out what your triggers are and either avoiding them all together or doing magic or energy work to protect yourself against them. Align your souls, ground your energy often, and work with a crystal ally to help supplement your energy body so that it has an easier time dealing with energies you find aggressive.

If you are someone who works with clients or ritual groups where you might interact with people who have little to no control, you have to be prepared to respond to this. In a one-on-one setting, I like to invite my spirit guides and familiar to join us and help prevent unnecessary spiritual stress. I keep my auric field dense, sometimes even forming it into the shape of an impenetrable diamond or a thick wall of iron. The violet flame auric shield we practiced in the previous chapter makes for an excellent personal shield when working in these situations. To that end, I also like to keep iron handy, as it can help to ground and center etheric energy. Having a piece to offer those experiencing overload in ritual has made all the difference in the past.

For those who struggle with staying anchored once they have grounded, there is a trick I developed to help myself many years ago involving a small fetish.

The Grounding Fetish

Make a fetish of yourself by combining moist earth from your land or neighborhood and toenail clippings from both feet until they make a firm ball. Take a piece of root from any plant ally that you work with for psychic awareness and then pack the clay mixture around the root; when complete it should be about fist size. Wrap this with brown fabric, dress with items that you feel represent you, and keep on your altar. Replace every six months or as needed.

This will ground, as well as bind, your etheric body to that environment, so be sure to disassemble it if you move or you run the risk of being tied to the location where the soil came from. This fetish can also be made to help you stay in your body when you are sleeping for those who travel too easily at night.

Being self-possessed means that you are in control of your actions, and anything that might hinder that should be avoided. We cannot allow foreign agents (be they spiritual or chemical) to have control over our actions or alter our free will. We must fully inhabit our minds, bodies, and spirits as active participants and living agents, and that means we must be willing to devote ourselves wholly to their partnership and maintenance.

The best way I have found to do this is through radical self-love and respect. Loving yourself enough to set boundaries when they are needed, creating paths to power when you feel weakness, and investing in a healthy lifestyle make all the difference when cultivating self-possession. For this to work, we need to be able to create discipline and devote ourselves entirely to it.

Self-possession is gained through an intense understanding of your strengths and weaknesses, working through or avoiding triggers that disempower you, establishing control over the energy body and spiritual gifts, having lots of patience and self-respect, and, most importantly, discipline.

Perceive and Discern Energy
Though not always easy for everyone, the practices of perception are vital for successful growth as a magician. Psychic perception not only allows you to tap into them but also to sense when dangerous or malicious energies might be afoot. You cannot safely lead a ritual without this ability, and you cannot safely live without it as a witch who walks between the worlds. Of equal importance, being sensitive in this way is the first step before we channel energy, and we cannot channel energy if we can't sense it.

Sensible energy comes in all shapes and sizes; it could come from a spirit, an object, another person, or a location, and knowing the difference is vital! To develop this set of skills, I like to play games with my psychic abilities, which at the very least keeps me interested. I go to different places like the zoo or the beach, and I connect with the energies within the space. Once I have a decent survey of the environment, I then break down the components of the environment and approach each one separately. As psychics, we are like connoisseurs of wine; we take a sip of the psychic vibrations and then must do our best to explore the bouquet of flavors that are present. Approach your psychic senses like a fine wine, and the more exposure you have to the different characteristics and flavors of psychic energy, the more refined your palate will become.

Discernment is key for us. We can sense energy, but can we tell if that energy is coming from a spirit or the crystal sitting next to you? This is a skill that develops over time, like all the rest of them, because it is an intuitive skill, one that can only be gained through experience. I keep a journal with me so that when I encounter new energy that feels unrecognizable to me, I can profile it later. I also keep a record of how I meet spirits and where I feel energy pooling in locations. By taking the time to map out and record our psychic experiences, we are essentially allowing ourselves to construct a user manual, complete with references and all!

Scanning the Environment

You can scan your environment at any time by merely extending your awareness outward in all directions and actively feeling it out with your mind. I do this by closing my eyes and focusing on the way my skin feels, then the way my skin feels against my clothes, then the way my clothes feel against the air, and then how the air feels against the walls. I then prompt myself with a series of questions and meditate on the answer like one might meditate on a math problem.

- Is there anything unusual about my environment?
- Is there energy present here that usually isn't?
- What spirits or spiritual energies are currently around me? If any, who are they? Are they familiar or foreign to me?

- Do I feel safe?

- Do I feel in control?

If your souls are aligned, you can send pulses of your white flame (the energy that forms within you as a result of soul alignment) outward in all directions and use it like sonar to determine what energies are there. This method works well especially for those moments when we aren't feeling the most connected spiritually. Simply send out tiny bursts and follow the flow of energy throughout the space; if energy bounces back to you, then zero in on that location and repeat the process. Each time allow your senses to fill in the blanks and create a picture of what is there with you at the moment.

During this exercise be aware of all of your senses and how they are responding. Perhaps you smell something. Maybe you taste something while you are doing this. It's possible to physically feel a sensation during this process. We each work a little differently, and we all respond uniquely to different types of energy. This is most displayed in our five senses.

In this series we have discussed many different types of energy and how to sense them. We have discussed the energies of the self and the planets, of our spiritual allies and the planes of being they come from; we talked about mediumship and other forms of psychic sensitivity, and so on. But there are still other forms of energy that have yet to make it fully into our work together, energies that exist further still, even beyond the reaches of our subtle awareness. As we move throughout these pages, keep in mind that one of our primary goals will be to sense and savor as many different types of energy as possible.

Channeling Energy

Once we can sense energy, we can channel that energy. Channeling essentially is the ability to act as a faucet for energy pouring through your etheric body via a secondary source. In some instances channeling can be considered a form of light possession. When we channel spirits, we become their mouthpiece; when we channel energy, such as when we draw down the moon or call upon the power of our ancestry, we become the conduit through which those powers coalesce in the physical world. When all three souls are aligned, it is believed that you are channeling the power of your divine will. We can channel just about any sort of power or frequency as long as we can tune into it.

Not every witch must know how to be a channeling intermediary for the spirit world, but we all need to know how to tune into energy and draw it into this world. This is how we charge objects like candles and stones, how we imprint our will upon our environment, and how we send energy through our hands when we perform healing magic. You can't get too far as a witch without the ability to make energy move from one place to the next.

The following exercises will introduce you to the theory behind channeling. Some of us do this naturally, others pick the skill up as they advance, but what is most important is that we observe the techniques and the theory behind them.

PART ONE: TUNING IN AND PROJECTING ENERGY

To tune in to a signal, you merely need to perceive that signal. Simply extend your consciousness so that it makes contact with whatever energy you want to draw from. You may need the help of sensory aids and tools to do this, and this is ultimately why we have magical tools: something always tuned in to these forces so you don't have to be. Tuning in is more natural than a lot of people think it is. For example, let's say we were going to channel the energy of joy. We would remember a moment when we were really happy and clear-minded and then use that memory and the feelings attached to that moment to hone in on the frequency of the memory. As we tune in to that frequency, I like to envision that it is coalescing into a sphere over my moon hand; this just helps me determine how well I am receiving the signal. With a few exceptions, we humans each have a dominant or projective (sun) hand

and a passive or receptive (moon) hand. If you are right handed, your sun hand is on the right and moon hand is on your left; if you are left-handed, the sun is on your left and the moon is on your right. If you are one of those super cool, naturally ambidextrous people, you just get to pick a team!

The clearer the signal I am tuning in to gets, the clearer the sphere becomes. Once I feel that I have a good connection and that the sphere of energy in my hand is as resistance-free as possible, I draw from that energy to initiate the active channeling process by moving my focus beyond the sphere and into the signal transmitting through that sphere.

To do this expeditiously, you must think of yourself as a multi-dimensional wormhole. I know it sounds a little fantastical, but you are likely tuning in to an energy source that exists somewhere else, possibly even outside of space and time, and to get it here you have to be able to be in two places at once. Allow the palm of your moon hand to relax and open up, revealing the first side of this wormhole, and then allow the palm of your sun hand to do the same, revealing the second half. Whatever enters one will exit out the other, but because your natural energy flows in one direction, there are natural currents of power inside this wormhole that create their own gravity. Whatever energy comes near the moon hand will be instantly sucked into a wormhole and shot out through the sun hand with force.

Visualize that your moon hand is like a grounding rod and antenna where the energies of this frequency gather. As they gather they are instantly collected by your moon hand, and as they travel the current of your own power they make their exit from their origin and traverse the worlds to make their way into our own. As it exits your sun hand, it will take the shape of whatever it is filtered into and enrich it with its essence. Try this again with different emotions and document the changes you sense internally as you experiment.

PART TWO: TUNING IN AND PROJECTING ENERGY

Using the same principles as the first part, this time work with the polar channels of energy within your body. Allow the energy to enter through your crown and to exit either through your hands, using them both as sources of projection, or run through you and exit via your root. This method works best if you envision a waterfall of the energy above you. As the water spills, it enters through your crown and travels to your third eye, where it splits into two rivers. One river of energy flows through each arm and then is distributed through the hands, taking the form of whatever it is channeled into and imbuing it with its essence.

To end the session, close the moon hand, breaking the channel, and visualize the connected energy source fading. Take three deep breaths, disconnecting from all currents of power and grounding all remaining energy.

Z Energy and the Nine Flames

Z energy, that perfect frequency that comprises all of space, time, matter, and energy, is the source of all things. Its consciousness is the Star Goddess, its power is omnipresent, and its range is infinite. Z energy is what contains the whole, and if we were to distill it into a single wavelength, it would go on forever. Our known universe is but a piece of this energy. It is the greatest mystery and the most profound secret. It is life and death and the cycles of being, it is light and darkness and matter, it is all that has come to pass and all that will be. Its opposite is what we call the void. The void is emptiness and nothingness; it is a place, a realm, another universe even, where all that we know or ever will know never existed. We see Z energy as a frequency that extends and travels through the void, the void being more substantial and massive than Z energy.

The problem, however, is that we cannot channel all of Z energy, so we need to be able to divide it up into various recognizable bands of psychic frequency. In doing so, we can better access the parts of Z energy that we need and channel only those specific frequencies. Some witches use the popular system of light rays from Theosophy, others delineate by working with the planes of being, but most witches I know are experienced in channeling energy from a direct source, like that of a crystal or deity. We can, however, channel a lot more than just that!

The concept of energy is something that we will discuss a lot in this book because it takes on many forms and many shapes, and each one of them is accessible for us to work with, at least sympathetically. It is an easy thing to say "energy" and not have much depth to our intention; this is something that I am guilty of in my own speech. When channeling energy, it doesn't seem to be enough for us to merely mentally focus; somehow we need to engage more than just the mind, but also the body (primal self) and the soul (the higher self). We find that when we have moments of spontaneous channeling, it is usually done so via an emotional or physical response. Think of when you get angry and strange things happen (a common occurrence reported by witches). This can happen spiritually as well through means of the higher self, such as when someone is possessed by a deity. The access points and type of energy may change, but usually all three aspects of the soul are expressing the energy being channeled.

As you can see, energy is something we are working with constantly. Unless you are trained in a tradition where you are taught to work with a specific type of energy, such as those seen in Peruvian shamanism, Reiki, and a small handful of witchcraft traditions, the specifics can be difficult to navigate beyond the essential elements. The way that I like to channel is to engage all three soul components by working with a series of psychic frequencies that have triggers rooted in our daily experiences. I refer to them as the nine flames, and they can be channeled by visualizing a liquid flame of a particular color and tapping into a unique set of imagery and emotional/psychic nuances to bring that energy forward into our working.

The White Flame

The white flame is perfect love and perfect trust in the flow of universal power and complete surrender to self-governance and authority. It is the flame most associated with the higher self. We call this flame the "holy flame." We tap into this frequency during souls alignment.

The Violet Flame

The violet flame is a bit tricky. This flame is connected to the spiritual experience and spiritual forces that make up creation. It is a flame of order and memory and is related to the higher self, psychic abilities, and past/parallel/future life data. We tap into this flame every time we feel "called" or divinely inspired to do something.

The Indigo Flame

The indigo flame is used to both keep us safe in the spirit worlds as well as to give us passage through them and is often worked with in spirit conjuration, mediumship, and soul flight. Intimately connected to the dead, it is a flame of extrasensory perception, spiritual protection, and travel. We tap into it when we visit a cemetery.

The Blue Flame

The blue flame is psychic projection, wisdom, willpower, and creativity. It is the flame of consciousness and the limitless possibilities of the mind. It is connected to reason and illusion, knowledge and mystery, science and religion. We tap into it when we say "So mote it be" at the end of our work.

The Green Flame

The green flame is the force behind the grass that grows between the cracks of pavement, the forest that reclaims a forgotten homestead, and the medicinal properties found in plants. It is a flame of growth, abundance, sustenance, intoxication, and the feral, and it is felt in the cycles of life, the tides of war, and the changing of seasons. We tap into it when we work with the plant kingdom.

The Yellow Flame

A flame of wisdom through experience, the yellow flame is the power present in every moment of graduation and evolution and is felt as pride, joy, and success. It is the active force behind all acts of clarity, commitment, and the ego soul. We tap into it when we see through lies and find the truth or when we are feeling righteous.

The Orange Flame

We think of the orange flame as the flame of the physical realm because most fires that occur naturally here burn with an orange hue. It is a flame of focus and intensification, and it is the active force behind metamorphic change. It is through the orange flame that we learn to take the old and make it new again, to burn away all that does not serve us, and to restore what is tired. We tap into this flame when we work with elemental fire.

The Red Flame

The red flame is primordial power, ancestry, and life force. This is the power and animating force of the primal soul, the flame of bestial life. It is instinct and compulsion, the strength within you that rises each day, eagerness, passion, sexual desire, hunger, regeneration, and feeling. We tap into this frequency when we connect physically with another person during sex.

The Black Flame

The black flame also contains every flame but the white flame. This flame is chaotic to the untrained and unfocused. Its force is that of decay, destruction, and the rejuvenation that ultimately comes from that. Think of it as a black hole: things get sucked in but are spit out as something else. We tap into this frequency when we undergo initiation.

Now, go ahead and think about each of those flames and the emotions or mental connections that come up when you do. Use those sparks to light the flame by homing in on them and sensing the energy behind the moment. Try the tuning in and projecting energy exercises from earlier in this chapter with these flames and see if one in particular calls to you. You might want to look at magic and spiritual practices that are thematically related to them as potential sources for gnosis. Throughout this book when we talk about channeling or sensing energy, I will often refer to one of these colored flames. Feel free to mark this section for easy reference later.

Raising Energy

Sensing and channeling energy is one thing, but raising energy is something different altogether. Without the ability to raise energy, our spells and other workings fall flat. One of my favorite ways to raise energy, besides practicing breath work techniques or dance, is to tread the mill.

Treading the Mill and Crossing the Hedge

From what I understand, the term "treading the mill" was coined by Robert Cochrane in the *Cochrane Letters*. It is a practice in raising power, not unlike how Wiccans cast a circle. In truth, this is one of those parts of my traditional Wiccan education that stuck with me far after training; however, its application is slightly different from how I use it today. Treading the mill is a lot like turning a crank. It is a way of building up energy and then using that energy to move between the worlds or to bring focus to all the worlds, a practice also known as "crossing the hedge" or "hedge crossing."

"Crossing the hedge" is a term we use to describe the act of slipping from our world to the others through a state of trance or ecstasy. Aligning your souls, performing ecstatic dance and breath, and working with hallucinogenic herbs and mushrooms are each examples of different types of hedge crossing. Generally speaking, treading the mill is used as a way to cross the hedge as well as to raise energy for magical purposes.

The energy from treading the mill can be channeled and poured into spell and ritual work or employed to raise large amounts of energy for protection. Traditionally, this is done with a coven or a group of practitioners, but contrary to popular belief you can most certainly perform it on your own.

Simple and precise, this working merely requires an article of fascination and room enough to walk around it in a complete circle. In some traditions the article of fascination is a stang, others an altar, and in my tradition we have used any number of items such as bones, lamps, candles, plants, and even crystals. Depending on your intention, once enough energy has been raised, the vibration of whatever you place in the center will become entirely mutable. Because of this, the sky is the limit with how you might go about using the energy therein. You can place a spell candle in the center and then use this method to charge and imprint your will upon it before lighting. You can program a stone so that it is attuned to a spirit and then summon that spirit using this method. You can put the bones of an animal in the center and use this method to conjure its totemic presence. You can do this around a ritual fire to initiate ecstatic union with the numinous.

PART ONE: TREADING THE MILL

Place the object in the center of the space. Stand at least three feet away from it so that your right shoulder is facing inward toward the object. Align your souls and ignite your holy fire. Then, with your palms facing the ground, turn your head to the right to gaze upon the object. Remember that your holy fire is unlimited energy, one that is the product of divine connection and a powerful tool to use for almost any purpose.

Look at the object with your power and see the power within it. Allow your holy fire to pour from your hands like liquid and then begin walking in a circle around the object. To use the metaphor of a wheel, the idea here is that the object of fascination is the central hub, you are the outer rim, and your gaze is a spoke that connects the two. Stand up straight, with your shoulders square and your head as high as the gaze will allow. Feel the power of your holy fire and the connection between yourself and the point of fascination and then begin to move forward with a metered step.

Some witches gallop, some squat and stomp, others simply walk; however you move around the circle, your steps must have a rhythm of some kind, even if it is a simple steady beat. As you move, do so with command and with purpose, and allow the liquid white fire to fall from your palms and hit the ground beneath you.

As it touches the ground, envision it spreading out like a forest fire, slowly filling the surrounding area. Know that all energy it produces only feeds this magical act, so as the fire spreads so too does the effectiveness of the working. As you circle the object, do your best not to speed up or slow down but to remain constant and steady.

Chant:

White flame falling, red flame rising, black flame always near.
Power stirring, lines are blurring, power gather here!

Continue to move in a clockwise motion, chanting, until you begin to feel the energy in the space around you change. It might grow thicker, it might become thinner, or perhaps it cools down or even heats up; notice the way this shift happens for you. That shift is coalescing energy and is the very thing we are farming. Continue to move and focus your gaze on the article of fascination, and with each cycle feel the energy grow more intense. Once you feel that the energy within the space has reached its peak, cease channeling the white flame. Instead, now as you move, you will be collecting the energy and using your gaze to transmit it directly into the article of fascination. I do this in three revolutions and while doing so recite any incantations necessary to charge the object.

PART TWO: VARIATIONS ON TREADING THE MILL

You might have figured out that this exercise is perfect for circle casting, and indeed it is. You will hear me mention throughout the book that I do not like casting a circle for most of my magical work. That being said, when I do cast a circle, it is either using the mill method, which we refer to as "laying the compass" (see chapter 6), or the slightly more ceremonial method that implores the Grigori (see chapter 10). I am purposefully putting those in different sections of this book.

Alternatively, this method is often employed to cross the hedge between the realms and walk between the worlds. Place your stang or altar at the center, and as you pour the white flame onto the ground, do so for only one revolution as if laying a path. Continue to follow this path of white flame for some time, knowing that it has no end and no beginning. It is common for some degree of chanting to go on, which aligns your path to its final destination. Some traditions chant the name of familial spirits or beastly allies for this, while others recite secret prayers. The goal is to lose yourself in the procession, to become one with the cyclical motion, and to transcend the physical plane.

PART THREE: TREADING THE MILL IN GROUPS

Working in groups to this end is sometimes a more powerful method. Though I have had success independently, I have felt palpable shifts while imploring these methods in groups. All members stand with their right shoulder to the center and then link hands; placing their right hand before them and their left behind. The circular procession is then commenced and energy raised. Another variation has all members moving only after placing their hands on the shoulders of those in front of them to build the desired energy.

Don't Rely on Whimsy

I will admit, this is likely my greatest flaw as a witch. I go with the flow a little too much and don't always plan ahead; even when I do, I tend to deviate from the plan. I also have a hard time finding discipline in the day-to-day aspects of life with the witch power. As we will discuss a bit later in this book, the ability to have and maintain discipline is of major importance once traveling the deeper planes. I tend to do the initial work to get me to where I need or want to go, and then once I am there I stop investing. Unfortunately, I know I am not alone in this! The good news is, neither are you.

What does it mean to be a disciplined witch? That is a question that will have a different answer depending on who you ask and depending on what you want your witchcraft to become. What is for certain is that however you define it, discipline always comes back to diligent practice and study.

We have to struggle through our lack of discipline to truly know what we are capable of. If I can do it with my monkey brain, I know you can do it.

Prioritizing What Matters

It all starts by auditing your relationship to the craft and your current practice. Take out your journal and follow along. Ask yourself if you are happy with where you are at, what you would like to see yourself become more proficient at, and what you think you need in order to make that happen.

The next three questions are important. Do you feel fulfilled by your craft? Do you feel challenged by your craft? Do you feel your witchcraft is helping to improve your life? If you aren't feeling fulfilled by your craft, then you know you are in need of change. If you aren't feeling challenged by your craft, then that means you have stopped growing. Lastly, knowing that your spiritual efforts, beliefs, and practices are helping you and your situation is critical to feeling invested in the long term. Fulfillment and growth are both essential for our over-all health as spiritual beings, but so is feeling like all of this is helping you live the best life possible.

Next, I want you to ask yourself where you want to go with your witchcraft and what you could be using witchcraft to change in your life right now. During our first meeting, I always ask my students where they see themselves as a witch in ten years. I want them to tell me what their ideal life looks like. We always adjust this as time goes on, but without a series of goals to work toward, we can easily get lost. It isn't enough to say "I want to be a powerful witch" or "I want to develop my psychic abilities so I am the best I can be." What do those things really mean to you? You need to be able to spell it out for your-self, and the more detail, the better. Remember, energy follows the path of least resistance, and when we think these things through and plan ahead, we are effectively carving a path for that energy to flow.

Take a look at what you've written out and divide those goals into three sections. The first section is for those goals that you have which will require more thought and planning. These are the goals that you know you need to tackle, but you aren't sure how to do that just yet. Let's call this section A. Section B is for those goals that you have and know what you need to do but haven't motivated yourself to tackle yet. These are goals you are actively working on or attempting to work on that are already experiencing resistance in your life. These are the goals we failed to complete, have neglected, or that have remained uninitiated. Lastly, section C is for those goals that you are actively working on and intend to continue working on.

Once you have your goals placed in their appropriate sections, go through and prioritize them. As you do this, be sure to place them in order of overall importance to you. It doesn't matter if you find them silly or profound, just list them honestly and realistically according to your life and your needs.

When each section is prioritized, see if any goals overlap or correspond. For instance, if you have a goal in section A that requires you to figure out more about your psychic abilities and a goal in section B that involves setting more time aside for research and psychic practice, then we would consider these to be corresponding goals. Or, let's say you have a goal in section B to become better at money and prosperity magic, and you have a goal in section C that involves performing daily offerings to the goddess Fortuna; these would be overlapping goals. Any overlapping or corresponding goals should be highlighted or starred. These are goals that we can approach together as one practice, and because they appear in multiple categories, they are reliable indicators of where to begin building our practice.

Once you know what the important things are and where those crucial things overlap on your map, you can begin the process of finding ways for them to fit into your lifestyle. This is difficult for some people. I am often accused of giving people too much homework, so tread lightly. As you try to find ways for these goals to fit in your life, you have to think long term and short term, and you might have to make sacrifices or adjust them to manifest the results you seek.

Building a Stronger Path

Sometimes it is helpful for people to have a template for how to do this. Keeping your journal handy, on a separate piece of paper make three more categories: list them as daily practices, weekly practices, and monthly practices. Under these categories we are going to list practices that will help you achieve your goals. As you reach them, you will want to go back to the original lists you made in the previous section to update the lists we are making in this section and keep them relevant.

How do you know what practices to do or which ones to prioritize? If you're a busy person, then looking for shortcuts is the answer. I want to perform practices that will cover as much ground as possible.

Often we can condense goals that correspond or overlap, but we can also find synchronicity in the methods employed to achieve our goals. For instance, I presented two examples in the last section where goals could overlap. Both of those examples could be combined into a single practice; we could set time aside to perform weekly divination that can inform us as to the best way to strategically handle our finances and do it as a devotional to the goddess Fortuna. Take a look at the list carefully and think creatively.

So, as a general rule of thumb, there are a few things we should add to our template before we fill it in. Under the corresponding sections list the following:

DAILY PRACTICES	WEEKLY PRACTICES	MONTHLY PRACTICES
quick alignment	full alignment	ritual work
quick energy clearing	full energy clearing	space clearing
quick altar work	2 x spell work	monthly intention
quick energy shielding	weekly intention	2 x 30 min. meditation
daily intention	weekly altar work	monthly altar work
check in with guides		

Don't be too alarmed; most of these will overlap. For instance, if you visited your altar four times a week for ten minutes, you could knock out half the list. As you go through your goals, try to fit them into this structure. Remember, be creative *and* be practical. Let's go through and flesh out the ideas in the template.

Everything listed under the daily practices category can be performed all at once or at different times throughout the day. These are things that should help you check in with your goals and your magic and should help build the witch power. Even if you only walk up to your altar, place your hands on it, and say a prayer to your gods or spirits on your way to bed for two minutes, that counts! These daily practices can be abbreviated and are meant to keep you tuned in. You can do all of these except for checking in at your altar in the shower every morning! Again, these don't need to be elaborate by any means; keep them practical and repeatable according to your life. If you cannot do anything else, at the very least set a magical intention for yourself each day that helps bring your goals further to fruition. Sometimes waking up in the morning and setting the intention to be more conscious of your finances or to be more open to the preternatural and occult can make all the difference.

The weekly practices category is where you will likely need to break out your planner. It doesn't matter when you are able to fit these in, just find a way. Again, you can combine practices into one by doing everything but one of the spells in one sitting. Some goals will take more time and focus; they will require you to set up a formal practice rather than an informal one. The spells can be done at your altar or at your kitchen sink; it doesn't matter as long as you are performing two spells a week that are aimed at either helping yourself or helping someone else. As you set your daily intention, you will want to set an intention for the week.

Lastly, monthly practices are pretty self-explanatory if you have been following along. Again, break out your calendar and see when you can fit these things in. Of course, you can combine them with other practices, do most of them in one sitting, or spread them out throughout the month. You will notice that thirty minutes of meditation is suggested twice a month. This can be guided meditation, freestyle, or intentional, but it should again be something that is oriented toward meeting your goals. For instance, if you want to magically master your finances, listening to a guided meditation that is designed for help with prosperity would be ideal.

Creating a discipline for yourself can be really hard, I know all too well. As I said before, this is something I have struggled with, but it is not insurmountable; it is something that requires patience and planning. My great inspiration to make these changes came when I saw a friend of mine who is a single mother of two, a small-business owner, and a community leader finding time to do all these things. She found a way to fuse her lifestyle and her magical goals together in a way that allowed her witch power to thrive. I knew if she had figured it out, I could too. So even if it all looks a bit overwhelming, give it your best and try to make it work. I challenge you to ninety days of this regimen. Try to make it three months following the plan we just made together and see if you don't feel like you have more control and are more in tune with the energies you are trying to manifest.

In conclusion, the abilities to remain self-possessed, be perceptive, channel power, raise power, and mold power through discipline are skills every witch really should strive to master every day if they are practicing at an advanced level. As you can see, there are plenty of ways to apply these skills and plenty of places in your craft where they are useful. If you aren't feeling confident with your witchcraft or don't know where to start revamping your practice from a practical level, I strongly encourage you to place your attention within the pages of this chapter.

Journal Topics

Meditating on the topics presented here in this chapter, respond to the following questions in your journal:

1. Which of these practices did you find were the most natural for you?

2. Which of these practices were the most difficult or unnatural feeling to you? Are they ordinarily tricky for you? What are some ways that you can improve upon this?

3. Other than what I listed here, what are some other practices that you have added to your arsenal as an advanced level practicing witch, and how have those impacted your work?

Chapter Three

The Mysteries of Orientation

*The self is not something ready-made, but something
in continuous formation through choice of action.*

—

John Dewey

Every witch has a set of rituals, spells, and customs within their arsenal that allows them to interact with the spirit world and engage quintessence. The unfortunate truth is that not all witches have an effective practice, or at least it isn't as effective as they would like. Yes, for some of us this is easier than others, but most of the time our inadequacies as witches have more to do with our lack of discipline and an over-familiarity with what we assume the craft is.

I know I tend to go on and on about the importance of having your shit together, and it is for good reason; if you feel weak, lost, broken, and confused, your magic will be unpredictable and unreliable. You leave yourself open to spiritual influence from unsavory channels, and you set yourself up for a tough time, especially if you are a solitary practitioner. Witchcraft *is* dangerous, most especially for those who lack discipline. There is so much to be gained as a witch by doing your own demon work, healing the old wounds from the past, unflinchingly looking at the things that make you feel powerless, and pushing your limits when it is safe to do so. The more confident you are in your life and your life choices, the sturdier your resolve is when it comes to your ability to thrive, the more powerful you grow in all denominations of your life and circumstance, and the richer and more rewarding your magic will be.

As an experienced witch exploring your own mysteries, I recommend that you focus not only on the sensation and development of a personal relationship, but also on what differences you find developing in your life because of them. Certain practices will sharpen your witch power, others will amplify it, and you might see that the spirits you already work with respond differently to you because of them. Even the simplest ritual, such as consecrating a chalice of wine for an offering, is meant to strengthen your bond with the other side.

The following rites, rituals, prayers, and customs should be a part of every witch's repertoire in some variation. As spiritual technology, their themes may not appear to be new in the craft, but I like to think that the way I approach them includes some upgrades and a fresh (Sacred Fires–oriented) perspective that I hope better suits the modern world. What I include are only the essentials; however, as you can imagine, the craft has produced a lot of art over the years, and showcasing a complete compendium is utterly impossible. In the back of the book, check out the bibliography and recommended reading section, where I list books that will introduce you to a wide range of magical practices so you can further explore your witch power and the secrets others have shared.

Keeping the concepts I presented in the first chapter in mind, let's take a more in-depth look at the mysteries of self-orientation and how mapping the flow of power and energy in your life can increase your effectiveness in the craft. To put it simply, self-orientation is the practice of orienting energies and correspondences so that they flow in accordance with your own natural flow and the natural flow of your environment. This ability will allow you the necessary flexibility to take your craft deeper than you ever thought possible and will be a staple in the work to come.

The Secret of Directionality

We all have a different take on the subject of directionality. Many use a standard system with fixed points of correspondence (earth in the north, fire in the south, air in the east, water in the west), and then there are others like myself who approach directionality in a more personalized manner. The theory with directionality is that different elemental frequencies and other types of energy such as those of the angelic or demonic realm are related to specific points on a compass and can be invoked by using that direction as a gateway. The supposed benefit is that this falls neatly into a standard system of ceremonially based magic and should allow us to use aspects of ceremonial magic in our common, or lower, forms of magic.

The problem with this is that the points are fixed, which means if you live in the middle of a continent and the nearest body of water is in the south, or if you live in the southern hemisphere, you are out of luck. The system just doesn't work for you because it wasn't made with you in mind. You either have to adjust to it or not use it to have an association with its corresponding energy.

The secrets of directionality don't just apply to the points on a compass, either! Directionality also pertains to the way energy moves in and out of being, and moving energy in the wrong direction can nullify the effectiveness of our magic. Most of us are taught that energy is received through the left hand/side of the body and released on the right. This isn't true for everyone, especially those who are left-handed.

Notice in the previous chapter we used terms like sun hand and moon hand to replace the traditional left/right hand because it doesn't work the same way for everyone. We are also taught that our personal polarity is set to exhaust life force from the crown chakra and to reabsorb it through the root. That also isn't true for everyone; some people (usually those whom we refer to as energy vampires) are naturally programmed to have their energy run the other way. These people aren't doing anything malicious, however; their stream just runs differently from our own.

We often want to take the easy road and use the recipe right out of the book. But anyone who has baked a cake 3,000 feet above sea level will tell you that the directions in the book just aren't right. One of the things I have found to be absolutely necessary is that I allow myself to break from tradition and identify my own personal directionality so that my witchcraft is rooted in my unique individual circumstance.

To do this, there are a few things we need to figure out.

The Direction of Your Resonance

Each of us sends out a signal in all directions, as we are effectively walking/talking psychic beacons that are constantly transmitting a signal. That signal is what we refer to as resonance. Understanding how your personal resonance is transmitted is a significant and often overlooked type of directional awareness to have. Not all of us have the same energetic physiology, and when we try to force someone who is not made from the same mold to function as though they were, we are dooming them to a tough road. If you have felt stumbling blocks as you work with energy, it very well could be that you were applying the wrong method.

Traditionally we are taught that energy moves through our bodies similarly to how the electromagnetic energy of the planet runs from one pole to the other. The idea is that we have a natural flow of essentially four-dimensional (or more) life force that moves through and around our physical bodies, delivering much-needed energy to the various parts of our being. It is not dissimilar to how blood running through our circulatory system carries oxygen and other nutrients to the body. Traditionally it is thought that when the energy is inside the body, it is being cleansed and revitalized. It then delivers nutrients throughout your anatomy and leaves the body, and as it travels outward and down, it transmits your signal and then travels down toward your root chakra and is once again reabsorbed, at which point the whole process starts over.

This is a perfectly acceptable theory on paper, but in reality, these poles aren't set for all of us in the same way; furthermore, the jury is still out as to whether or not the energy ever actually leaves your body to begin with. Over the years as I have seen clients and worked with other witches I have discovered that some people's energy flows backward from the standard model; some people even receive from their solar plexus chakra and send from their heart chakra. The majority of us are born with the standard model fitting quite nicely, but not all of us are and not all of us stay that way. People whose energy flows counter to our own or originates from a different point than our own often get branded as "psychic vampires" and can make the rest of us feel quite uneasy to be around them. This is for a good reason, as our energy flows in one direction and theirs goes in the other and essentially becomes a cup that just collects what we are pouring out. It isn't their fault; they often have no clue.

On the other hand, if you are one of these people who happen to flow a bit differently, then being around the rest of us can be overwhelming, unnerving, and make you uneasy for an entirely different set of reasons. A lot of people who are empathic often have a different type of plumbing system than the rest of us, and because of it have spent their lives struggling to find solid ground as they move from system to system looking for answers. It may seem simple, but something as simple as the direction in which your life force travels through your body can have a significant effect on how you move through life as a witch and how you see others move through life. If this is you, there is nothing wrong with you; you just have the added homework.

Sometimes these things can be adjusted or amended over time through therapies and energy work. If these things develop later in life, there is a good chance that there was some sort of trauma experienced. With the right kind of healing practice, the natural flow of life force through the body can be restored. We will not cover this here as the practices for this sort of restoration can be found in common witchcraft and occultism under "energy healing." If you are naturally programmed to flow a bit differently than the rest of us, you will want to make sure you are figuring out your own unique flow. It is okay to be different; just know what makes you different and use it to your advantage!

Mapping Your Flow

This is a practice that can be done solo or with a partner. I find that working with a partner is the easiest way to get results, as doing this alone can be difficult if you aren't taking your time and really using your senses. Find a competent energy practitioner in your area and have them do a scan of you and have them use whatever system they are comfortable with. Using your witch skills, create an energy ball at the top of your head and allow it to get caught up in your natural flow of energy. Have your partner follow this ball through your body, paying particular attention to directionality and, of course, anywhere the ball gets stuck or changes direction. After each time, allow the ball of energy to be reabsorbed at the point of its origin. Do this at least three times, check for consistency and patterns, and draw a map of it. If you are doing this alone, I would suggest that you perform this three times over the course of a week and that you compare your results from each experience.

Yes, we want to know the map of your natural flow, but what we really want to learn from this experience pertains to the directionality. Does it pour out of your head and travel back down through your feet and/or the base of your spine or does it spill out from the bottom of your spine and then travel up to the top of your head? If your energy body flows from crown to root, then you are in luck, but if it is the latter, then you need to work on creating a denser aura. This will help with your almost empathic ability to soak up other people's energy, as it will make it less likely for negative spiritual forces to attach themselves to you, and it will help you to have less of a splash radius with your own energy.

The rest of the information you gather as a result of this should be used to help you figure out where energy in your body accumulates, needlessly or otherwise. Why does energy get stuck in certain places? Think of energy like water. Being an active element, water naturally wants to flow. The only reason for water to pool is if it cannot flow on its own. If energy is getting stuck in a part of your body, then it is collecting in that location for a reason and should not be ignored. Energy pools when the flow is corrupted, and that only happens when there is some sort of trauma related to the area via direct or sympathetic means. We should interpret this as a cry for help from the energy body akin to a knot in a muscle; the way to resolve it is through therapeutic means.

Raising Power in the Energy Body

Ultimately, the reason we need to know which way our energy flows is that for us to raise the large amounts of power often required for active engagement with quintessence, we need to know which direction to turn the crank. Let's go back a step and think about that ball of energy that we allowed to float on the current of your energy body. This same technique can be applied to both help you raise energy as well as ground that energy when necessary.

Perform the practice again, but this time let's tweak it a bit. First, when you form that ball of energy, get more specific. Make that ball of energy a ball of blue fire, which symbolizes willpower in my tradition. Second, do not allow the ball to be reabsorbed when it travels back to the point of its origin; instead, let it grow more prominent and more intense with each pass. Lastly, release this ball on the third and final pass. Allow it to burst like a firework in all directions and then encompass you in a sphere of blue fire. After a few moments of feeling out the sensation of the sphere, reabsorb it back into your energy body.

Try this two different ways. As the ball travels through the energy body, do your best to keep the same speed with each rotation. Do not allow the ball to speed up as it moves, but instead force it to remain consistent. Next, let the ball speed up with each pass as it grows in intensity. Out of these two methods, which do you prefer? Which feels stronger?

Place a sigil inside of the blue fireball and then, instead of releasing it so that it encompasses you, send it into an item like a candle or a poppet to charge the item for spell work. This practice can help in many ways, and we will revisit it later.

Your Compass

I mentioned earlier in this chapter that the points on the compass don't always line up to where their correspondent energies lie. Sometimes we live with a lake in the east, a desert in the north, and mountains in the south, so going with the traditional model of directionality may not always be the best for you. When connecting to the magic of our planet and the power within it, it is absolutely essential that as witches we draw upon the powers of earth, air, fire, water, and spirit. These alchemical elements not only represent the power and frequencies found within the universe most known to us but are also significant pieces of our magical heritage. A seasoned witch likely will have gone through several rounds of training related to them, and though these aren't the only elements that we work with in the occult, our forebears have deeply rooted them in the craft. For many of us, we will no doubt be familiar with them in relation to the points on a compass.

Furthermore, let us not forget that there are six points, not four; we can't neglect above and below. These last two take our magic from being a two-dimensional work of art to a three-dimensional master-piece.

As a witch, we should always be looking for what works, what is practical, and what makes sense. When those things aren't obtainable, then we can move on to the less efficient means to make our magic manifest, but there is something to be said about simplicity. We want to make sure that the energies we are working with have as few obsta-cles to move through on their way to us, and, above all else, we want to be working with the powers and spirits that are local to us.

Drafting Your Compass

When it comes to directionality, I think it is most essential to orient the compass so that it works with you and these forces. To do this, you need to know the local terrain, which often means getting a map. First, think about the places associated with each element. Earth is often associated with mountains and hills; water with oceans, lakes, rivers, etc.; air with plains and fields (areas free of obstruction); and fire with deserts and dry places. Look on your map for these places around your area. In what direction is the most substantial body of water? The highest peak? The flattest land? The hottest valley?

Now, draw a compass and place the corresponding elements in the appropriate areas. If you run into an area with multiple elements pres-ent in a major way, like wetlands and mountains, then you will default to the most predominant element available. If you are in a historically dry place and water is not something readily available, then perhaps the direction to invoke it is above or below you, and it is acceptable for you to invoke multiple elements in the same direction. When all things are present, it won't matter where they came from. Use your critical thinking skills to place the most appropriate alchemical elemental correspondent in each direction.

When you perform your next elemental invocation, work with this specialized personal compass instead. In Sacred Fires each of us works with our own unique compass.

The Mysteries of the Genius Loci

I grew up in the wetlands of Appalachian Ohio. We experienced each of the four seasons in all their full glory. Tornadoes and torrential rain in the spring. Snowstorms that would blanket the landscape with so much white that you couldn't leave your house for days in the winter. Humid summers that made me think I was sprouting gills because the air was so thick. Those beautiful stormy autumns that brought a breathtaking array of golds, reds, oranges, and browns still sweetly haunt me to this day. We lived our lives by the weather and the seasons. We depended on the snow and rain to fill the reservoirs, swamps, and lakes, and to flood the river valley every year. As a witch, it was essential for me to harmonize with this yearly cycle and even to aid it along at times by working magic to bring rains during drought or to stop it when it was too much. My life and my magic there were deeply connected to the seasonal shifts I experienced.

Then one day I moved to the northeasternmost tip of the San Francisco Bay Area, and all that changed. Despite the name, the SF Bay Area isn't actually a place known for its abundant fresh water, and where I ended up was about two hours from the ocean. The first few years here, there were what felt like maybe three seasons. Winter and spring ran into each other, summer was king, and autumn was incredibly short. When we went through a record-breaking drought for several years, the seasonal shifts felt even less drastic: summer raged on for most of the year, and there was a bit of an autumn-like winter that brought basically no rain. This went on and on for years, and I started to lose my grip on the shifts that our planet underwent. The already blurry lines became riddled with smudge marks, and the animal inside me became very disoriented. I grew up depending on rain, playing in it, swimming in lakes and flooded streams; to be somewhere where there was almost no fresh water and basically no rain for several years was a nightmare!

I learned a valuable lesson because of this; the seasons are the planet's natural breathing cycle, and each part of our planet experiences them differently. This cycle regulates the flow of life and death within an area, and the primal elements of ourselves are directly connected to this flow. Our ancestors were attuned to it, lived with it, and raised crops according to it, so knowing it is just as much a part of us as anything else. Regardless of the intensity of the season, we still must acknowledge the effects of the shifts and work with the natural flow of life and death. Sometimes this is going to be easy, but other times this is going to be hard.

What I neglected to do when I moved here was make a connection with the spirits in the area. In the craft we refer to this type of spirit as "genius loci" or "local spirit," and had I connected with them upon arrival, I likely would have been able to withstand the transition with much more grace. I also would have been able to deal with the several years' long drought, which is something that happens here every decade or so. I may have been new, but the genius loci have been here since the mountains formed and the valleys settled. I also have a sneaking suspicion that the weather magic I continued to do during the drought would have been more successful had I consulted them.

The spirits in the Bay Area are much different from the ones where I come from originally. The energies here feel much different in general, but this is most visible in the spirit population. Upon visiting me here, my longtime friend from Ohio said that the difference in energy was that Ohio felt more earth and fire and the California coast felt more like air and water. This really stuck with me even at a cultural level.

Ohio is known for its agriculture and steel work; my part of California is most known for Silicon Valley and being a port city. The elements I grew up learning to thrive within were not the dominant frequencies here, and not knowing that put me at a disadvantage. I decided to change that and developed a little system to help start the process of harmonizing with the local spirits.

Contacting the Genius Loci

The genius loci of your particular area can be any number of spirit types. The term doesn't apply to a sub-genus of spirits, merely the radius in which those spirits are found. It actually can be a bit difficult to find and work with them, especially if you don't know where to look. There are four ways I recommend starting your search.

1. **Look up local history and local legends.** No matter where you live in the civilized world, someone has stepped foot there before you, and every area has its own folklore, myths, legends, and history. Where I grew up, in addition to the fae spirits who lived in the swamps, knolls, and forests, we also had the spirits of American First Nations peoples as there was once a vast group of people there known as the Mound Builders, the spirits of deceased soldiers from the French, Indian, and Civil Wars, and—most memorable for me—the spirits of escaped slaves who traveled the Underground Railroad, as there were multiple locations within the area that were known stops. Each spirit had its own work for me, and each one that I got to work with bestowed upon me its own blessing.

    There were also spirits that I learned I should stay away from because of the history. I learned not to work with the ghosts of Utopia, Ohio, who suffered a great tragedy at the hands of a severe flood, but instead to honor the trek they embarked upon nightly. I learned not to work with the spirits in the woods at Indian Lake because they didn't care much for white people, and I learned that the spirits of the coal mines in Athens, Ohio, were more likely to come out in the fall than any other season, so doing ritual there meant changing locations during those four months.

I learned the ebb and flow of spirits—which ones stayed year-round, which ones floated in and out with the changing seasons—and I learned which ones were friendly and who to stay away from. The majority of the need-to-know information is already out there; you just need to look for it.

Before we move on, I want to stress the absolute importance of having a relationship with the spirits and current descendants of the Native and indigenous cultures of the area you live in. In my experience as an American witch living on land that once belonged to another people, I cannot be settled and indeed plugged in unless I am living in harmony with the First Nations people and their beliefs. For me, this takes the form of providing monetary support to Native tribal craft persons, meeting and maintaining a relationship with tribal elders and other members of their community and providing support when needed and I am able, and lastly, using my privilege (yes, I said it!) to shed light on issues that affect the preservation and continuation of Native cultural heritage.

2. **Look for natural or historic landmarks and crossroads** such as parks, old buildings, cemeteries, battlefields, plateaus, forests, public transit lines, etc. In general, spirits like to hang out where they won't be disturbed, so you may have to take a hike to get to them, but they are always there. If you live in an urban setting, your local spirits are going to be indigenous to not only your city and its surrounding landscape but to individual blocks and neighborhoods, too. Anywhere that is remote and relatively undisturbed is likely to house genius loci, but places like subway stations and main streets also attract their own kind of genius

loci. Here in California I work with the spirits of the mountain and the bay as well as the spirits of the BART train.

3. **Look for ley lines and other lines of energy.** You will always find spirits like the fae and the dead following ley lines, so if you can find these energy lines, they are hotbeds for activity, especially where they intersect. These areas are usually places where local legends occur, so start there, but some areas also have organizations who have already mapped them out. Dowsing with a pendulum or rods is useful when discerning them, as well as muscle testing and of course following the natural terrain of surrounding geography and looking for areas with drastic change, such as where the forest meets a desert. Once you find them, follow them, and use your witch power to reach out and find where the spirits rest.

   In addition, follow the power lines. Spirits are also attracted to energy, so they can usually be found wherever there is a lot of easily convertible power. Power lines, electrical boxes, and electrical towers are basically buffets for some spirits, so if you can safely get close, you will likely run into some genius loci.

4. **Notice the local wildlife and its patterns.** Lastly, an often overlooked method of making contact with genius loci is to study the animal and plant life of your area as well as any folk or medicinal lore related to them. The local spirit population is 100 percent connected to the local animal and plant life, so the more familiar you are with them, the better. A butterfly or a hummingbird that is out of season could bring a message. Finding an early bloom on an apple tree could signal an omenic transmission. You wouldn't know, though, if you weren't familiar with the area. Knowing when local plants come into season and timing magic to coordinate with that energy can be quite powerful if done right. Timing protection spells to coincide with a local deer rut

can add beneficial stag juju to the working. There are so many allies waiting for you; you just have to pay attention and do right by them.

The genius loci are just as important to the effectiveness of our power as the elements are. We need them not just to be allies in our magic, but to be mediators between ourselves and the natural forces within the land. If we can develop a relationship with them, then we are more likely to be informed about spiritual matters impacting the area and are likely to gain access to information about the environment we live in.

Working with the Genius Loci

After we orient ourselves by discerning our own compass, we need to reach out to these genius loci and build a bridge of cooperation and understanding with them. As I said in the beginning, these spirits can be any type of spirit, so be careful and be sure to proceed with caution and respect. You may find that they have a lot to teach you, even things that are not related at all to the local environment.

There are many ways to ritually connect with the genius loci, the most appropriate being entirely dependent on the type of spirit they are. For guidance on working with these specific types, you should check out my previous book. There is, however, a general and direct way of making contact with them by way of an introduction and an offering.

Once you know what genius loci you want to contact, select an offering that would be most appropriate for them. For spirits such as fae, offerings of milk and honey usually go over very well. For the dead, offerings of milk, wine, and bread will do the trick. For spirits such as demons, an offering of candy, tobacco, or spicy alcohol will get their attention. Keep in mind that whatever you leave out as an offering will likely get picked up by animals or even people, so you should always have a designated offering spot, and in the case of things like candy, a place to bury it. Place your offering in a circle of local stones and recite the following prayer.

> *I beseech you, (insert name of spirit here), and align my will to your*
>   *own.*
> *I make this offering of (insert your offering here) to you in hopes*
>   *that you would receive it well.*
> *This is not pity or a handout, a means to trick or to harm you.*
> *This offering is a token of my awareness and appreciation; though*
>   *it may not be as mighty as you, I pray that you receive it still.*
> *Know that I see your greatness, I feel your presence, and I hear your*
>   *whispers on the wind.*
> *Know that I am an ally, a kindred flame, and another spirit who*
>   *lives in this place, not just another human who ignores you and*
>   *takes advantage of this place.*
> *I make this offering to you and ask that you receive it well. May you*
>   *see this as an act of peace and friendship. Blessed be.*

The Secret Mysteries of Now

As occultists, we tend to thrive on the philosophical. We write tomes about how ritual intersects psychology and about the connections between primitive peoples and modern-day magic and do our very best to wrap our minds around science and spiritual experience. Modern witchcraft is full of philosophy and anthropology, full of all the mental trappings required for someone to spend their entire life exploring, but where we are headed requires us to let go of all this. The cost of admission for this particular ride is that we do our very best to release the burdens on the mind as much as possible and allow the primitive and bestial aspects of our being to take control for a while.

When we allow our primal souls to drive the car for a while, we are given glimpses into aspects of our environment that are otherwise undetectable. At this stage in the game, I am going to assume that you are a witch who is versed enough in the fundamentals to understand the basics of meditation, brain waves, and all of the other stuff required to get your ego on board with the broader operations of witchcraft. You can comprehend all of it academically, you can understand the concepts behind the things I am about to explain, but for you to have the experience I hope you have, you don't need any of the philosophy or psychology.

Lifting the Veil

What *is* required of you now, as a first step in allowing that bestial part of you to take the wheel, is that you show up entirely to this moment. I need you to stop whatever it is that you are doing, take a deep breath, and release anything that is on your mind. Just be here with me, be here with your breath, and be present with your awareness.

Focus on the way your body feels as you read this. Are you comfortable and free of aggravation? How do your muscles feel right now? Your back? Scan your body; start with your feet and work your way up to the top of your head. Take a moment and inventory the sensations you experience when you really focus on the different parts of your physical body. How are they different? How are they similar? Which parts of your body draw more of your attention than others?

Take a few deep breaths. Each time you exhale, expand your consciousness so that it is allowed to perceive each of these various sensations at once. Right here, right now, strive to achieve a moment of absolute physical awareness. If you are anything like me, this may take a few attempts, but don't give up. If this is too difficult, then try to imagine what it would feel like if you were to have a moment of absolute physical awareness.

Continue to take deep breaths, but this time as you exhale allow your consciousness to slip from your body, slowly pouring out of that moment of absolute physical awareness and into the air around you. As you breathe in, let the quintessence that fills the air fill you, and as you exhale, let that same quintessence wash your awareness out into space.

Extend that awareness outward in all directions until it fills the space around you. Take a moment, continuing to breathe deeply and fully, and do another inventory. How does it feel to touch the walls or the boundaries of your space? What part of the space draws your attention the most?

After you have taken inventory, allow your consciousness to slowly settle back into your body. Over the next several breaths, work to release this awareness and return to a normal, open, and active state of mind.

· · · · · · · · ·

One of the most important traits to have as a witch is flexibility. When we build a practice that allows us to be flexible, we can be better prepared to roll with the punches and make the absolute most of what is presented to us. In addition to creating the mindset required for contact with the quintessential, we also must focus on allowing ourselves to build the bridges necessary between ourselves and what is quintessent. The best way to do this is to orient ourselves with our surroundings, partner with the genius loci, and exist one hundred percent in the moment.

Apply these practices, take your time, don't rush them, but do make sure to do them. These are cornerstones of the witch's art that are often overlooked and taken for granted but must be understood and applied to have a healthy and vibrant witchcraft practice.

Meditating on the topics presented here in this chapter, answer the following questions in your journal:

1. How do you find energy moves differently for you than it does for others in your life?

2. Draw a map or diagram of the directional flow of energy in your environment and within your body. How do these two flows of energy relate?

3. Have you met with the genius loci of your area? If so, who are they, and what was it they wanted to share with you? Do you know how to locate them again?

4. What are some of the things that keep you from being able to be in the moment, and what can you do to keep them from distracting you?

Chapter Four

The Eye and the Dream

*It is the mark of the mind untrained to take its own processes as
valid for all men, and its own judgments for absolute truth.*

——

Aleister Crowley

I listened to every word that came out of her mouth as if it were the only thing that could give me life. There were five of us huddled around her feet, ears perked and poised like schoolchildren at story time. She had a strange demeanor—as if she was half in our world and half in another; present in body but not entirely in mind. I felt as though she were speaking only to me—we all did—but she had this way of connecting us to something that was just beyond our usual grasp. It was a wisdom, a power, an influence that took us over and filled us with awe.

Behind her I could sense spirits moving in the incense smoke, indicating conversations she was having that we would not be privy to.

The room was full of altars and candles, every wall a mural of photos and paintings, each corner the home of statues and offerings. Fetishes and talismans hung from the ceiling. She sat on an antique wooden chair that was carved with ornate detail and resembled a throne. She was the queen of this place, and all who entered knew it.

As we stepped out of the Voodoo Queen's temple, we all felt a cold snap of reality like a crashing tsunami. The sun hit our faces and we each looked at one another with confusion, as if waking up from some shared psychedelic trip.

"How long were we in there?" my friend asked.

"About forty minutes or so. It feels like we were there for hours, though," I responded as I glanced at my watch.

"We were only in there for forty minutes?" another friend asked. "That must have been some spell we were under!"

"Yeah, we were definitely taken away by the spirits, and so was she! She was a fascinating person to be around," my partner said.

That was an understatement; the Voodoo Queen was intense and majestic, exuding spiritual power from every pore. "It was like she was in her own dream and we stepped into it for a minute," I replied, nodding in agreement. "She is one powerful witch!"

As we discuss taking our witchcraft more in-depth, we should also consider the importance of creating a practice that allows us to do so. My experience with the Voodoo Queen left me with the realization that I wasn't doing all I could be to take my work further. My psychic abilities and my spiritual practices were not as integrated as I had seen hers be, and I quickly realized that I was functioning at half capacity. She had created a way of life that made it easy for her to live her truth as a mediator for the spirit world, and I needed to find a way to do the same. In the last chapter we discussed practical steps and ways of doing this. In this chapter we are going to discuss the practices that will help us do this in our world as well as within others.

My search for better witchcraft led me to two unique practices that totally changed my spirituality forever. They are called the witch's eye and the witch's dream, and both of them lay the foundation for the development of a transcendental practice deeply rooted in your personal gnosis. A transcendental practice is one that places your connection to the spiritual or nonphysical realm at the forefront of your understanding of life. For me, this was groundbreaking; it shattered my notions of what being spiritually connected meant. What we discuss here will open the door not just for our work with the witch's sabbat that will come later, but also for our work exploring the soul and its connection to God Herself in part 2.

As separate studies, these three parts can monumentally reshape your practice, but combined they set the stage for the most profound mysteries I believe we can explore in the craft.

The Witch's Eye

The witch's eye (or witch eye) is a term used to define the psychic abilities that come with witch power. Your extrasensory perceptions, regardless of what they might be, give you the ability to perceive or "see" into the hidden world. The witch eye comes with our witch power, and as I discussed in *The Witch's Book of Power*, each of us is likely to possess multiple psychic skill sets as a result.[3] Generally, we use these skills as an extension of our power, but rarely do we get the chance to integrate them into our personal spiritual development beyond learning to control them to some degree. In my experience, however, learning to control them had not resulted in those psychic abilities serving a higher purpose early on in my work. Sure, I could use them to help and serve others, and that was nice enough, but they weren't really taking my witchcraft anywhere. Working with the model of the witch eye, however, changed all that.

---

3   Hunter, *The Witch's Book of Power*, 17.

To possess the witch eye means that your psychic abilities are in alignment with your work as a witch. It comes from having those psychic abilities rooted in your personal gnosis and using them to construct its paradigm. It may seem simple, but when our psychic abilities aren't allowed to serve us, they often take on a life of their own. I believe that many witches who struggle with their psychic abilities usually do so because they are not giving purpose to them and have adopted untrained psychism into their gnosis. Not all of us come equipped to be expert-level psychics, and some of us have gifts that would be difficult to use with other people, but by giving our psychic abilities a purpose and a direction, no matter what they are or what combination of them you might possess, we are ensuring that they will always be working for us, whether or not they are working for others. This keeps them as supportive aspects of our gnosis rather than destructive ones.

The other benefit from this is that by integrating our psychic abilities into our spiritual practices, we are given the ability to continually develop them with the aid of spiritual forces like those I discussed in *The Witch's Book of Spirits* and even the Creator Spirit itself.

The witch eye must be opened for this to happen. By this, I mean that we must actually awaken and align our psychic abilities to our cause. The following ritual to open the witch's eye is both an activation and a baptism of sorts that rededicates your psychic abilities to your path.

Opening the Witch's Eye
You will need:
- White or black candles—one or three is appropriate; you need an odd number of candles. We also want to be able to see but at the same time have no backlighting.

- A compact mirror—the kind with two mirrors on the inside. Make sure that no one has recently looked into it, including you. If they have, you will need to perform a cleansing on the mirror.

Find yourself seated in the darkness, the candle(s) lit before you and the compact at your side. Activate your witch power by aligning your souls and reaching out with your senses as a white fire blazes around you. Call upon your own guides and allies, as well as Aradia, the tutelary spirit of the witch power, and ask her to be here as you cross the threshold and open your witch eye. Know that thousands of witches before you have done something similar and that you are not alone. Take a moment to feel your spirit allies and draw your entire focus to this moment.

Open the compact, pass the mirrored surface over the candle flame, and say the following incantation:

By this fire a sacred blessing, a gift from witches long ago.
To see the eye and have the sight, power to feed and grow.
Open my mind, open my eye, let me see the one.
This is my right, this is my power, it cannot be undone.

Bend the mirror so that it is at about a 160- to 170-degree angle and place it directly in front of your eyes. Allow your eyes to focus and then slowly move the compact away from your face about three to four inches. If done right, what you should see is that a third eye will be brought into focus. Stare directly into that eye, so much so that you find yourself looking through that eye and into your very soul.

Chant:

Between two worlds the eye of I, transfixed within my gaze.
Between two worlds the eye of I, free from fog and haze.

Stare into the compact mirror and chant in this way until you feel a shift in the air around you. When you feel the energy settle, conclude by saying:

Blessed be this opened eye, holy in her name.
Blessed be this opened eye, my path, and sight the same!

Keep the compact wrapped in black fabric, and store it somewhere where it will be undisturbed by anyone other than yourself.

The Witch's Dream

The witch's dream is not unlike shamanic reality, but it does differ in some ways. The idea is that when we are in the right state of being, we enter a type of consciousness (trance) where symbolism and spiritual experience come together as one. We see and communicate with spirits, receive visions of the future, even explore some of our deepest internal recesses while in this state of mind. The only problem is that it is not always accessible, and this is where the witch's dream diverges from shamanic reality. The witch's dream is something that we create and can learn to access at any time. As a construct, it is not unlike a "mind palace," a place that you visit in your mind to store and house information or to have a particular experience. Our goal within the witch's dream isn't to construct something that we just go and visit from time to time, but a place that we are always connected to and are at least partially aware of at all times.

It isn't exactly as simple as that, but it also doesn't need to be more complicated. Think of it as a place you can visit that is solely dedicated to your witch power and sculpted by your gnosis. You can build this place and tune into it like any other energy, and its uses are endless. It will look different for each of us, and it will ultimately be one of the most unique things about your craft because of its connection to gnosis. For me, it looks like an ordinary living room in a regular one-story house in suburbia. For others, it looks like a castle in the sky or a fortress in the ground. What matters is that this place becomes the staging ground for your shamanic and psychic interactions—a place that represents the part of you that is forever connected to life on the astral plane.

Through the witch's eye, we construct and engage the witch's dream. What we see as a result of our psychic and spiritual interactions is reflected in the witch's dream. Like all good mysteries, the dream will continue to reveal more and more, leading us to pockets of truth that rest within quintessence. It isn't enough to visit the dream from time to time or just once a month when the moon is full; we must find a way to anchor ourselves in the dream full time so that we can better engage quintessence. Every day we have to be tuned in to the spirits we work with, the gods we have aligned ourselves with, and the subtle energies of the witch's tree.

Personal gnosis and the witch's dream are essentially the same things. As is the case with the witch eye, the witch's dream is a dedicated, aligned, and intentional variation of personal gnosis. We all have personal gnosis, but the witch's dream is personal gnosis with witch power. This means that our gnosis is capable of not only constructing our reality, but constructing a reality on other planes as well as within someone else's gnosis. This is the part of the witch power that plugs into the universe and allows us access to not only see the unseen, but to touch it as well.

In my previous work, I have mentioned the concept of setting presets along the psychic radio dial. These presets can help us jump to a frequency with ease, escaping the need to scan for the right station and minimizing the potential of accidentally tuning in to the wrong one. To effectively anchor the dream, we have to discover the presets that automatically come with our witch power; our psychic abilities, quintessential heritage,[4] and other forces that are uniquely influential as to how our power manifests (like personal astrology). The witch's dream is the nexus where all of these presets join together to produce beautiful music.

---

4 Referring to familial magic and ties that would automatically bring about the witch power, such as being the descendant of a witch.

To understand the nuts and bolts of the dream, you have to think of it as a symphony. Each preset is an instrument, and you are the conductor. Each instrument is capable of evoking a unique response from its listener. A trumpet can signal the entrance of a regal grand waltz or the somber memento mori of "Taps"; a violin can be the soft pad that lightens the mood or a melodic driving vehicle; the timpani can build suspense or carry a beat. When these instruments are brought together and given an arrangement of music, then something that is greater than the sum of its parts is created. In this way, we as witches bring the components of our craft together and create the dream.

For me, it is essential to understand that even though these instruments are vastly different in comparison, from design to sound, somehow when they are given the proper instruction they can come together to do incredible things. That being said, any band geek can tell you that when a bunch of musicians gets together and warms up, it isn't exactly a pleasant sound. Each instrument playing its own thing and there's no synchronicity in the whole room; the sound can be quite overwhelming and unpleasant. To get that special magic, we have to give members of the orchestra a piece of music and instruct them on how to play together. In this way, we as conductors must take up the baton and guide the pieces of our dream to work in tandem in order to produce the sort of environment where the quiescent can be influenced. This can only happen through discipline. Without it, our witch's dream will be more like a seventh-grade band room at the start of practice and less like that symphonic orchestra. For those of us who take magic seriously and want to see what we are capable of as witches, we have to take the role of conductor seriously.

To do this, we have to make sure we are doing the prep work necessary; we have to remove the residue of past experience and what we have taken for granted so that we can see clearly through the witch's eye. Luckily, in the last two chapters we have already been working on the prep work, so if you have been applying the methods so far, this next exercise should be a breeze.

The first step in navigating the dream is to figure out what your presets are and then, if needed, install some more! You should have a thorough understanding of your strengths and weaknesses as a person, including those parts of you that are spiritual and psychological. Let's take a quick look at a few advantages and weaknesses we should be aware of before we start to map out the dreamscape.

Your Mental State

It is critical to be of sound mind and to have the ability to critically think within the dream. Any aspect of your life, be it stress, anxiety, or mental illness, can skew the way you perceive the dream. I know a lot of authors won't touch this, but I think it is an important thing to discuss because aspects of the dream will be entirely fantastical, mental creations meant to drive you deeper into the spirit world. It is barely safe for someone who suffers from depression to perform this magic, let alone someone with schizophrenia or paranoid delusions.

Being in a sound state of mind will keep you in the driver's seat and give you the single most important strength of all: the ability to create a dream, not a nightmare. If you are one of the millions of people who have been diagnosed with any type of mental disorder, there is no shame in that, nor does it have to be a handicap when practicing the craft. Stay medicated, stay in touch with your doctors and support team, and continue to thrive. You can be a witch who explores this more in-depth work and still be on medication, but it's likely this work will eat you alive if you aren't on your medication. I have been witness to more than one case of individuals who chose to be off their medications who enter the dream and never come back. It is a terrifying thing to watch. We want to be the conductors of the symphony, not the audience.

How strong do you feel mentally? Do you have stress or anxiety? If so, how does that affect your ability to do magic? Do you suffer from other instabilities that might interfere with your ability to practice magic effectively? If so, how do you plan to practice the aspects of the craft that go deeper and bring into question the very nature of reality? Is that a safe thing for you to experience?

Who Your Allies Really Are

The other must-know strength is who has your back in the spirit world and who will be informing you while you are there. The dream will no doubt be connected to the spirit world; it is essentially the platform where your world and theirs collide. It is important to know who your spirit guides and/or familiar spirits are and have a well-developed relationship with them, as well as the gods you serve. In my tradition we serve the Star Goddess, whom we see as the creator spirit; the Queen of Witches, whom we refer to as Diana; and her concomitant Dianus, the King of Witches. We also work with several of the great witch chieftains and permutations of the witch power, such as Aradia, Hecate, Macha, Janus, and Lucifer, to name a few. Our relationship to them informs the unfolding of the dream and beckons us to explore different parts of the map, inspiring us to devote entire decades of our lives in dedication to harmonizing with their unique frequencies.

We recognize that our spirit allies are more than presets, but when we are talking about anchors within the dream, they possess their own strain of gravity, prompting us to see the dream through a particular lens. Our allies are like a source of news, and each news outlet has its own way of spinning a story. Ultimately, it will be the spirits that shape our experience within the dream, so knowing and having an intimate relationship with a few friends and contacts will only benefit you in the long run.

Consider these three points:

1. Up to this point, what allies have presented themselves to you as reliable and trustworthy?

2. Do you feel confident in your ability to work with spirits in general? If not, what steps will you take to better acquaint yourself with the practices and methods related to them?

3. Do you feel you have room to actively pursue a relationship with a spirit at this time in your life?

Let's say you have a hard time staying grounded or you have difficulty making out what a spirit is trying to express to you. This is where adding a few instruments comes in handy. Any deficit that you feel you have energetically can be adjusted through some sort of energy work or energetic interference. Working with crystals, herbal allies, and different meditation techniques are all excellent tools to have in your arsenal, but for them to actually be a tool you can use, you have to be acquainted with how they work. Take a look at those three points I made; if any of them made you perceive an aspect of personal weakness, then work with these tools to alter the way those things manifest in your life. If you find that one of those areas needs some love, then give it some love!

The Mundane Trappings of Living the Dream

In addition to a few key aspects of yourself that must be understood to have a healthy and fruitful relationship to the witch's dream, we also must take steps in the day-to-day to ensure that we are setting ourselves and our dream up for success. Living the dream can be difficult, but if you follow these pointers, it should be a little easier to merge the worlds and watch the dream unfold before your eyes. These mundane and straightforward things might seem like trappings, but they are vital to how you live in the dream.

Believe in yourself unconditionally. This is essential to life within the witch's dream. To believe in yourself is to put fuel in the tank, so to speak. It may be a weird reference, but in Peter Pan, the children must recite "I do, I do, I *do* believe in fairies!" over and over to give life to the fallen Tink. In this way, we too must believe in fairies and spirits and ancient beings just as much as we believe in ourselves. Without belief in your ability to perceive the other worlds and the inhabitants that reside in them, you cannot tune in to them, just like without confidence in your godhood, you cannot be a god.

You must take "perfect love and perfect trust" to the next level. To live within the dream and take from the wells of creation, we must surrender to the fluid nature of quintessence. We have to be like the root that grows around the stone, the light that bends in the prism, the water that follows the path of least resistance, and the winds that diverge in the meadow. To be this malleable, we must be many things at once, and we must be open to many experiences at once. We must be both in love with quintessence while simultaneously trusting enough in ourselves (and it) to keep the relationship beneficial and the dream active.

To make the dream real, you must allow it to be real. Stay out of your own way and keep yourself from being bogged down with self-sabotaging resistance by regularly performing acts of magic, ritual, and cleansing. This will be echoed in the next chapter, but I urge you to not wait for the "right moment"—when in the dream, all moments are the right moment. Engage your problems with magic and find ways to keep magic as an essential aspect of your day.

The witch's dream must be seen as a state of mind as well as a plane of being. It is essentially a pocket plane— one suspended in the etheric, right within the realms of preternatural perception but outside those of normal if we were to get technical. If we remain anchored in the dream, then a piece of us will always stay suspended within another world, and we can access it like any other preset.

Establish your code. Create methods of discernment for navigating the hedge and the dream. Have a personal set of omens or signs that when seen in the wild (whether in the dream or outside of it) inform your experience and let you know when it is time to pay attention to the dream and tune in. For me, this is seeing a hummingbird, a symbol from the hallowed plane, or seeing a floating cottonwood seed, which signals a message from the angelic realms. These are kind of like personal superstitions that keep you queued into what is happening in dream and are going to be totally unique between you and the spirit world. Each of us has a unique code, some more extensive than others, but regardless of how well established, the code is a token of your relationship to the spirit world and should be cherished. Throughout this section we will address ways of spotting this connection and how to plug into the coding, but for now think of ways you already do this instinctively.

The witch's dream is a sacred space. Not unlike the enchanted Isle of Avalon that the sorceress Morgan Le Fey found herself visiting for the first time, the dream is full of amazing secrets that are both relics of a time past as well as those that are of newer discovery. We must remember that this place is a secret all unto itself, one that must be treated as sacred and worthy of our time and energy. It is so sacred, in fact, that it can only ever be known by you.

Don't overcomplicate the witch's dream. As complicated as it all can look on paper, don't get spooked and overcomplicate the transcendental nature of the dream. Just tune in to the dream, live within the dream, and continue to expand its borders as you flush out your personal gnosis surrounding quintessence. The spirits and planes you interact with there are extensions of your own witch power and manifestations from the quintessential; they are pieces of the dream but not the dream themselves.

Waypoints and Relics

The witch's dream is made up of several interchangeable parts, and like our thumbprint, no two dreams are alike. This doesn't mean that we don't have a lot of overlap in our dreams as a collective; however, our dreams rub off on one another like cooties. The minute we start to share our thoughts about the craft with another, the second we begin to digest a book or step in a circle at a public ritual, our dream becomes tainted by someone else's. This isn't always a bad thing, but it does mean that we have the added burden of making sure that we only share the dream with those whom we feel are a good influence upon it. The dream is the birthplace of our secrets and should be protected at all cost. Even without the pieces that become personal, there are lots of pieces that simply become part of the dream because they are part of our culture.

The witches who have walked before us, those who forged a way through the oppressive overgrowth of spiritual oppression and survived to tell the tale, such as Doreen Valiente, Gerald Gardner, Victor Anderson, etc., are all excellent guides within the dream. Our contemporary craft is loaded with their influences. Their work is almost inescapable, and their discoveries along these frontiers helped to shape a commonly accepted map of witchcraft for the twenty-first century.

Relics are the stepping stones we first must follow to cross the stream and become excellent waypoints along our route. Waypoints within the witch's dream give us access to territories that have already been discovered. By traveling to these waypoints, we can access otherwise untouchable regions of the dream and we would be void of the basic tools required to engage quintessence.

These teachings come with spirit names, sacred rituals, special prayers, and much secrecy. Each tradition serves a different set of spirits, keeping the mysteries related to them close and preserving that spirit for all of time. For me, these secrets revealed a pathway toward many essential experiences in my life that allowed me to put pieces together I never thought were connected. I have found that those who have been fortunate enough to join a tradition and have a positive experience can attest to a similar phenomenon. While this isn't an option for everyone, those interested in the secrets of the witch's dream need not look too far, as the clues are spelled out plainly in any number of volumes on the craft.

Symbols and Power

When your spirituality or religious practice is steeped in symbolism, you must wonder what all the fuss is about. In the same way that waypoints and relics help us hone in on the witch's dream, symbols and sigils help us to navigate specific aspects of the dream and anchor them into our waking reality. The idea is that if we can see a symbol in the witch's dream and then see it in our waking life, thanks to some special dynamics (which we will discuss in the following chapter), any energy directed toward the symbol within the witch's dream will then be present in the same symbol on the physical plane.

As above, so below; what we do on the other planes shall be done on our own.

The agents within the witch's dream, those spirits and energies that reach out and communicate to us through its field of perception, will do so most commonly through symbolism. Instead of telling you to stop, they might show you a big red truck. Instead of telling you to start a family, they may just show you a house. And sometimes it gets way more complicated. Instead of telling you what type of spell would be best to resolve an issue, they may just show you a sigil from some book you read once or they may leave a tool for you in the dreamscape, and you don't know if it's something of more profound symbolism or precisely what it looks like. Sometimes it's hard to know when a hammer is just a hammer and not a rocket launcher.

Part of working within the realm of the witch's dream involves the creation of your own code so that you can avoid unneeded confusion. Indeed, this will be perhaps the most valuable of your secrets, as this code is the key that unlocks the hidden language between the dream and the physical plane. Later, this same symbolism will be used and expanded upon when we go deeper into the witch's dream and do the dreamwork that is required to take us to the witch's sabbat.

Some witches use an extensive code, others a simpler code, but you can't go far in the craft without finding the potency of symbols and other languages of the dream. My teachers were adamant that I learned Theban fluently and was able to transcribe it into English at a glance. Many witches I know carry this tradition and only write in Theban script when writing in their Book of Shadows or on spell paper. Nowadays, I mostly use Theban to write messages to spirits or for the occasionally written spell that I really want to be anchored. Theban is known the world over as the witch's script and has been used by our kind for quite some time. It is highly popular among witches, and as you could imagine it is a very charged script and thus is quite useful.

In the beginning it is necessary to start off simple and over time slowly allow yourself to develop your code. I recommend starting off using bits of code that already exist out in the wild and elaborating upon them and their use. For instance, magical alphabets like Elder Futhark and Theban (which I just mentioned) make an excellent starting point for the work of programming your code. They aren't typically something that you see out in the world, so when you do see them, they will be recognized as a magical language and tune you in to the witch's dream.

I found working with the Elder Futhark system to be particularly compelling because there was a vocal component to it. It is both a language and a divination system that is believed to have been gifted to us by the god Odin himself. In addition to the subtle and divinatory meaning of each glyph, each is its own sort of spell, and you can invoke the presence of that energy by toning or singing its name; this process is known as *galdring*. I have found myself haunted by their power for days after an intense galdring session, which gives them a little something extra when connecting the worlds.

To this end, I have also had much luck in working with the Greek alphabet and its oracular component. What makes the Greek alphabet just as exciting is that it is perhaps the oldest living system of divination and has an extensive history of evidence to support its use. This means that tapping into the energy within each of the letters is actually quite easy. I invite you to search out these alphabets and include them in your witchcraft if you haven't already.

Eventually, however, you might want to take it to the next step and create a script that is all your own. The easiest way to do this is to work with what we refer to as sigils, which are essentially compounded words or phrases that have been condensed into one symbol. That symbol can then be used in your code as a trigger or conduit for magic.

Creating Sigils

Like the magical alphabets, sigils can be used as a type of magical language within the witch's dream. I personally find the application of sigils to be a bit easier than working with the alphabets alone, as sigils are symbols that we create and are loaded with the specific energy of whatever it is we might be working toward magically. Sometimes using a sigil like those in this book or creating your own to use in the witch's dream can reduce a lot of the searching and waiting. Like the nine flames we discussed in the second chapter, sigils are capable of representing thoughts, feelings, sensations, etc., much more than a letter or number typically can on their own.

There are some sigils that will be shown to you by the spirit world. Some sigils, however, you must forge and empower all your own. This comes in handy when you know you will be working with an energy long-term or even if you want to add an extra degree of focus to your intention. Truth be told, there isn't enough room in this book to give you a proper education on sigil magic, but you only need to know the basics and have a little creativity to do this successfully and apply it to your work in the witch's dream.

The following process can be applied to any word or phrase in the same manner. Use it to access a plane of being you want to visit, further propel a spell, attract spirits and allies to you, or even to draw specific types of energy to you in the witch's dream. For the sake of example, let's say we want our witch's dream to be connected to the witch's sabbat.

Step One: Working with the term WITCH'S SABBATH, remove all vowels, punctuation, and duplicate letters from the term. What we have left is WTCHSB.

Step Two: From the remaining letters, assemble the sigil by stacking each letter on top of one another or within each other, by arranging the letters in whatever pattern or shape you find the most pleasing, or by condensing the letters further.

To continue condensing, look for letters that appear within other letters and omit those as well. For instance, T is a letter that is hidden in the bottom portion of the letter H, and the letter C is hidden backwards within the letter B. With a little creativity, if you bend the top and bottom of the letter H, it becomes a B. B also contains the letter S in its shape. If the letter B were tilted on its side, it would also include a W. So, in this case, all of the letters that are found within our original set can be found in the letter B.

Step Three: Fluff it up. B on its own is something that we will see out in the world and is completely unavoidable, so it can't be a B. If we were to get a little creative, the letter B could easily take the shape of a lemniscus (∞). Therefore, we have condensed each of the original letters into one symbol that represents the witch's sabbat.

You can tweak your sigils in any way you want, as long as they contain each of the original components and the sigil makes sense to you. Feel free to add lines or embellishments, just make sure it is something that you can immediately identify. For this reason, I think it is usually better to stand on the simpler side of the fence, but to each their own!

After you have created your sigil, use it often. Part of what makes it work is that it immediately registers in your brain and becomes part of your language system. This is only going to effectively happen if you are using it on a regular basis. Even if the sigil represents something that you rarely work with, you still need to visit that sigil and reinforce its connection. Eventually you won't need to do this because the groundwork has already been laid, but in the beginning it is imperative that each sigil receive the appropriate amount of mental attention.

When I am installing a sigil or symbol of any kind for the purpose of becoming a part of my witch's dream, I take five minutes twice a day to sit and focus on the sigil and its energy each day for a week. Sometimes I break that into two weeks with five-minute sessions each day if I am busy or having difficulty following through.

As part of the witch's dream, symbolism is vital in understanding and commanding the energies we work with. Sometimes all we need to do in order to stand out in an interview is to weave a sigil for success into our aura, place a sigil for protection on the inside of the engine hood to avoid an unwanted accident, or draw a sigil for summoning your allies in the air when you feel spiritually vulnerable. As long as your sigils have power in your witch's dream, their influence can extend over anything they are attached to, including the other reaches of your personal gnosis that don't directly correspond to the witch power.

In the appendix you will find a collection of helpful sigils and symbols. Feel free to work with them and to add them to your practice.

Journal Topics

Meditating on the topics presented in this chapter, answer the following questions in your journal:

1. What was your experience like performing the witch's eye working at the beginning of the chapter? Did you see anything immediately or soon after? If so, what?

2. How do you perceive the witch's dream?

3. What are the blocks you perceive that exist between you and the witch's dream? What can you do to remove these blocks?

4. Do you naturally encounter the witch's dream? If so, what is it like to you?

Chapter Five

Programming the Dream and Awakening Gnosis

The general function of dreams is to try to restore our psychological balance by producing dream material that re-establishes, in a subtle way, the total psychic equilibrium.

———

Carl Jung, *Man and His Symbol*

Sometimes we want to work with symbolism outside of our own sigil work. For me, this comes in handy when identifying messages from specific guides and just about all of the gods I work with. The symbols we find ourselves using can come from anywhere and be just about anything: a crown, a crow, a lamp, a computer, a person, etc. I may be able to call upon the energies and allies I work with using a sigil, but that doesn't mean they will show up in the form of a sigil to get my attention! For instance, why would the spirit of stag show up as anything else other than a stag? Why would a god who has a particular affinity for a butterfly show up as anything other than a butterfly to get your attention? There very well might already be symbols associated with your personal spirits and the spirits you work with; knowing those is going to be essential when identifying the messenger and its authenticity.

By programming symbols into our dream, we will immediately know what they mean and what to look for because we wrote the code. For example, I use a nail to represent boundaries. When I see a nail in my witch's dream, I know that somehow my boundaries were crossed or are being crossed. In this way, I know that when I see an apple, it is the right time to move on to a big project; when I see a broken mirror, I know to end a relationship. These are symbols that I have programmed into my dream because they already have a specific meaning to me.

The process of programming these is not so different from programming sigils; it's all about mental investment. I do think, however, that programming these types of symbols into your dream requires less of an investment. If your god comes to you as a horse, you should be able to figure that out; there would be no need for you to program that awareness into you. Instead, you just need to clarify the terms of your communication.

If they are going to come to you as a horse, you should get the specifics: What color is it going to be? How big is it? What is it doing? This way you know if the horse you see while walking your dog is indeed a messenger from your horse god or if it is a total coincidence that you should run into a horse that day. Planning matters in these situations, so be sure to include a little extra strategy when you are bringing spiritual allies into your practice who will be part of your witch's dream.

Symbolism in the Witch's Dream
and the Common Code

Dreams are highly personal, so there is never a one-size-fits-all option when it comes to interpretation. Dream symbolism and shamanic symbolism, the kind that we use when engaging the witch's dream, are uniquely tied together and likely will be identical if not similar to each other for many of us. Unless you have a personal connection to the symbols listed here, you are likely to rely on background symbolism (the symbols we pick up via culture and society) and can use the common code established from background symbolism to interpret your dreams. Included in this section are those symbols that I have personally added to my own interpretations and come from years of having an active dream life. Your unique connection to a symbol should always override background symbolism.

Plants and Fungi

Plant allies appear to us in dreams and symbolize life force, growth, and spiritual pursuits. Depending on the type presented in your dreams, plants also represent food and other forms of prosperity such as wealth. To our most basic instincts, plant life is intrinsically connected to earth and its cycles. On the other hand, fungi represent the opposite, usually indicating otherworldly or extraterrestrial information. Both are seen as healing forces within dreams that bring sacred knowledge from, and even the need for a journey to, the other side of the hedge.

It is not uncommon for witches to dream of plant allies that they have made a bond with. Because of the fluid nature of communication in dreams, many witches find it easier to access and work with their plant allies while dreaming. My experience has been that when a plant appears to me in a dream, it usually indicates that I am in need of supplemental energy, the kind that my physical or etheric bodies cannot produce on their own. In addition to the interpretation listed here, it also might be a good idea for you to look up the herb's holistic properties. If the herb has holistic properties that could be beneficial, talk to your doctor and see if it is something that can be added to your regimen. If you dream of toxic or poisonous plants, that could indicate the need for purification work and/or shielding work on your behalf.

Common plants and fungi that appear in a witch's dream include:

General Meanings

Flower: A gift from the other side, a message hidden in plain sight, spiritual attraction, and new beginnings or remembrances.

Fruit: Sex and death, rebirth through initiation or deep mysteries (especially when accompanied by a snake), a contract with the spirit world. Rotten fruit indicates someone is going back on their word of a spiritual pact or vow.

Shrub: Being accompanied by spirits and other beings who watch over you. The veil between worlds and the witch power.

Tree: Spiritual teachers, generational knowledge passed through families or close groups of people, and the inheritance of spiritual information or power gained through study.

Vine: Protection and aggression in spiritual matters, forces moving in the background, and unseen allies both in this world and the others.

Specific Meanings

Apple: Children, childhood, and academic knowledge.

Ash: Secrets and hidden meanings.

Birch: Ghosts and familiar spirits. Crone and hag power/wisdom.

Cactus: Survival and defense. Someone is trying to take your resources.

Catnip/Catmint: Attraction, playfulness or experimentation, the need to change perspective.

Cedar/Fur: Ancient mysteries from spirit teachers are being revealed.

Cinnamon: Recent ancestors are reaching out to you.

Clover: Blessings and luck. Fairies or land spirits are on your side.

Cypress: Gods or significant spirits from another age are watching over you and have a hand in things.

Datura: Be careful not to be seduced by your impulses or misled because of them. Do a reading and look into the matters at hand before acting.

Ivy: Protection from spiritual harm. A safe place or trustworthy friend will soon come.

Lavender: Go back to the basics and call upon the fundamental forces to provide clarity. This could also indicate the overcomplication of a matter and the need for a relaxed approach.

Lily: Sex and relationships are essential right now even if you don't know it. Pay attention to what your body is saying to you. Avoid conflict.

Mandrake: You are being initiated by the spirits and are being led to new mysteries where your three souls can thrive doing the work they need. Look within for answers.

Mint/Spearmint/Camphor: Illness or bad energy are on their way. Act quick and fortify your mind, body, and spirit.

Mushrooms: Wisdom and answers can only be obtained through trance and meditation. Other-planar forces are at work at this time.

Oak: The time to act is now; listen to the spirits and strike while the iron is hot. Answers to the problems at hand can be found by studying the ancient past. This is a cycle that has repeated itself before.

Orchid: Travel or a traveler will bring inspiration. Psychic wisdom is being revealed.

Poison Ivy/Poison Sumac/Poison Oak: Pay attention to your actions and study every step before taking it. Things are not as they appear.

Pomegranate: Death and sex, contracts with the other side. A message is waiting for you from the other side.

Rose: Love and commitment, contracts and marriage. Past or future lovers are on their way to you.

Rosemary: Your grandparents are reaching out.

Rue: Goddess is calling; pick up the phone! Time to spend time at your altar. There is sacred knowledge waiting to be revealed about your destiny.

Sage: Your primal soul is not comfortable in your environment; it senses spiritual disturbance.

Thorn/Hawthorn: You are being psychically or spiritually provoked; protect yourself.

Wheat/Grain/Corn: Food or resources.

Willow: The dead are reaching out for contact. Someone from your past is on the way.

Animals, Insects, and Cryptids

When animals appear in our dreams, they are thought to be representatives of the primal soul and its fight for survival. Animals are often harbingers of wisdom from our physical and emotional selves and should be seen as messengers bringing important information forward regarding the current state of those selves. Animals also can bring forth information from other planes of being, especially if you spot that particular animal while traveling to that plane often. It is believed by some witches that the guardian spirits, or Grigori, often present themselves as animals when making contact with humans. Spirits and astral projections will also take the shape of animals, as we do when visiting the witch's sabbat, and can even take on the shape of cryptids and mythological creatures such as the hellhound, bigfoot, kraken, or thunderbird.

In shamanic cultures the connection between the practitioner and the animal kingdom is seen as a necessary skill and practice. The same can be said for those who practice traditional witchcraft, with the animal kingdom being of chief importance when connecting with the spirits of the land and their counterparts. Visitations from the animal kingdom come with directions, informing us of shifts within and around ourselves and endings and beginnings, and are seen as guides through wild terrain both within and around.

Common animals and cryptids that appear in a witch's dream include:

General Meanings

Bird: Direct messages from spirits, gods, or people.

PASSIVE: You are being comforted.

AGGRESSIVE: You are being warned.

Fish: Indicate wealth of some kind; something valuable.

PASSIVE: Something or someone is revealing a gift.

AGGRESSIVE: Something is threatening your livelihood.

Mammal: Nutriment and resources.

PASSIVE: A friend or ally will soon reveal themselves.

AGGRESSIVE: The time is now; do not hesitate to protect yourself.

Reptile: Trust and mistrust.

PASSIVE: Be wary of your surroundings and keep your guard up.

AGGRESSIVE: Your suspicions are being confirmed; proceed with caution.

Specific Meanings

Alligator/Crocodile: Hidden instincts and the unconscious/subconscious. Shadow work.

Bat: Rebirth and the potential of the unseen world. May also represent demons and demonic communication—divine for this.

Bear: Independence and the cycles of life. May indicate the need for protection.

Butterfly: Messages from the spirit world. Heralds a new wave of energy and focus.

Camel: Stress and the need to conserve your energy at this time.

Cat (House): Sex and feminine power; also suggestive of spell and magic work.

Caterpillar: You have undiscovered natural abilities that require discipline.

Dog: Your friends need you or you need a friend.

Donkey/Mule: You feel lost or confused or stressed. Take time to come up with a plan before proceeding.

Dove: Peace is on the way; keep the faith.

Elephant: Memories and memory; the need to look into the past for answers.

Goat: Stubbornness will get the best of you or your peers.

Hawk/Falcon: You have a message from a spirit guide or teacher that is being revealed along the journey.

Horse: You don't feel free or you are feeling stuck. Time to find a way out of a sticky situation.

Kangaroo: Your parents are calling out to you for attention or you should go to your parents for help.

Lamb: Sacrifice is needed to obtain enlightenment.

Leopard: It is crucial to remain unseen by others now and to hang back and watch as others reveal their spots.

Lion: You are being called to leadership. Focus and remain steadfast; others need you.

Mantis: A subtle but radical shift is underway. Pay attention to your surroundings.

Moth: The power for change is in your hands; you must choose how this change will manifest. To remain safe, stay in the shadows.

Mountain Lion/Snow Leopard: To discover the truth, you must turn inward for answers.

Mouse/Rats: Your resources are being threatened; someone is smearing your reputation.

Rabbit/Hare: Think fast and avoid detection. Now is the time to listen to all your senses.

Snake: The truth regarding an accepted lie is revealed. Initiation.

Shark: Your financial resources are at risk. Watch for bad deals.

Tiger: Discipline is the only way through the matter at hand. Be brave and stay focused on the task at hand.

Turtle/Tortoise: Things will move slower than expected, but it is better this way.

Wolf: You crave the accompaniment of others for a reason. Locate your pack and find the answers you seek.

Zebra: Things are shifting into balance at this time.

Cryptids and Mythological Creatures

Bigfoot/Sasquatch: You have misguided yourself or are misrepresenting yourself to others. Be aware of the lies you tell yourself.

Dragon: There is a fine line between passion and obsession, and you or someone close may be crossing it. Alternatively, dreaming of a dragon can suggest luck, the discovery of the hidden, and wealth. Divine for further interpretation if unsure.

Griffin: The changes happening in your life are filled with positive energy and potential. Use your mind as well as your might as you plot a course forward.

Hellhound: Your past mistakes and misdeeds that negatively affected others are coming to haunt you. Taking responsibility for your actions is the only way out. May also suggest a spirit contract has been broken on your end.

Kraken: The elemental world is making contact; divine for more information. Alternatively, the kraken suggests there is deeply hidden anger and mistrust that is violently making its way up to the surface.

Phoenix: It is time to embrace the powers of renewal and change that are present in your life. The old you is no more; it is time to discover what the new you is all about.

Sphinx: The mysteries within are complex as a puzzle. You require more experiential information to unlock and reveal the unseen.

Thunderbird: The gods of men are angry, and the spirit world is upset. The powers of creation are moving to correct the course.

Metals, Minerals, and Gemstones

Metals, minerals, and gemstones are seen as messengers from the deep earth and deep space. They represent our spiritual connection to the planet as well as the cosmos and bring information to us about our desires and hidden qualities. They also can be symbols of strength and resilience, representing the durability of specific situations, events, or traits. The key word with these materials is hidden, as the information they represent is rarely something easily obtained or found.

If these materials develop as a tool, then it is essential to investigate the meaning of that specific tool. For instance, if you dream of a silver spoon or a quartz hammer, it is as essential to know what that tool is used for as it is to know what it is made of. In the case of jewelry, such as an emerald necklace or gold earrings, generally, these things are seen as something that is either coveted or that makes a statement about status.

Common metals, minerals, and gemstones that appear in a witch's dream include:

Metals

Brass: Everything is not as it appears to be; proceed with caution. Alternatively, this can indicate that spirits related to high magic are reaching out.

Bronze: Something precious in your life requires more care, attention, and protection. It is important to reinvest in what you love and ward your home.

Copper: Health and security take center stage now, especially for yourself and those you love. This can also indicate a small financial windfall through simple means.

Gold: Success is at your fingertips. You have been blessed by the spirits for all your hard work. Don't give up now; the race is almost over!

Silver: Energy is inconstant at this time. You must rely on your intuition and have faith in your ability to make it through anything.

Steel: The time has come to more aggressively approach the matter at hand. Go to war against the forces that disempower you, and only accept victory.

Titanium: You are not prepared for the task at hand. Strengthen and fortify yourself before proceeding with the plan.

Minerals and Gemstones

Agate: You require balance of mind, body, and spirit at this time. Do not hesitate.

Amethyst: Your intuition and psychic senses are not clear at this time. You are receiving a message from a higher or greater power, but you are not able to receive it.

Citrine: Your energy body and aura are in need of purification and cleansing. Dreaming of citrine may also indicate an overabundant empathic force. Use your head, not your heart, at this time.

Diamond: You require fidelity from your allies and loved ones. Reinforce the bonds you feel matter the most at this time.

Emerald: There is an esoteric knowledge that is waiting for you to construct it. Put the pieces together one at a time and look at the big picture. All will be revealed once the many are brought together to make the whole.

Garnet: Primal connections are calling out. Talk to your ancestors; they have wisdom to share.

Granite: Stability is something of great importance now, and the spirit world is at your side helping to provide it. Check in with your foundations and reinforce those fundamental aspects of your life such as love, friendship, and the connections that are important to all of us.

Jasper: It is time for a little relaxation and downtime as you work toward nurturing yourself. If you don't take some time to love yourself, no one else will.

Lapis Lazuli: The Grigori are reaching out. Meditation will bring the calm you need to solve the puzzle and develop gnosis. Wisdom is obtained through introspection with the gods.

Lava/Magma: Your primal soul is draining while you work toward something new. It is okay; move through the tiredness and condition yourself to your surroundings. This won't last forever.

Limestone/River Rock: Memories from your past contain clues to your future. Pay attention to your intuition and wondering mind—they are leading you to inspired wisdom and epiphany.

Marble: You have a lot of work to do at this time, but the results will be magnanimous. Continue to build and sculpt; the power is in your hands.

Moonstone: Trust your intuition and the witch's dream; what you see there is real and just for you.

Opal: You have stumbled upon a hidden vein of magic and quintessence in your life. Tap into the forces that surround you to gain access and gnosis.

Pearl: Your innocence and light are essential at this time. Stand for what is right.

Pyrite: Not everything that looks precious is precious, and not everything that looks familiar is familiar. Take time to carefully survey those aspects of your life that you stopped paying attention to.

Quartz

CLEAR: You are in need of clarity and meditation before you can make the right decision.

SMOKEY: Your power is growing, but you must study it to learn what you are capable of.

ROSE: Emotions run high, and you seek validation from external sources when you should be looking inward.

Ruby: You are about to stumble upon something new and exciting. Keep your eyes peeled and respond swiftly to invitations of adventure.

Sand: You long for something that is missing but can't quite put your finger on it. Divination will yield answers.

Sapphire: You don't understand a situation with the depth required. Take time to review the facts and to see all sides.

Shungite: You are experiencing mental and spiritual interference from technology and media that is keeping you from being authentic. Disconnect so you can reconnect with what matters.

Tiger's Eye: You don't feel safe and may not be making the best decisions at this time. Find comfort before making your next move.

Topaz: You must forgive and seek forgiveness.

Tourmaline: You must reinforce the three souls and work toward alignment on a daily basis. Your daily practice is suffering at this time.

Places

Locations are often linked to personal experiences and represent our connection to the past. If you dream of a location you have never been to, these experiences are often seen as temples for specific psychic frequencies or vibrations known through cultural references. For example, if you dreamt of the pyramids in Egypt but have never been to them, one would interpret their appearance as a connection to the esoteric past. Locations can also be places we have visited in past lives. If you dream of a mystical garden that you know could not be real, paying attention to the plants, architecture, and landscape could lend clues as to what energies manifest within this place. For all of these reasons, doing your best to retain or record as much information about the locations you visit in your dreams is of particular importance.

Common places that appear in a witch's dream include:

Airport/Bus Station/Train Station: Your goals are beginning to feel too heavy, and anxiety is creeping in. Have faith that you can see things through and make necessary changes to ensure you can still reach your destination.

Castle: You are moving into a place of power or currently hold one. It is vital to secure and protect that power at this time.

Cemetery: The dead are reaching out and require your attention. Alternatively, this may also indicate a fear of death or of those that are dead. Face your mortality.

Church: Your higher self is seeking union with a larger force but is blocked by illusion or false truths. Connect to the spiritual forces in your life to find the necessary wisdom you seek.

City: You are becoming more aware of the deeds and motivations of those around you and are worried that you will get lost in the crowd. Your success has to do with your individuality, not your compliance.

Desert: You feel lost and need to preserve your resources at this time. Do not go with the flow; instead, divine for answers to help you find security.

Different Planet: You are being led away from what you know to discover something new. Alternatively, this may indicate higher spiritual forces at work.

Forest/Jungle: Resources are not scarce at this time, but know-how is. Research into the matter at hand is necessary for success.

Garden: You are craving social interaction at this time, are subconsciously reaching out for friends, or a friend is reaching out to you.

Grocery Store: You need to prepare for a future rough patch. Divine for specifics.

Grove of Trees/Circle of Trees: The other worlds are reaching out and have a message for you. Journey to this grove of trees when awake and retrieve it there.

Home: Your home feels foreign to you or there is a foreign energy within the home. If you are afraid during the dream, do a banishing and cleansing on the home. If you do not have an emotional response or feel comforted by it, reach out to the foreign energy for more information.

Childhood Home: You long to be connected to your roots and aspects of your life that are innocent or naive. Indicates stress. If parents are deceased, could indicate contact.

Grandparent's Home: You feel the structures and bonds in your family are fading. Indicates a sense of possible loneliness or feeling of neglect. If grandparents are deceased, could indicate contact.

Hospital: Your fear of transition keeps you from making necessary changes in your life. Alternatively, you require support at this time.

Hospice: It is time to let something important go, but in the process, you will make it holy.

Island: You require alone time for reflection and recovery. Alternatively, this indicates a new type of awareness opening up for you.

Lake: You will find answers in seclusion and meditation. Look within and go deep into the parts of you that remain unmoved. Could indicate a need for hermitage or sacred pilgrimage.

Library: Knowledge is being revealed to you. Slow down and savor the story being told right now.

Mountain: You feel overwhelmed at this time because you have a lot on your plate and feel alone in the process. Reach out for companionship at this time.

Ocean: There are deep and hidden truths that are coming to your attention. Focus on your thoughts and fears at this time, and work through those things that make you feel powerless.

Pond: You have recently obtained knowledge but have not applied it to your life. The time to apply it is now.

Plains/Grassland: The inner world is vast and endless, and you are getting lost within it. Spend time outside of your normal routine to find much-needed mental balance.

Prison: You are stuck or feel wrongfully accused of something. If you see a person in prison from your waking life, this indicates a lack of trust or a need to proceed with caution.

Pyramid: What you are building or creating now will last for a very long time. This can also suggest that significant changes will happen quickly if we feel stuck.

River: You are being told to leave something behind in order to move forward.

Road: It is time to move on. Remember your past for inspiration but keep looking forward.

Temple: You seek knowledge from an institution or tradition but should look for it within.

Waterfall: You are holding on to your emotions. It is time to talk to someone about what is going on in your life.

Work: You have anxiety about your current task and should call in spirits to help at this time.

Events

Events are complicated in dreams as there are different types of event experiences that we might have and they all have different roads for us to travel when looking for clues to their meaning. Dreams that include events in your life that you have already experienced, such as those related to past trauma or emotion, indicate a need for some sort of soul retrieval; a piece of you is stuck in that event and needs to be brought back for that wounding to heal. If you dream of positive events that you once experienced, that indicates your soul is craving the energy it felt there and is essentially showing you what it needs. Some dreams showcase events from past lives, again suggesting the need for soul retrieval. On the other hand, we can also dream of tests, meetings, protests, and all manner of hypothetical situations.

Common events and scenarios that appear in a witch's dream include:

Automobile Accident: You feel like things are moving too fast but don't have the control to slow them down or possibly the resources to ease the pressure they bring on. This indicates severe stress that is now affecting you on a spiritual level. You must find the time to slow down now; this is a dream that warns of impending catastrophe if things continue the way they are.

Being Chased: There is something you fear is unconquerable, and you are avoiding it to the point of creating stress and discomfort in your life. If you cannot see who is chasing you, this indicates that you are running away from yourself; you need to focus, center your energy body, and call upon your allies for help. If you are being chased by someone you know, that indicates unsettled business; it is likely that the astral thread connecting you is being stimulated. They are either thinking of you or you are thinking of them. If this is someone who has caused you harm in the past, you should perform protection magic and speak with someone about the related trauma. If you do not know the person but clearly see them, this is suggestive of otherworldly contact. To be the one chasing indicates that you are after something that person represents or that you covet a trait the person possesses.

Birth: There is new energy coming into your life in the form of a person or project that will change your life forever. Dreaming of your own birth suggests initiation of some sort. Dreaming of giving birth indicates you are prepared to pass along wisdom and knowledge or embark on/complete an important project. To dream of watching a birth suggests that you are to play the role of observer to a significant change in someone's life or in society.

Death: You have come to the point of no return and must allow something to come to an end. If you dream of your own death, you are likely to be soon undergoing a drastic change in identity. If you dream of someone else's death, this is suggestive of the end of an era in your life or the need to allow for a peaceful transition. If you dream of causing death to an animal or person, this is indicative of high stress and an emotional outburst on your part toward that person/animal or what they represent.

Divorce: This suggests an official separation from a person or a way of thinking and a reassessment of their importance.

Dreaming: To dream about dreaming or to be in a dream within a dream indicates that you have information buried in your subconscious that requires exploration as it will help you resolve current issues. Seeing a hypnotherapist, shaman, or teacher can help to achieve this.

Earthquake: There is a major disturbance in the flow of things that is affecting your ability to feel stable and secure in life right now. Alternatively, you may need to really "shake things up" to accomplish your goals.

Falling: To dream about falling and not experience fear can indicate that your consciousness is leaving the body. To dream of falling and experience fear suggests that you feel out of control at the moment.

Famine: You feel resources are limited and that you or someone/something you love is in danger due to this lack of resources. Alternatively, this can indicate intentional negative energy being directed at you.

Faulty Machinery: If machinery or equipment breaks while you are using it, this suggests that you are afraid of your own stubbornness. To dream of fixing defective machinery indicates that you are about to have a breakthrough regarding a problem.

Fire: Fire symbolizes great change and discipline. To dream of starting a fire suggests that there is a new opportunity on the horizon. To dream of being caught on fire indicates some form of initiation or renewal. To dream of arson suggests rage and pent-up emotion that stems from organizational oppression. To dream of dancing around a fire is suggestive of spirit contact.

Flood: There is sexual or creative energy that is causing tension in your life. Pay attention to it and satiate its call.

Funeral: There is a need for closure. Allow yourself to focus on the completion of long-term projects or relationships that you have been meaning to wrap up. Alternatively, this can also suggest that you need to confront an aspect of yourself that you do not find value in.

Getting Fired: The end of an era is coming and not by your hand. Secretively, you have been hoping for this for a long time but likely do not know what to do in response. Divine for more information.

Graduation: You have completed a cycle in your life and are "leveling up" because of it. Your hard work is finally paying off. This also indicates that you will likely soon be stepping into new and exciting territory in life that you are uniquely suited for.

Hunting: There is a strong desire or need for something very personal to you. What you require can only be obtained through study, focus, and quick reflexes. If you dream of being hunted, this suggests that you are under attack because you possess a desired spiritual virtue.

Interview: There is a need for you to explain yourself for others to take you seriously, and you feel judged by your peers for your decisions.

Kidnapped: Your attention is being diverted away from your current tasks and is being invested in distraction.

Public Speaking: There is something important for you to convey to others right now, but you do not know how to verbalize it. Now would be a good time to journal about what brings stress into your life and to mentally work through how you feel about your stresses.

Ritual: You are being invited to make contact with a new or beloved spirit. Alternatively, this can suggest that you are being either reminded of a spirit contract or that you must use magic to overcome an obstacle.

Shapeshifting: You are being reminded of your power and of your true self—the self that only the spirits know, not the self you pretend to be around others. Alternatively, this can be a warning about deceit. Divine for more answers.

Wedding: You are feeling the need to connect to and be part of something other than yourself. This can also indicate a spirit contract or agreement that has been made or currently is being made.

The Body

When parts of the body show up in your dreams, they can be a literal message about that body part and/or its particular system of the body, but it can also allude to shifts within the energy body that might be going on unnoticed. For instance, dreaming of teeth is often a sign of root chakra energy activating or kundalini rising.

Common parts of the body that appear in a witch's dream include;

Arms: The caring and nurturing aspects of your personality are important at this time. Reach out for those you love (this should include you) and give them the needed attention required at this time.

Back/Shoulders: The world is heavy, and right now you feel every bit of it. See this burden not as punishment but as necessary for your goals to manifest. You cannot be broken.

Chest: You are feeling smothered or closed in and need to formulate a plan of action to remove yourself from oppressive forces at this time.

Ears: You have been sensing spirits and messages from beyond but haven't known what they meant. Now is an excellent time to ask and wait for an answer. Divination may help.

Eyes: It is essential to believe the things you see for yourself first-hand and to question those that come through the grapevine. You can only trust yourself at this time.

Feet: Your path requires your attention. Do not blindly move forward but instead pay attention to where you are placing each step.

Hair: Your strength and power are being tested. Dig deep at this time and pull from the infinite well within.

Head: Everything has become too mental and confusing. It is just as essential to feel the answer as it is to know it.

Heel: You are afraid of a weakness being exposed.

Navel: You crave the connection and bond of family, be it what you are a part of or what you might build yourself.

Neck: There is an overabundance of psychic energy in your body that needs to be released. Communicate with spirits and gods, practice more magic, and exhaust more of that energy.

Nudity: You crave freedom from judgment.

Stomach: Your internal process is conflicted, and it is time to slow down and sort out the facts.

Teeth: The energy of your primal soul is moving on its own. Now is the time for serpent magic and for shedding old skin.

Tools, Technology, and Transportation

We have a strange connection to technology. It is in our nature to build tools that make our lives easier, and in modern times that generally means objects like cell phones, computers, and forms of transportation, but it also includes tools for the construction or demolition of goals and the things that block us from them. When modern technology appears in our dreams, it generally represents our need for connectivity, the act of connection, or modes of information. On the other hand, when we find manual tools such as a shovel or a sickle, this usually indicates the need for action on your behalf.

Common tools, technologies, and modes of transport that appear in a witch's dream include:

Tools and Technology

Anvil: The process will be difficult, but you have in your hands the ability to create success and beauty. You only need to realize it and allow the potential to be revealed through intention.

Athame: It is important to focus right now on what matters most and to not lose sight of the goals you have set for yourself. Success requires deliberate intention at this time.

Broom: Lower-frequency energies have settled in your life, and it is time to clean house.

Candle: You are searching for guidance. Trust in someone whom you know only wants the best for you, as others may covet what you have.

Cauldron: It is important to savor the moments being presented to you and have your fill of laughter and love. In the future there will be a time when those things feel scarce, and you will need deep reserves to see yourself through. Alternatively, a cauldron suggests renewal and an abundance of resources, as well as mystery and resourcefulness.

Cell Phone/Tablet: You are receiving new information at this time that you will want to keep close.

Chalice: Good news is on the way!

Computer: You are finding life to be a bit cold and unfeeling at the moment. Human connection is important at this time.

Hammer: You are required to act swiftly on new opportunities; they won't last long.

Radio: Spirits are reaching out to you; make time to listen to them.

Shield: You are emotionally, mentally, and spiritually protected at this time. Have faith.

Shovel: You are searching for intellectual inspiration but are having a difficult time obtaining it. Keep looking!

Stang: The Witch King is reaching out to you. Alternatively, keep those things that matter most to you safe at this time.

Sword: Your willpower requires focus and determination. Don't worry about the competitive aspect of life at this time; instead, pay attention to the technique that you use to navigate it.

Sickle: It is time to harvest those things that you have planted to make way for new growth in all aspects of your life.

Television: You will receive important news regarding your community soon.

Transportation

Airplane/Helicopter: You will soon rise above those blocks and obstacles that you face and will achieve a new level of consciousness as a result.

Bicycle: Your path requires you to focus and find balance at this time.

Boat/Ship: There are aspects of your personality and subconscious that are now being revealed to you. Making a study of yourself and your growth at this time may yield great personal results.

Bus: Your friends or community are in transition. New discussions about the future are soon to take place.

Car: Your ambition and determination will take you far at this time. Enjoy the ride.

Limousine: You're craving the finer things in life right now and will likely find yourself enjoying them. An opportunity for you to see life from a different perspective is on the way.

Spaceship: You are being contacted by higher-vibrational spirits such as those who are teachers and muses. This is an excellent time to explore creative pursuits, connect with those things that bring you inspiration, and practice new forms of magic.

When Symbols Aren't Symbols at All

You could have the most thorough system of symbols and magical scripts of any witch in the world and spend countless hours programming them into your witch's dream, but there will come a day when none of that matters. In my case, it was the day when I learned that sometimes a bird is just a bird. Just because a symbol means something to us doesn't mean it always has a message for us.

To discern whether or not a symbol is indeed an omen or some message from an ally sent to you through the witch's dream, you have to do a gut check and never be afraid to ask for confirmation. Generally, I find there is an instant understanding on my end that what I am seeing is indeed of the witch's dream; it comes with a sense of recognition, as if my witch power was excited by the discovery. It usually perks me up a bit, and I feel drawn to it.

If you are unsure you are getting a message, then ask for the sign to be shown to you again. Ask for clarity one more time if you still aren't sure, but if after the second time you haven't received a clear message, then move on. Whatever you do, don't make it too hard—and don't let it be too easy, either!

If you want even more clarity on the matter, then do a reading or ask your guides for help. It is always better to double check yourself and your gut than to just assume and miss out on a message or, worse, think you're getting a message and really, you aren't! You are in control of the witch's dream and make all the rules; don't forget that you can adjust your practice to suit your needs.

Degrees of Dream

Up to this point, I have been urging you to push your limits as you explore the unmapped territory of the witch's dream. I've basically told you just to accept all of this stuff about a make-believe world called the witch's dream that will give you magical powers and pointed out that all the cool witches are doing it. But just because we may want to be like the witch in the woods doesn't always mean we can be her. Our witch's dream may be beautiful and empowering and an excellent way to meet spirits to help us along our journey, but it isn't necessarily something that every reader can jump into unencumbered.

Not all of us can go full-throttle all the time, and even if you could be, it doesn't necessarily mean that being engaged with the dream is appropriate for the particular time and place. You might not want to have part of your consciousness floating off in the ether while driving or operating heavy machinery, for example. You also might get burnt out from time to time, like I tend to do, and need to be able to either position yourself at a lighter level of interaction with it or remove yourself from it altogether. As witches and architects, we can gauge our degree of involvement with the dream and the depth of surrender to quintessence. I commonly break them down to four levels.

Level One

Not in a trance state but aware of and sensitive to the psychic environment around them. The mind is sharp and focused on life at the moment, and the individual has to actively tune into or call upon a spirit to make contact. Though quintessence is observable, the dreamscape is limited in influence but approachable, and the individual is energetically rooted predominantly if not entirely in our plane.

Level Two

This is a light to intermediate state of trance that consists of steady breathing, a focused and task-oriented mind, artistic motivations or philosophical thought process, and a general feeling of being in the flow and connected to quintessence. Spirits are easier to perceive, and we are likely to make contact with them directly through divination or quintessential manipulation. We are capable of basic candle magic and simple spells, meditation, most forms of divination, and astral travel or soul flight during this degree of dream.

Level Three

This is a deep to advanced state of trance that consists of steady breathing and experiencing the spiritual in the moment as the witch power communes fully with the spirit worlds. Acts of voluntary possession can take place with more ease, as well as great acts of spiritual command. High ceremonial magic, ecstatic trance work, elaborate forms of divination and spirit contact, as well as travel to the witch's sabbat and total submersion within quintessence are all possible at this degree.

Level Four

To achieve this degree of dream, we must literally be dreaming. Later I will dive into lucid dreaming, a practice that allows you to be an active participant in your dreams. Many traditional witches rely on their dreams to provide instruction and the useful insight required to navigate life within and outside of the witch's dream; we call this oneiric praxis. Like most of the terms in traditional witchcraft, this one sounds very fancy, and because it is so, it is easily dismissed as fluff. *Oneiric* refers to what is of the dream—the knowledge and power that comes from the spirit world and the subconscious—and *praxis* simply means practice. An oneiric practice is one that is led by the teachings presented to us while dreaming, and it requires us to have faith in the power of those dreams.

We don't need to be at a three all the time, but we should try to toggle between levels one and two as often as possible, reserving the fourth level for special occasions. Staying within those confines gives us a lot of access without going too far for too long. From a psychic health perspective, one of the risks of the dream is the longevity of time spent there at the deeper levels. It wouldn't be safe for someone to stay at a level three longer than a few days maximum, so keeping it on the lighter side is best, especially for those extended periods of time.

Toggling between a two and three tends to be what those of us who are in the priesthood of the craft spend most of our time experiencing. A requirement of the priesthood is personal devotion and investment when communing with the spirits we work with. Being in these stretches of the dream can be dangerous when you don't understand what you are doing, but for the well-practiced witch, it can be quite a comfortable and informative experience.

Journal Topics

Meditating on the topics presented here in this chapter, answer the following questions in your journal:

1. What are three things you can do daily to ground yourself in the witch's dream?

2. What symbols often appear to you in meditation, trance, and dreams? How do you think those could be related to the witch's dream? Might they benefit your work within the witch's dream?

3. On a scale of one to ten (one being with little effort and ten being with maximum effort), how easily do you enter each of the dream levels? What could you do in your practice to increase that?

Chapter Six

Protocols of Quintessence

*We must all be aware that protocol
takes precedence over procedure.*

——

Irwin Corey

There are four steps to the operation of every ritual or spell: preparation, ingress, congress, and egress.[5] In our tradition we like to
think of magic as something that is woven or sewn into and out of the
fabric of the universe. The four steps will guide us as we weave and
link our strands together. Generally, each part of a more considerable
ritual working will contain various spells, invocations, charms, incantations, etc., and each of those (whether part of a bigger working or
not) will contain some variation of each of the four steps. It is a micro/
macro thing. The larger workings are made up of smaller workings.

5   In his book *Azoetia,* the late occultist Andrew Chumbley introduces these concepts
    to us as an outline for interaction with the witch's sabbat. Ingress, congress, and
    egress are all presented as rituals in the book and provide their own unique support
    for the particular magic observed within his *Cultus Sabbati.*

Preparation is the first step in magic. As a part of our weaving, this not only includes the collection of all of our supplies but also the laying out of our warp. It is around this warp that the strands will be woven, so placing them in the right spots and making sure they are strong will provide a reinforced and sturdy final product. Lastly, it is the drawing of the first strand and lining it up in just the right spot so that the weaving can begin.

An act of ingress is like taking that strand and inserting it into the warp once it has been lined up. Acts of ingress take us into the misty curtain; they bring us into the frequency of whatever it is we are working with, and they merge our world with another. Ingress means to enter.

Next, congress: the weaving has begun, and the strand becomes live with power and intention. To hold congress is to commune with the power if only for a moment, to feel it and become alive with it, to channel it and see it emerge into being. This is where we align with the powers. Congress means to be within the domain or presence of active quintessence.

Lastly, egress, which is to take the strand and close the first loop in the pattern of the weave. This is us disconnecting from the frequency and returning to the place of origin. To perform an act of egress is to come full circle, to cross the veil once more, and to enter our world. Egress should be so smooth that it acts as part of your preparation, performing the last step of lining the strand up to make another loop in the pattern.

I was taught by my teachers that a good spell or ritual should be written like a story. It needs to have an exposition, complication, climax, and then a resolution. Either way we look at it, acts of magic—be they spells or rituals or ceremonies—should include at least these four parts. We should always make sure that we finish the pattern, close the loop, and seal the weave to keep it from unraveling, and this is how we do it.

Preparation

The entire first section of this book is all about preparation. It is showing you how to flip your way of thinking, to use the witch's eye to pierce the veils of perception and view the threads of magic that extend from you in all directions. After that, the sky is the limit. The most significant hurdle for most of us is in switching to a mindset that allows magic to be engaged to begin with. This is why we spend so much time developing our perception and connection to the spirit world. It isn't easy, and it isn't something that will happen all at once; quite the opposite. If you are anything like me, you will likely find that the moment you feel prepared and capable, the tides shift and a new lesson unlocks, educating you to the fact that you will always be in a place of preparation. The whole thing can be a bit discouraging sometimes.

What I believe to be the most important thing to hold to the heart is that our whole life is preparation for the next, and the next life is simply preparation for the following. This life isn't "it"; life doesn't just all end; it continues, as will we. We must see our momentary existence as a giant act of preparation or, better yet, of becoming. For us to become what we are meant to be, we must prepare for what is to come.

I know a lot of witches who feel disconnected from their spirits and their magic. In my experience, this is because they stopped preparing their lives to include them. As I mentioned in the first part of the book, we have to approach our problems with magic, not drop magic when our problems come knocking. We simply cannot only be available for the powers when it feels sunny outside. If we want real magic to exist in our lives every day, we need to make way for it. If you take what we discussed in the first section of this book and apply it to the following practices, you will already be more prepared than the average witch.

In addition to this sort of preparedness that comes with the everyday engagement of your witch power, there will likely be other varying degrees of work you will need to do before engaging in the act of magic. When preparing to jump into magic, you should be asking yourself if you have everything you need. Do you have the tools, the allies, and the environment necessary to do the magic you want to do? If not, then can you work with what you have? How would that change your magic? Sometimes being prepared is all about looking at your goal, then taking stock of your resources and doing the best with what you have. There are, of course, other ways to become prepared and to always have the best resources available when needed so that every act of magic can benefit from preparedness, even when it must be performed on the fly.

Preparation is all about knowing what you need, having what you need, and knowing how to use it when you need to. In the craft this extends to doing divination and laying out a plan. For now, whatever divination system you are most comfortable with should work. Before casting any spell, divine the following:

- What do I not know about the situation?
- What is the best approach to handling the situation?
- What will be the outcome if I don't do a working?
- (Optional) What can I do to change the outcome?
- What will be the outcome if I do a working?
- What are the blocks in the way of my working?
- What can I do to remove those blocks?
- What can I do mundanely to help support my magical working?
- Are there any spirits that I should be working with?'
- Are there any special precautions I should take
  (such as casting a circle or setting a container)?

Again, this entire first section is all about preparation. Being prepared is a lifelong journey, so don't get overwhelmed; embrace it and learn to love to journey. Once you get into the flow of things, get a decent idea of what you're working with, and are able to pull from those wells of energy, you are ready for magic!

Ingress

The rites of ingress take us into the veil that separates the worlds and sets us upon our course for magic. If we were sewing, this is when the needle plunges through the fabric, and like a needle, we have to be sharp to pierce the veil. There are different ways of doing this, each tradition favoring their own unique take. Acts of ingress generally come in two parts.

Part One: Purification and Consecration

The first act of ingress opens the way for all of the magic we will carry out in our working. It syncopates our environment with the environment of the witch's dream and simultaneously clears the path for more magic to follow. This is done in various ways, but in Sacred Fires it goes as follows:

For Consecration Without a Circle

Find yourself at the center of the space intended for magic and activate your holy fire as previously instructed. Take three deep breaths, and as you exhale, envision your holy fire pouring down from your body. Allow it to fill the floor or ground of the space around you in a perfect circle, cleansing the space around you for at least three feet in all directions. Focus on merely maintaining this image for a few moments, and then allow the flames to slowly sink into the ground beneath you. When you feel the energy, dedicate the space to the art:

> *By the powers of the triple soul, by the powers of a sacred flame,*
> *I dedicate this space to the witch's art!*
> *Hear me, spirits; hear me keen: be here now or be unseen.*
> *What soon comes does so with might;*
> *I dedicate this space to my sacred rite!*

Stomp your foot to seal the energy remaining.

For Consecration With a Circle

Not all witches cast circles. For me what determines this is comfort, need, and taste. Over time you will get used to the sensation of having an open magical space, but you may find yourself in a situation that requires you to have a sealed space, or you may just be entirely put off by the idea of not having one altogether. Once the witch's tree is invoked, you are surrounded by your spirit guides and allies and the powers sworn to guard our rites. Not casting a circle does provide a particular type of energetic breathing to happen within the space, one that I found to be incredibly invigorating in ritual. If I am going to be doing a heavy working or working with people I am unfamiliar with, then I always cast a circle. I also always make sure to cast a circle if I need to be engaging spiritual energy that I am unfamiliar with. Again, this is all about comfort, need, and taste.

Find yourself at the center of the space intended for magic and activate your holy fire as previously instructed. Take three deep breaths, and as you exhale, envision your holy fire pouring down from your body. Move so that you are in the east, with your right shoulder facing inside the space that is to be the center of your circle and your left hand tilted down with your palm upwards at a 45-degree angle. Remember that your holy fire is unlimited energy, one that is the product of divine connection. Keep your head forward at all times. From the easternmost point of your circle, begin to steadily and with intent walk around the parameter of your circle space three times. Lift your right hand up into the air as if to catch the flow of white fire and continue to pour its liquid flame from your left hand as you slowly raise it into the air over the course of your three revolutions. As you do this you must envision that a perfect sphere of white flame is forming around you. Say:

I cast this circle thrice about to keep unwanted spirits out!
Sphere of power, sphere of the art, I conjure you by beating heart.
I bid you rise and contain; be a vessel for rites arcane.
From the shadows and light, I cast this circle with flame of white!

At the end of your third trip around the circle, you should again be in the east, facing the south. Turn so that you are facing the center of the circle space. When you feel the energy settle, dedicate the space to the art:

By the powers of the triple soul, by the powers of a sacred flame,
I dedicate this space to the witch's art!
Hear me, spirits; hear me keen: be here now or be unseen.
What soon comes does so with might,
I dedicate this space to my sacred rite!

Stomp your foot to seal the energy remaining.

Part Two: Laying the Compass and Invoking the Witch's Tree

In our tradition the following is more than sufficient to effectively pierce the veil and keep the space safe during any working. We tend to work a lot with our spirit guides and familiars, as well as a set of guardian spirits, and we enjoy the ability to produce spirit traffic during ritual, so casting a circle or container usually is not preferable. Because circles are designed to keep some things out and other things in, creating one will likely be anathema to working with the spirits in a less restrictive manner.

In our tradition we summon a field of energy known as the witch's compass, and from it we erect the witch's tree. The compass is a ceremonial fixture designed to give us access to specific energies we encounter as we walk our path on the lonely road. The lines of energy we lay down truly are the metaphorical and symbolic paths of the lonely road itself. What makes the compass so powerful is that it is composed of the symbolism from our tradition, so as it is conjured into the space, we are drawing upon the spirits and powers behind our tradition. At the center of the compass is a giant tree, known to us as the witch's tree, which is the personification of your own witch power made manifest through the world tree. It is a symbol of our reach as witches: roots that dig deep into the underworld, a trunk that is tall and wise and extends through the middle world, and a canopy that extends into the overworld. For us, this tree is the altar from which all of our work will be done. It is the stang of creation.

Find yourself at the center of your working space and direct yourself so you are facing the northeast. Raise your arms so that your hands are over your head, slightly in front of your body, with your palms facing out. Say:

> *I stand at the center of four roads*
> *Between the apex and vertex of time and space.*
> *I conjure the witch's tree from the black flame of God Herself*
> *And look upon the void's own face.*
> *Before me and behind me lies the sovereign path,*
> *The road of those who wear the crown.*
> *At my side lies the crooked path,*
> *The road of those who keep the way.*
> *From north and south, the left-hand path,*
> *The road of poisoners and the self-redeemed.*
> *From east and west, the right-hand path,*
> *The road of healers and the artists unseen.*
> *Let eight be four and four be one*
> *And the black flame eclipse the sun.*
> *From the one, I call the tree,*
> *And from the trunk unlock the three.*
> *By the compass and the powers,*
> *By the Grigori and the towers,*
> *What is within is now without,*
> *May all our enemies be turned about.*

Brothers, sisters, others of the art,
Together in blood we ne'er shall part.
Spirits, allies, imps who don't stray,
The witch's blood opens the way.
Let three be one, and one be eight,
I blur the lines of life and fate.
By the black flame so must it be,
Of all worlds the witch's tree.

Take a few moments and breathe slowly and deeply. See your spirit guides and familiars standing with you around the compass.

Congress

Ingress allows us to open the way and set the stage for our work. I liken it to stepping aboard the bridge of a starship: once you're there and have set your course, you can go anywhere and do just about anything, from transcending the realms of humanity to summoning ancient spirits. We are now ready to boldly go where no one has gone before.

During congress, the meat of the working is performed. At this stage we will invoke our gods, conjure our spirits, raise energy, tread the mill, summon up quintessence to use in spells, and carry out our secret operations. Each ritual will be different and have its own requirements, so the only thing to focus on at this time is your operation!

If you are doing a ceremony of any kind, it is generally customary to invoke your deities. I included invocational prayers in chapter 7 to the different emanations of the Witch Queen and King; if you aren't working exclusively with your own deity, check out mine! Otherwise, different traditions don't really agree on if you should invoke the gods before every working or not. Unless I am working with them directly or performing a working that is ceremonial, I tend to leave them out. They get plenty of devotional time at my personal altar, so I only call them into magic space when I need them. Some traditions will invoke their gods during each working as a matter of respect. Again, this is one of those things that is up to the practitioner; there is no right or wrong way.

The only things you really need to keep in mind are to respect the boundary you made if you cast a circle and to release or ask the spirit you invoke to continue with you outside of ritual space. You have to play crossing guard and give clear instructions to any and everything that is brought into the ritual space. Don't forget about someone and leave them hanging. It is also a good idea to leave offerings to these spirits after you work with them ceremonially, especially those who are gods.

If you cast a circle, in theory, the energies you invoked or summoned should leave once you have closed the space. This, however, doesn't always happen. If you forget to tell a spirit where to go, usually they just follow you out of the space or will go back to where they came from and be less likely to show up next time. It's a bit like being called to a party by your friend and then having them ditch you.

Once you have performed your ritual working, it is time to close up shop!

Egress

Just like camping, whatever you bring in, you take back with you. The rites of egress allow us to make our way back home once our magical workings have been completed during congress. Before you leave, however, it is essential to acknowledge the completion of the working and take a moment to think about how you will ground those energies in your life and the witch's dream once you are finished with the main working.

When we are ready to leave, we merely follow the same procedures but retrace our steps to get back to the other side.

There are a few ways to approach this. Some traditions will merely acknowledge and release the energies they conjured during ingress, while others absorb those energies. I fall into the latter category. By the time you make it to egress, you are usually spent energetically, and absorbing energies back into your energy body once you are finished with them is an excellent way of restoring your power.

To Release the Witch's Tree and Compass

The witch's tree can actually be left up if you choose. This is usually a good idea if you did a positive working, as it will remain potent for a few days and continue to attract positive energies. The same cannot be said, however, for negative workings. If you do something intense or on the not-too-positive side, you will want to take it down! The decision is entirely yours. However, to release the witch's tree, you simply need to face the center of the space, take three deep breaths to ground yourself in the energy, and then visualize the tree and compass dissolving into a billion little grains of white sand and being absorbed into your etheric body as you command it to release by saying:

> Witch's tree, whose power is of all planes,
> I release thee now and take the reins.
> Into my body, into my mind, into my soul a place you'll find.
> As without so within, with my breath I draw you in.
> As without so within, with my breath I draw you in.
> As without so within, with my breath I draw you in. Blessed be.

To Release the Circle

Move so that you are in the west, with your right shoulder facing the outside of your circle, both hands up in the air in a Y formation, palms toward the ground. Keep your head forward at all times. From the westernmost point of your circle begin to steadily, and with intent, walk around the parameter of your circle space three times. Slowly lower your arms to your sides as you move around the circle and envision the power of the circle being absorbed into your fingertips. Use that energy to reinforce your own personal magical shields. As you move counterclockwise and absorb the energy, say:

Sphere of power with no start, vessel of the ancient art.
I release you, circle, and take back the flame;
Your power is mine to claim.
As without so within, with my breath I draw you in.
As without so within, with my breath I draw you in.
As without so within, with my breath I draw you in. Blessed be.

What to Look For As You Weave

At any point in the process of performing magic, you might receive a message or impression from your spirit allies. One of the traits all parents or caregivers share is the ability to be focused on one thing while simultaneously focusing on their children or ward. We have to possess that same degree of multifaceted attention during our workings and keep ourselves always at least partially tuned in to our spirits, especially our familiars. They will be letting us know what is going on and if any changes need to be made to the work, and, perhaps most importantly, they will be able to let you know the safety of your surroundings.

As I mentioned before, more significant workings require more substantial buildup, and the more energy you are going to be working with, the more reinforcements you are going to need. Be prepared for that by planning things out in advance. Most of our workings should be simple and won't require a lot of buildup, so ingress might be as simple as aligning your souls and igniting your holy fire. Congress might merely be a wishing spell. Egress could just be an acknowledgment that the wish has been made and is out of your hands. But sometimes it's a lot bigger than a wishing spell, and you have to pull out all the stops like the ones I discussed in this chapter. Planning ahead will let you know what you are going to need to do to make the working effective.

Make sure that you can feel the energy of the working at all times. From the moment you initiate ingress until the very last second of egress, you should feel energy moving; at the very least you should feel your own energy moving. If you don't feel it moving and aren't feeling energy projecting from you, then take a few moments to realign your souls and perhaps perform a quick cleansing on yourself before you continue. Magic isn't a race; no one wins if they speed through it. Magic requires us to feel and experience, and it should be something that we savor.

As we explore the feast days and other rituals in the coming chapters, make sure that you have these four stages woven into your plan and that they are present in the working. What I will present is the bare bones of the ceremonial system, but you are the one who has to write the ceremonies should you choose to engage the powers therein.

JOURNAL TOPICS

In addition to the prompts from within this chapter, meditate on the following questions and answer them in your journal:

1. How do your spells and rituals compare to the outline presented in this chapter? Are all four parts evident in your work?

2. Write a spell that follows this method and then perform it. How did the energy feel in the beginning, middle, and end of the working?

3. Sketch some of your most affirming ritual experiences.

Chapter Seven

Activating Quintessence

Man is a microcosm, or a little world, because he is an extract
from all the stars and planets of the whole firmament, from
the earth and the elements; and so, he is their quintessence.

———

Paracelsus

Every component of a spell, from the words you say to the ingredients you use, is an anchor of quintessence. Many witches skip the vital process of tapping into and calling upon the magical energy found within these components, assuming that magic is solely about intent and that somehow the universe will figure it all out. Before something becomes an agent of magic or a source of power that we might draw from, we have to first tap the wellspring found within. We refer to this process as awakening or activating quintessence, and it is a lot easier than you might think.

One of the beautiful things about the witch power is that it is naturally drawn to quintessence, and it comes with a sense for where to find it. To find the quintessence within a spell component, all you need to do is tune into the frequency resonating from the item and then hone in on the source to clarify the channel. We do this by allowing our consciousness to follow the frequency until we meet the point of its origins. It is akin to looking down a straw to see what is on the other side. Once we find it, we focus on increasing its intensity by coaxing or pulling the energy out through the other side, like taking a sip through the straw. Once the flow of energy starts moving, that source is accessible until you tune out of it.

Sometimes, such as in the case of herbs and crystals, this power lies on the other side of a master spirit such as a deva or plant spirit. In this case, we actually communicate with them and inform them as to what it is that we want them to do on our behalf. For example, if working with rue, a favorite of mine, I would approach its master spirit psychically, inform it of the situation, and then ask for it to allow me access to its power to make this happen. The more you work with the master spirit, the faster this process becomes, which is why many witches prefer to grow their own magical herbs or work with a limited amount of them. It is better to work with five herbs and know their spirits well than have access to a hundred herbs and not know them at all.

I would also suggest that to keep you and your materials at the ready, spend time getting to know the things that are already in your cabinet. Take ten to fifteen minutes every day for a week tapping into and connecting with the spirits of your herbs, oils, stones, and other materials. When you get new materials, tap into them and introduce them to your environment. Get to know them and let them get to know you; this way, if you do need them on the fly, they will be more likely to work with you. For those witches who have a difficult time with their spells being effective, this simple trick may just be the fix.

Once you grow accustomed to connecting to the quintessence within your materials and spell components, you will be able to take it to the next level, which is to essentially distill that power into a readily applicable form. This is usually done by drawing the essence of the material into another substance, such as water or oil.

In the case of crystals and metals, the most common practice is to empower fresh water with the essence of the stone. This is done by placing the stone or metal in a glass container full of spring or distilled water and then placing that in direct sunlight for three to five days. After it has been charged, the stone or metal is removed, and the water can be drank, applied to baths, used in mists, etc. Obviously, not all stones and metals are safe for this, so please do your research. Stones like malachite and certain metals like copper can be toxic if worked with in this way, so it is always best to check before preparing a condensed form of quintessence and make sure that its application will work with your plans. Crystals and metals can be added to oils for the same purpose but should be charged ahead of time, as oil should not be left out in the sun.

Herbs are much more versatile when it comes to working with the quintessence they provide. Stones and metals are solid and aren't likely to completely dissolve, but herbs are malleable in this way. In addition to working with essential oils, which are extracted from a plant and generally resonate with the purest vibration of the plant or flower, we can also work with the raw plant matter itself.

Every piece of a plant contains a different aspect of the plant's overall frequency. The roots have its most base frequency, resonating into the underworlds. The stems and leaves resonate with the energy of that plant's middle-world frequencies. And, as you might guess, flowers are thought to contain the plant's highest vibration. Whenever possible, keep this in mind when accessing the quintessential power, as these different layers will act as a prism, refracting the original frequency of the plant into its higher, middle, and lower-level frequencies. Think of these as notes in a chord: when all three are played, it produces a harmonic sound of the whole plant, but these notes can also be played individually to produce a melody or, in our case, create the desired flow of quintessence.

Sometimes we will want to work with the highest vibration of a plant and sometimes we will want to work with the lowest. Generally, the high frequency produced by flowers brings about the blessings of the plant. The mid-frequency of the plant is thought to bring about wisdom, knowledge, and durability, and can be found by working with stem, wood, or bark. The root is believed to bring about the more aggressive and/or baneful aspects of the plant's frequency. This isn't always true for an herb; for instance, the roots of a belladonna plant are less likely to aid in a curse than its flowers or fruit, but in general this is an excellent guide to follow. Roots move through the soil and push things aside so that they can reach whatever nutrients they need. This makes them formidable vibrations to work with in magic.

The same process of awakening or activating quintessence can be performed on anything, even manmade objects. Mainly all we are doing with this process is tuning in to the psychic frequency resonating from the material, finding its source, and then putting a tap into it so we can capture the quintessence. Once it starts to flow, all we need to do is direct it.

To direct this energy, we are mostly going to program it to do a specific thing on our behalf. This same technique works for everything from stones to herbs to ritual tools; once you have hold of its essence, you very clearly state what you desire it to do. Form a short sentence, like "Rue, protect me from psychic attack" or "Hyssop, guide me to clarity." Whatever it is, make it a direct and singular instruction. Avoid saying anything complicated, like "Mint, purge my aura of negative vibrations and clear my second sight so I may see the witch's dream better!" or "Mandrake, bring me all the wisdom and knowledge of the craft and help me become a master of the arts!" Once you start to put the components together when you cast the actual spell, you will give them further instruction and can get specific as to how you want them to work as a team. In the initial activation of the herb, however, you want to merely draw upon the aspect of the plant or spell component you will be working with directly.

Condensing Crystal Quintessence

Once the quintessence has been activated, we can direct its energy into just about anything we desire. Sometimes, though, the quintessence we seek must be conjured up beforehand to be used in our magic. How might one access the essence of a specific alchemical element without having direct access to it in the moment? These are energies we work with often in the craft, so having multiple ways to access them is always a good thing.

Some witches work with crystal grids, which are made with stones and minerals that are placed in a specific geometric pattern, with a main stone (or an object to be charged with energy) in the middle acting as an amplifier for specific energies as they manifest. Fed by the surrounding stones, the energy output by the main stone is usually palpable and recognizable. Creating one with stones that are specific to the element of fire would allow you to channel that energy—likewise for any of the other elements or correspondent properties possessed by the crystal. All you need to do is awaken the quintessence in each of them, program them by psychically implanting instructions, and then place the stones in a pattern that corresponds to your work. Once all the stones around the main stone have been activated, you will need to give the larger, more complex set of instructions to the main stone in the middle.

Example Patterns

Each grid on its own, if correctly set up, is capable of pumping out the same energy as another witch and makes an excellent anchor for larger, more vivacious energies. Most often we use crystal grids to either help us manifest a spell quicker, as they really do make excellent batteries, or to amplify a specific frequency that we require to be present. For the alchemical elements, making a grid from one, some, or all of the following crystals should plug you into these powers.

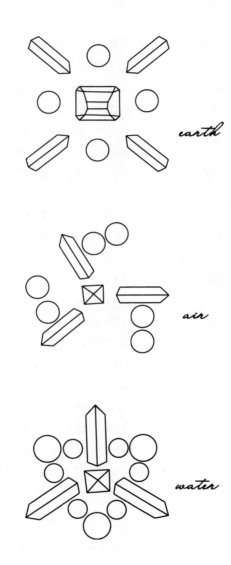

earth

air

water

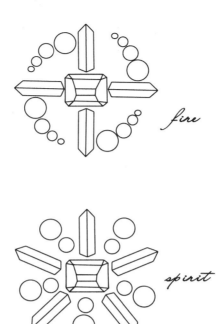

fire

spirit

By using crystal grids, we are essentially condensing quintessence into a refined source of power and using the natural flow of energy that crystals possess to make that happen. With herbs, however, it can be a bit trickier. Yes, you can make herbal grids, which essentially carry the same idea as crystal grids. Instead of working with a main stone, an item is placed in the center for charging. The herbs are then collected and either blended into incense that can be burned to invoke that power or a tea to do the same.

Condensing Herbal Quintessence

We can also create what is called a *fluid condenser*, or *decoction*, which is a technique that allows you to extract quintessence from an element or location. According to Nigel Pearson, a fluid condenser "refers to the non-physical (fluid) energy that is the essence of each element, which is incorporated into a liquid that can be used in the work of spell crafting."[6] The idea is to collect the appropriate plant matter, add it to water, and then boil it down into a thick, almost syrup-like consistency without burning it. The result is a concoction that contains the distilled quintessence of its ingredients.

You would use these in invocations to the elements, add a drop or two to poppets and fetishes for extra oomph and to give them the power contained therein, and can even dress candles with them. Basically, a condenser is useful anywhere you might benefit from the fluid energy that is the essence of each element.

EARTH
Equal parts mushroom, patchouli, and decaying leaves from a forest floor. *Do not consume.*

AIR
Equal parts dried eucalyptus leaves, catnip, and apple. *Do not consume.*

FIRE
Equal parts clove, sandalwood, and rosemary. *Do not consume.*

WATER
Equal parts willow, sage, and basil. *Do not consume.*

SPIRIT
Equal parts rue, oak, and honeysuckle. *Do not consume.*

I also make a different type of condenser that I refer to as a *spatial condenser* as it cues me into a location rather than a specific element. This is done by making a decoction from material harvested under a full moon from three trees that are local to a particular area. This can be bark, leaves, wood, twigs, etc. Instead of damaging a living tree, I typically use something it has shed. For instance, I have made one

6 Pearson, *Treading the Mill.*

for my home, which allows me to tap into the location and the spirits found there whenever I travel. I made one for the mountain that is close by because I work so often with the spirits there, and it gives me access to them regardless of where I am.

Condensing Divine Quintessence

As a witch, you will likely make some special connections with divine beings. Our gods are our friends, our allies, and on occasion our masters, depending on your type of devotion. As you have guessed by now, I work with Diana and Dianus as the Witch Queen and the Witch King. I have done my best to describe them in my previous writings, but it is really quite difficult to express who these beings are to anyone. No two witches are alike, and no two connections to the divine are alike. I can present them to my readers archetypally, I can describe them down to every detail, but I could never find the words to describe them intimately. Another Dianist (someone who holds Diana as a central goddess) who has an equally intimate connection to Diana will likely describe her in very different terms. Even though we worship the same goddess, she is known differently by us both.

I remember watching two people who were both devoted to Hecate get into an intense argument over the right way to pronounce her name. Before too long they were cussing each other out and developed a years-long feud between the two of them. What bothered me the most about all of it is that they were both wrong—wrong because they felt they knew Hecate so well that they denied the other's relationship to her as valid. In the end, it didn't matter who was pronouncing her name correctly; they both came out losers from this one. Both of them had a relationship to Hecate, but relationships are intimate, and they both knew a different side of her or were at least tapping into the egregore of Hecate in different ways.

The way a divine being presents itself to you will change as you change, and your first and only priority is to watch and interact with it as it unfolds. These individual expressions are what we refer to as your "personal gods" or "personal spirits." The mysteries between your personal spirits are yours and yours alone, and you should always keep in mind that others will have the same. My Diana, the Witch Queen that I know, is and should be different from the one you know. I have had over twenty years of praying to her, working through life's issues with her, and developing something unique. You can never have what I have, but you can have something better: your own connection to her.

I bring this all up because personal spirits are our lifeline to the Divine. Once you have bonded with a spirit and have a personal connection with them, you can work with that connection to further your craft. Divinity is all around us, but when we want to tap into the specific divine frequency that we are personally working with, we must first condense or distill it. This helps us to better define the frequency we are psychically tapping into, and, as with crystals or herbs, helps us to anchor that specific energy into our work. We can condense divine quintessence by creating what we refer to as a *simulacrum*.

Simulacrums are like fetishes or statues that are constructed to be the anchor for a divine spirit. Creating a simulacrum is no easy task, as it is done in several stages over one year and one day of devotional work to that spirit. In my tradition we create two simulacrums, one for both the Witch King and the Witch Queen. Channeling and then condensing divine quintessence is no quick task, however. The idea is that over the course of that year and a day we are channeling and calling upon the power of our personal gods through prayer, service, and acts of devotion. During this time we are building those deeper bonds and are constructing the individual pieces of the simulacrum with the quintessence we find as a result of that study. When the working is complete, we have a miniature version of our personal gods, one constructed over time that harnesses different aspects of our gnosis and journey to better understand them. Simulacrums are like houses that embody our personal gods and resonate with their specific vibrations.

The following are instructions on how to make a simulacrum for the Witch Queen and Witch King. To be clear, they each get their own simulacrum! Don't be afraid to add to the things that represent your personal connection, and think of each stage as a step along the path to strengthening your bond to your personal gods. Altogether there are thirteen stages of making a simulacrum.

The Simulacrum of the Witch Queen

During the construction you will be asked to burn Witch Queen incense. This is easily made by combining equal parts myrrh and amber over charcoal.

You will need:

STAGE ONE

- A 12–16 ounce clear glass or black ceramic jar with lid

- Thirteen rose hips

- Snake shedding (at least a handful)

- Queen Elizabeth root

- Soot from a fireplace or ritual fire devoted to the Witch Queen (a few pinches will work)

- Myrrh (about an ounce)

witch queen's master sigil

- The Witch Queen's master sigil in black (as shown above), which has been drawn upon a square of parchment or brown paper (feel free to use a recycled brown paper bag for this) and is approximately 3 inches (8 cm) in width on all sides

- A small piece of moonstone or bone
- A drop of blood
- Witch Queen incense
- A white, a red, and a black candle

STAGES TWO THROUGH ELEVEN
- The nine collected symbols that have been drawn upon a single square of parchment or brown paper (feel free to use a recycled brown paper bag for this) and that are approximately 3 inches (8 cm) in width on all sides
- Witch Queen incense
- A white, a red, and a black candle

STAGE TWELVE
- Earthen clay (the fast-drying, no-bake kind that you can find in craft stores works fine)
- Witch Queen incense
- A white, a red, and a black candle

STAGE THIRTEEN
- White, red, black, and silver acrylic paint
- Paintbrush
- Witch Queen incense
- A white, a red, and a black candle

Her simulacrum is made in stages and should be assembled with great care and preparation. Each stage represents a different aspect of your relationship to her, and as you assemble it, you will be forging your bond with her and clarifying your connection, aka condensing her divine quintessence. In totality, it will not be completely functional until one year and a day after its consecration; though you will be able to use the simulacrum at any stage in your work, it just won't be completed until the final stage. This is because in the final stage you are dedicating your magic and your life to her, which only will be proven real after a solid year of real dedication. This means you have to show up, do the hard work of mediumship and soul flight, and truly devote yourself to her. Over this time, you will have many conversations with her, you will unravel incredible mysteries, and, most importantly, you will become a better witch.

In our tradition each simulacrum is unique and treated with the utmost respect. Specific blessings and rituals are performed over them by our clergy that further imbue them with power and magical strength, but before those rituals can happen, each student must first complete the year and a day of ritual work on their own and then present their simulacrum to their teacher. The teacher, having the skills to do so, taps into the simulacrum's energy and determines if it is powerful enough or if it needs more. This is because we are working with very tradition-specific entities with particular standards.

You will be working with your personal Witch Queen, who is unique to you. Again, the spirit of the Witch Queen that is fusing with this simulacrum is a unique emanation of her, one that is revealed to you and you only. Even in our tradition, with its strict rules surrounding the mysteries of the simulacrum and the specific spirits that go along with them, we still see this relationship as being of chief importance. Despite the other works we do, the work related to the identity of your personal Witch Queen is essential for further progression into the mysteries.

Stage One

Assuming you have aligned your energy and prepared yourself for magical work, light the Witch Queen incense and set it to the side but keep it close. Collect the rose hips, snake shedding, soot, Queen Elizabeth root, myrrh, moonstone or bone, and the parchment with her master sigil drawn in black; place them all to the side. Light the three candles and place them in the shape of a triangle before you. with the black candle to the bottom left, the white to the right, and the red to form the peak.

Note: You will be required to draw a drop of blood toward the end of this; be safe and sterile. I recommend the use of single-use diabetic lancets as they draw enough for just one drop of blood and are safe to throw away afterward. The only acceptable substitute for blood that is drawn as an act of personal sacrifice is semen or menstrual blood.

Place the jar in the center of the three candles and then gather your ingredients, which you have already placed off to the side.

Next, one by one put them in the jar, breaking only to wash your hands at the end. As you place the rose hips in the jar, say, "By the Throne of Within, I call her spirit." As you place the snake shedding in, say, "And see through the glamour of mankind." As you place the soot in the jar, say, "By the Throne of Below, I call her spirit." As you place the Queen Elizabeth root in the jar, say, "And raise it from the great abyss." Place the myrrh in the jar and say, "By the Throne of Above, I call her spirit." As you put the stone or bone in the jar, say, "And draw her light-darkness from between the stars."

After washing your hands, take her master sigil and place it before you, then draw a drop of your own blood and dress the center of the sigil with it. Fold the paper over four times, rotating clockwise each time and chanting "Witch Queen!" with every turn.

Place the folded parchment in the jar and say, "By the river of blood and the lonely road, I bring your spirit from my flesh. Be here now and make this your home!" Put the lid on the jar and then hover it over the smoke from the incense and say or sing her hymn.

The Hymn to the Witch Queen
From black to red and red to white, she is the mistress of the rite.
Part of one, but nine is she; the mother of the witch's tree.
Hail the crescent and circle round; she is the mother I have found.
From the crossroads and the sea, our lady sets me free!

From black to red and red to white, granting all the witch's sight.
Part of one but nine is she; the mother of the witch's tree.
Hail the crescent and circle round; she is the heavens and the ground.
From the crossroads and the sea, watching over and guiding me.
From black to red and red to white, guiding all souls in flight.
Part of one but nine is she, the mother of the witch's tree.
Hail the crescent and circle round, through her wisdom I am crowned.
From the crossroads and the sea, she is the sacred key.

Place the simulacrum on your altar, make an offering of alcohol or tobacco, and wait. You essentially have the seed of a spirit in this jar now. You will need to feed and care for it by giving it regular offerings, visiting it often, singing the hymn, meditating with it, and including it and the spirit within it in your magic.

Stages Two Through Eleven

Throughout the following year, you must come back to the simulacrum and work with it during trance under each full moon. During each working, ask the Witch Queen to present to you a symbol that you can use to place in the jar to help you construct your simulacrum. After you retrieve the symbol, light the incense, as well as her three candles, and then draw the symbol on the paper. Fold it twice, each time moving in a clockwise direction, and then add it to the simulacrum. Seal the simulacrum back up, run it over burning incense once more, and then say or sing the Hymn to the Witch Queen before placing it back on your altar.

Stage Twelve

After you have completed exactly one year and a day's worth of personal development and devotion to her, draw upon her essence by filling the remaining empty amount of the simulacrum with myrrh and seal the lid one final time, extra tight. Take the clay and use an appropriate amount to cover the lid and about one or two inches past the lid so that the lid will not be able to move once it has dried. Next, sculpt the face of a woman with a moon etched upon her brow and affix it to the top of the jar. As you do this, say or sing the Hymn to the Witch Queen. Place it back on your altar to dry for three days, visiting it and saying or singing the hymn each day.

Stage Thirteen

On the third day, if the clay feels dry to the touch, light the incense and the candles, and then paint the entire simulacrum white. As you do this, speak to the Witch Queen of your hopes and dreams and tell her what you need her help with. Let this dry. Next, paint the entire simulacrum red. As you do this, speak to the Witch Queen about your passions and the things you want more of. Let this dry. Paint the entire simulacrum black. As you do this, speak to the Witch Queen of your magical successes with her up to this point and your future plans. Let this dry.

Lastly, paint her master sigil on the front of the simulacrum in silver paint. Place this between her three candles and say or sing her hymn once again. The working is complete.

The Simulacrum of the Witch King

During the construction, you will be asked to burn Witch King incense. This is made by combining equal parts frankincense and amber.

You will need:

STAGE ONE
- A 12–16 oz jar clear glass or white ceramic jar with lid
- Thirteen acorns or other small to medium tree nuts that have freely fallen and been collected at dusk
- Peacock feather
- High John the Conqueror root
- Soot from a ritual fire devoted to the Witch King (a few pinches will work)
- Frankincense (about an ounce)

witch king's master sigil

- The Witch King's master sigil in white (above) that has been drawn upon a single square of parchment or brown paper (feel free to use a recycled brown paper bag for this) and that are approximately 1.5 inches (4 cm) in width on all sides

- A small piece of antler, horn, hoof, or bone

- A drop of blood

- Witch King incense

- A white, a red, and a black candle

Stages Two Through Eleven

- The nine collected symbols that have been drawn upon a single square of parchment or brown paper (feel free to use a recycled brown paper bag for this) and that are approximately 3 inches (8 cm) in width on all sides

- Witch King incense

- A white, a red, and a black candle

Stage Twelve

- Earthen clay (the fast-drying, no-bake kind that you can find in craft stores works fine)

- Witch King incense

- A white, a red, and a black candle

- White, red, black, and gold acrylic paint
- Paintbrush
- Witch King incense
- A white, a red, and a black candle

Like the simulacrum for the Witch Queen, his simulacrum is made in stages and should be assembled with great care and preparation; all the same rules apply. In totality, it will not be completely functional until a year and a day after its consecration. You have to show up, do the hard work of mediumship and soul flight, and truly devote yourself to him.

Stage One

Assuming you have aligned your energy and prepared yourself for magical work, light the Witch King incense and set it to the side but keep it close. Collect the acorns, feather, soot, High John root, frankincense, the piece of antler, and the parchment with his master sigil drawn in white, and place them to the side. Light the incense and then the three candles and place them in the shape of a triangle before you, with the white to the bottom left, the black to the right, and the red to form the peak.

Note: You will be required to draw a drop of blood toward the end of this; be safe and sterile. I recommend the use of single-use diabetic lancets as they draw enough for just one drop of blood and are safe to throw away afterward. The only acceptable substitute for blood that is drawn as an act of personal sacrifice is semen or menstrual blood.

Place the jar in the center of the three candles and then gather your ingredients, which you have placed off to the side.

Next, one by one put them in the jar. As you place the acorns in the jar, say, "By the Throne of Within, I call his spirit." As you place the feather, say, "And see through the glamour of mankind." As you place the soot in the jar, say, "By the Throne of Below, I call his spirit." As you place the High John root in the jar, say, "And raise it from the great abyss." Place the frankincense in the jar and say, "By the Throne of Above, I call his spirit." As you put the antler in the jar, say, "And draw his light down from the stars above."

Take his master sigil and place it before you, then draw a drop of your own blood and dress the center of the sigil with it. Fold the paper over four times, rotating clockwise each time and chanting "Witch King!" with every turn.

Place the folded parchment in the jar and say, "By the river of blood and the lonely road, I bring your spirit from my flesh. Be here now and make this your home!" Put the lid on the jar and then hover it over the smoke from the incense and say or sing his hymn.

THE HYMN TO THE WITCH KING

From white to red and red to black, from the gallows and the rack.
Part of one but nine is he; the father of the witch's tree.
Hail the hoof and hail the horn, he's the shade to which we're sworn.
From dusk till dawn and shadow's end, in his service I shall spend.
From white to red and red to black, from man to stag,
*   then wolf and back*
Part of one but nine is he; the father of the witch's tree.
Hail the hoof and hail the horn; he's the goat to which we're sworn.
From dusk till dawn and shadow's end, I am the Witch King's
*   humble friend.*
From white to red and red to black, he is the leader of our pack.
Part of one but nine is he; the father of the witch's tree.
Hail the hoof and hail the horn, the keeper of the oaths we've sworn.
From dusk till dawn and shadow's end, it is through him
*   that I transcend.*

Place the simulacrum on your altar, make an offering of alcohol or tobacco, and wait. You essentially have the seed of a spirit in this jar now. You will need to feed and care for it by giving it regular offerings, visiting it often, singing the hymn, meditating with it, and including it and the spirit within it in your magic.

Stages Two Through Eleven

Throughout the following year, you must come back to the simulacrum and work with it during trance during each new moon. During each working, ask the Witch King to present to you a symbol that you can use to place in the jar to help you construct your simulacrum. After you retrieve the symbol, light the incense as well as his three candles, then draw the symbol on the paper. Fold it twice, each time moving in a clockwise direction, and then add it to the simulacrum. Seal the simulacrum back up, run it over burning incense once more, and then say or sing the Hymn to the Witch King before placing it back on your altar.

Stage Twelve

After you have completed exactly one year and a day's worth of personal development and devotion to him, you draw upon his essence. Fill the remaining empty amount of the jar with frankincense and seal the lid one final time, extra tight. Take the clay and use an appropriate amount to cover the lid and about one or two inches past the lid so that the lid will not be able to move once it has dried. Next, sculpt the face of a horned man and affix it to the top of the jar. As you do this, say or sing the Hymn to the Witch King. Place it back on your altar to dry for three days, visiting it and saying or singing the hymn each day.

Stage Thirteen

On the third day, if the clay feels dry to the touch, light the incense and the candles, and then paint the entire simulacrum black. As you do this, speak to the Witch King of your magical successes with him and your future plans. Let this dry. Next, paint the entire simulacrum red. As you do this, speak to the Witch King about your passions and the things you want more of. Let this dry. Paint the entire simulacrum white. As you do this, speak to the Witch King of your hopes and dreams and tell him what you need his help with. Let this dry.

Lastly, paint his sigil (either common or master) on the front of the simulacrum in gold paint. Place this between his three candles and say or sing his hymn once again. The working is complete.

JOURNAL TOPICS

Meditating on the topics presented here in this chapter, answer the following questions in your journal:

1. In this chapter we talked about activating and condensing different types of quintessence. What are types of condensed quintessence that you have worked with in your practice?

2. Our goal with every practice is to deepen our gnosis. How have the practices discussed in this chapter helped to inform your gnosis and how you look at energy?

3. What are natural locations where quintessence might be found? How would you condense it?

Chapter Eight

The Tools of Quintessence

In order to perform any act of successful ritual witchcraft, you must have your basic traditional set of working tools. Without them, all but the most powerful born-witch or warlock is powerless when working at a distance from his victim. They are the tools of your trade, as much as an easel and brushes are of the artist.

———

Paul Huson, *Mastering Witchcraft*

Another one of those things I have wavered back and forth on in my work is the use of the traditional tools. There are two schools of thought when it comes to them, the first being that of a folk magic perspective, which says that you should be using practical implements in your magic: your chalice can be a teacup, your athame a butter knife, a kitchen pot your cauldron, etc. Their common use and practicality are said to imbue them with extra power, and this school of thought also emphasizes that anything that works, works. The second school suggests that magical tools should never be used for anything besides magic and that a degree of special attention must be placed on their preparation and preservation. I have come to believe that both of these schools are right and present perfectly functional approaches to magic.

The issue is, however, that neither school works well on their own. For starters, there is something to be said about practicality. We know it isn't likely that the folk magicians of old actually had access to fancy tools. They would have worked with whatever they had and would have used everyday objects found around the home. This would have either limited the number of tools used or perhaps made every available tool magical in its own right. Witches if anything are creatures of familiarity and would have instinctively sought out the quintessence in their environment. On the other hand, when you stumble into high magic, you see how tools that are treated with an elevated degree of intention and attention are capable of wielding great power on their own.

It is one thing to have never been exposed to this sort of power and not understand what is going on behind the scenes with the tools, possibly even forming the opinion that there is nothing more profound there. It is another thing altogether to dismiss the practice of working with special tools because you haven't been exposed to them and then assume that you have all the pieces of the puzzle. I was one of those witches who gave up on having special tools, mostly because I couldn't afford them or couldn't find them, but after realizing that my practice was missing something, I revisited the practice and found a hidden gem that often goes without notice.

Our tools are vehicles for quintessence that help connect the witch's dream to its power. As energy manifests within them, it is altered and changed so that by the time we are ready to use that tool, it has already been sculpted for our purpose. As you might imagine, specific materials and ways of preparing those materials might be more efficient than others when reaching for the best end result. A chalice can be a coffee cup, but a silver chalice will sculpt the energies of the goddess with much more ease, and a silver chalice that specifically has been consecrated for the purpose will provide almost perfect efficiency. The tools are just as much shortcuts to the wells of energy we must draw from as they are sensory aides to help us sync into the witch's dream, where we can better interact with quintessence.

Because our tools are vehicles for the energies we must summon and then weave together, we really must give advanced consideration as to the makeup of those tools. For me, the formula that works best is one rooted in the practical and the more fantastical. Tools that have a history and have been used for practical means have a particular sway over our world. Tools that have absorbed quintessential energies have a specific sway over the other worlds. It would make sense to have a tool that possessed influence over both sides of the veil; in theory, it would be in our best interest to procure such a tool.

Antiques! The most powerful tools I own are those which came from a friend or an antique store. I have an affinity for both copper and silver, and I started collecting pieces for magical use over a decade ago. I have a silver knife that I inherited from a grandmother of mine, a copper chalice that I picked up from a flea market, and an iron cauldron that was gifted to me, all of which came preloaded with plenty of juju. All I had to do was clear them of direct intention and voilà! I refer to these types of tools as being "wise" because if they could talk, they would likely have some good stories. Clearing them of direct intention simply erases any specific programming that might have come from foreign sources and resets the item back to its original purpose or frequency. This particular type of clearing removes the influence of past users while allowing you to tap into its history and is appropriate to perform on any object before its conversion to a magical tool.

Clearing Intention

All you need to perform this clearing is salt, spring water, and a white towel. Mix the salt and water. Visualize a white flame and send it into the water, activating the quintessence therein, and say:

> *I summon the oceans from between the worlds*
> *And imbue this water with their strength.*
> *By the King, Queen, and Sacred Other,*
> *I fuse the realms as the salt melts and*
> *Bring forth the sacred well of innocence!*

Pick up or place your hands on the object and visualize a thin blue haze, the remnants of someone else's willpower still barely active but present. Cleanse the tool with the freshly empowered spring water, using the towel to make sure you cover the whole surface. In the case that you are needing to cleanse a wood surface, such as a finished wand or altar table, add oil soap to the water once it has been charged and then use the solution without worry of damaging the wood. As you clean the object, send white fire out of your hands with every motion and visualize yourself polishing out the thin blue layer of energy. Once the whole object has been removed of this blue haze and is vibrating brightly with white fire, say:

> *By the three crowns and the sum of their parts,*
> *I reclaim this (insert tool name) in the name of all worlds*
> *And break the bonds of all former masters.*
> *IO, IO, SHAE-O, IO, IO HÉ-O. So must it be!*

Consecrating Tools

When we consecrate something, we are essentially doing two fundamental things. First, we are anchoring the witch's dream in mundanity. When we go to pick up that tool, we will be channeling the power of whatever that tool is programmed to channel instantly. My spirit allies taught me that we should be able to instantly tap into a ritual tool's power, and it should be so strong in this power that even someone who does not possess the witch blood should be able to feel the energy off of it. Think about that for a second. If someone who doesn't have the natural hardware to sense preternatural forces were able to detect the power coming off an item, that item has to be pretty potent. It also has to have the ability to pierce through the veils of perception. As instant access to the wells of power, our magical tools should possess that much strength on their own, which makes them unique and, in my opinion, deserving of a little extra-special attention.

The other essential thing that consecrating a tool or object does is prepare that object to actually wield this sort of power, sort of like tempering it for use. For this reason, we should be aware of the properties related to each unique part of the tool. Sometimes it is as simple as knowing the wood your wand is made of, but other times it is being able to identify multiple types of stones and metals or specific patterns and shapes. So if you get a wand that is made from willow and is adorned with crystals, you absolutely must be familiar with how the properties of willow and those stones work together. Each unique combination of properties will create a different frequency and produce a different set of principles when the tool is used. Whatever your tool is made of, do some research as to the properties its components carry and connect to the quintessential force within them before consecration.

Sometimes acts of consecration can take minutes, sometimes they take days or even months; depending on the specific energies you are working with, they may also require you to do a little traveling. Because we are programming these tools with particular sets of energies, we have to do the work related to their consecration when and where those energies are most available. For example, if you were consecrating a blade to the moon, the entire consecration would take place over a moon cycle. If you were going to consecrate a blade to the full moon, you would only need to do the working while the moon is full. Likewise, if you were binding the powers of the ocean to an object, you would need to actually travel to the ocean to do so. For a tool to be a substitute for higher power, you must first encounter that power and expose that item to it.

Consecration requires us to mark tools with specific sigils or runes, which will be used to instruct the flow of energy once the tool is drawn. These sigils are a code that instructs quintessence as to its direction and cues you as the user into the source of that quintessence. Different systems have different codes, and the goal of most advanced witches is to develop their own secret system that is known only to them and their spirit allies. Any one of the symbols you have seen in this book can be used as a piece of this operation, as well as any symbols that hold specific purpose to you or any sigil you make of your own accord.

At this point, I am going to assume you are well aware of what each tool is associated with and don't need me to go into great depth as to their implementation. However, since most books lack a set of consecration symbols and rituals, and not all witches have had the instruction on how to consecrate their own tools, the following, from my own tradition, is a brief introduction to the Lesser Rites of Consecration for each tool.

The Lesser Rites of Consecration

These rites are versatile and should be altered to fit the needs of each specific tool. As an act of preparation, perform the previously mentioned clearing of direct intention before moving onto inscribing. Each tool will have a specific act of ingress that will involve some sort of inscription, an act of congress that will align the powers and charge the object, and an act of egress that will seal the energies and complete the working.

The Athame

The athame is one of the most popular and beloved of the witching tools. It pierces the veil and cuts sharply into all worlds. It is a tool of air, of focus and clarity, of perception and willpower. The athame can be made of any material that can be rendered into a sharp edge, most commonly steel, bone, and brass. Again, different material responds differently to different energies. A steel blade is not going to be conducive to working with the fae due to its heavy iron content. A bone blade would not be appropriate for working with angels as it would vibrate too slowly. No matter what the material is made of, it must be sharp! Part of its effectiveness comes from its sharpness, and if it is going to pierce the veil, it better be razor sharp. Sharpen the edges to the best of your ability and be sure to keep it covered when it is not being used. It is a knife, so remember it is a tool and a weapon, and that is its purpose.

During ingress, if the blade is metal, the sigil would be engraved, but when not possible, draw the sigil with black marker (it works!) or with black water-resistant paint. If it is made from wood or bone, then burning the design into the medium is generally preferred.

athame sigil

Ingress

Place the above sigil on your blade. Visualize and draw upon a blue flame and allow it to circulate through your body for some time. When you feel a sufficient charge, take a deep breath and then blow over your athame, visualizing the blue fire pouring out from your breath and empowering the symbols on the tool.

Congress
Program the athame by cutting each of the following three times: a piece of flesh (meat or leather works best; sorry, vegans: the best option for you probably would be to use reclaimed leather), a piece of earth (stab the ground), and lastly by cutting through a knot that has been tied three times. With each cut visualize the pressure and force actually quickening the power within the blade and enlivening it.

As you cut through the flesh, say: "By the Queen of the Red Flame!"
As you cut through the earth, say: "By the Queen of the Black Flame!"
As you cut through the knot, say: "By the Queen of the White Flame!"
Draw upon the blue fire once again. Channel the energy through your athame, lift it up so it is pointing directly in the air, and visualize the blue fire shooting up toward the heavens with laser-like precision. Say:

By the witch's power and the triple queen,
I charge this blade to part the unseen.
Sharp and swift, like my will,
The witch's blade will tread the mill.
By these marks of sigil and spell,
May it part the worlds from heaven to hell!

Egress
Seal this rite of consecration by slowly bringing the blade down so that it is directly in front of your eyes, and then visualize the blue fire slowly calming and settling into a subtle burn. Kiss the tip of the blade on both sides, and then say:

Awakened now by my desire,
Always to burn with my blue fire.
So must it be.

The Boline

The boline is a crescent-shaped knife that is usually only sharpened on one side and traditionally has a white hilt. Much like the athame, the boline is used in magic to cut but is generally reserved specifically for use with herbs. The boline is also particularly excellent for working with the dead and the spirits of the lower worlds. Like the athame, the boline should be sharp along the edge used to cut.

Ingress

Place the following sigil on your blade. Visualize and draw upon an indigo-colored flame and allow it to circulate through your body for some time. When you feel a sufficient charge, take a deep breath and then blow over your boline, visualizing the indigo fire pouring out from your breath and empowering the symbols on the tool.

boline sigil

Congress

Program the boline by performing each of the following tasks: harvest a bundle of herbs with the boline under the dark moon, harvest a sliver of earth from a cemetery or crossroads, and harvest a piece of bark from a dying tree. With each cut visualize the pressure and force actually quickening the power within the boline and enlivening it.

As you cut through the herbs, say, "By the Queen of the Red Flame!"
As you cut through the earth, say, "By the Queen of the Black Flame!"
As you cut through the bark, say, "By the Queen of the White Flame!"

Draw upon the indigo fire once again, and channel the energy through your boline. Lift it up so it is pointing directly in the air and visualize the indigo fire shooting through the blade and bending toward the underworld with laser-like precision. Say:

> *By the witch's power and the triple queen,*
> *I charge this blade to part the unseen.*
> *Sharp and swift, like my will,*
> *The witch's scythe will tread the mill.*
> *By these marks of sigil and spell,*
> *May it part the worlds from heaven to hell!*

Egress

Seal this rite of consecration by slowly bringing the blade down so that it is at eye level and then visualize the indigo flame slowly calming and settling into a subtle burn. Kiss the blade on both sides and then say:

> *Awakened now by my desire,*
> *Always to burn with my indigo fire.*
> *So must it be.*

The Wand

Wands are tools of fire, representative of the male phallus (as are the athame and sword) and the potency of willpower. They are connected to the creative and regenerative forces in the universe. Traditionally made of wood, though frequently seen fashioned out of crystals or metal, wands are one of the oldest tools known to magic.

Ingress

Place the following sigil on the handle of your wand. Visualize and draw upon a blue flame, and allow it to circulate through your body for some time. When you feel a sufficient charge, take a deep breath and then blow over your wand, visualizing the blue fire pouring out from your breath and empowering the symbols on the tool. Pass the wand over an open flame three times.

wand sigil

Congress

Program the wand by performing the following tasks: draw a pentacle upon the earth with your wand, stir a bowl containing water clockwise until it creates a whirlpool, and, lastly, run the wand along the inseam of your thighs, allowing it to pass over your sexual organs. As you perform each action, visualize the motion and sensations empowering the tool.

As you pass the wand along your inseam, say: "By the King of the Red Flame!"

As you draw the pentagram upon the earth, say: "By the King of the Black Flame!"

As you stir the water, say: "By the King of the White Flame!"

Draw upon the blue fire once again. Channel the energy through your wand, lift it up so it is pointing directly in the air, and visualize the blue fire shooting up toward the heavens with laser-like precision. Say:

> By the witch's power and the triple king,
> I charge this wand to bare my sting.
> Sharp and swift, like my will,
> A witch's wand to tread the mill.
> By these marks of sigil and spell,
> May it travel the worlds from heaven to hell!

Egress

Seal this rite of consecration by slowly bringing the wand down so that it is directly in front of your eyes and then visualize the Blue Fire slowly calming and settling into a subtle burn. Kiss your wand and say:

> Awakened now by my desire,
> Always to burn with my blue fire.
> So must it be.

The Broom or Besom

Brooms are essential to our rites as they are used to cleanse space, to create borders or hedges, and for protection. They are especially loved by those of us in Sacred Fires, and we go to great lengths to learn how to work with their magic. Sacred to the Divine Other, they are tools of directionality and duality. The handle classically symbolizes the phallus, while the brush symbolizes the vagina; its combined power symbolizes the unification of the two halves of God Herself. Brooms used for the heavier magics, which would require consecration, should be made of wood and have some form of natural bristle. It isn't always possible to find a natural binding, but at the very least the handle and brush should be made of all-natural and simple materials. The metal brooms you get at the supermarket won't cut it in the long term. Part of what makes a broom powerful is that its handle was grown over time and comes with all the energy from that process.

Ingress

Place the following sigils on your handle. Visualize and draw upon an orange flame, and allow it to circulate through your body for some time. When you feel a sufficient charge, take a deep breath and then blow over your entire broom, visualizing the orange fire pouring out from your breath and empowering the symbols on the tool.

broom / besom sigil

Congress

Program the broom by performing the following acts: lift the broom so that the bristles are pointing toward the ceiling, then use it to draw a clockwise circle three times; flip it over and draw a counter-clockwise circle on the floor with the bristles; lastly, sweep a crossroads with the broom (or your front doorstep and back doorstep). With each motion visualize the pressure and force actually quickening the power within the broom and enlivening it. As you sweep the ground beneath you, say: "By the Queen of the Red Flame!" As you sweep the threshold or the crossroads, say: "By the Queen of the Black Flame!" As you draw a circle in the air with the bristles, say: "By the Queen of the White Flame!"

Draw upon the orange fire once again, and channel the energy through your broom. Lift it up so that it is perpendicular to the ground and the handle is pointing directly in the air, then visualize the orange fire shooting up toward the heavens with laser-like precision. Say:

By the witch's power and the Divine Other,
I charge this broom to uncover.
Sharp and swift, like my will,
The witch's broom shall tread the mill.
By these marks of sigil and spell,
May it part the worlds from heaven to hell!

Egress

Seal this rite of consecration by slowly bringing the broom down so that it is directly in front of your eyes, and then visualize the orange fire slowly calming and settling into a subtle burn. Kiss the tip of the broom handle and the bristles, then say:

Awakened now by my desire,
Always to burn with my orange fire.
So must it be.

The Stang and the Staff

Traditionally, a stang is a vertical altar that has been made from special wood that has a fork at the top, creating a Y shape. It is engraved with sigils, and then an iron nail is driven through the bottom to prevent any energy from draining out. The stang is considered to be masculine, another phallic symbol, whereas the horizontal altar is feminine. These vertical altars are supposed to be specific to the god force. I am, I guess, rebel enough to have a stang dedicated to the Witch Queen, and quite a sizable horizontal altar dedicated to the Witch King. In some traditions the stang represents the axis mundi and the Star Goddess.

A staff is similar to a stang, representing the axis mundi and the phallus, but it lacks the forked top and the iron nail. This is a tool that is more movable and can do much of the work of the wand with more weight. Similarly, the stang and staff can be made of any wood, the properties of that wood being the underlying energy of the tool. Commonly, these are made from oak, redwood, ash, thorn, and birch. Regardless, the related magic work is almost the same, save the sigils.

Ingress

Place the following sigils on your handle. Visualize and draw upon an orange flame once again, and allow it to circulate through your body for some time. When you feel a sufficient charge, take a deep breath and then blow over your entire stang/staff, visualizing the orange fire pouring out from your breath and empowering the symbols on the tool.

stang/staff sigil

Congress

Program the stang/staff by performing the following acts: hold the stang out as far as your sun hand will allow and drive the bottom into the earth. Using the stang/staff as a point of fascination, walk around it, creating a small circle with the stand in the center.

Draw upon the orange fire once again, and channel the energy through your stang/staff. Lift it up slightly but keep it perpendicular to the ground so the forked top is pointing directly in the air, then visualize the orange fire shooting up toward the heavens with laser-like precision from the two points. Say:

> By witch's will I charge this stang/staff to be
> The tree of all worlds, containing the three.
> By the thrones I imbue it with power, blessed by this sacred hour!
> By these marks of sigil and spell,
> May it align the worlds from heaven to hell!

Egress

Seal this rite of consecration by slowly bringing the stang/staff down so that it is directly in front of your eyes, and then visualize the orange fire slowly calming and settling into a subtle burn. Kiss the tip of the stang/staff and then its bottom. Say:

> Awakened now by my desire,
> Always to burn with my orange fire.
> So must it be.

The Cauldron

Cauldrons are probably my favorite magical tool as they are incredibly versatile and there really is just something extra witchy about chanting over a cauldron! Aside from aesthetics, the cauldron is traditionally made of cast iron and as such is incredibly heat tolerant. This is part of the energy we will be drawing from, so it is an important thing to keep in mind as you go cauldron shopping. You don't want a cauldron that will break if it gets too hot or if it gets accidentally dropped, so durability is also an issue.

My first cauldron was made of green glass, and I used it for years. It was more of an antique potpourri vase, but it had a large mouth and got the job done. I have used ceramic pots and ashtrays, mason jars and aluminum pie tins; all of these will work in a pinch, but nothing beats the real deal.

What makes a cauldron so unique is that they are vehicles for transformation and as such can transmute anything that goes into them into something else. Think of their original purpose of cooking: mixing various ingredients to make a meal that would sustain a family for days. Though traditionally a tool of female energies, mythology is full of gods and goddesses who are associated with the cauldron for this purpose, so we can't overlook this origin. All this being said, a cauldron is a powerful tool in the craft as it is the perfect vessel to contain our quintessential fusions.

cauldron sigil

Ingress

Place the above sigils on your cauldron. Visualize and draw upon a blue flame and allow it to circulate through your body for some time. When you feel a sufficient charge, take a deep breath and then blow it into the cauldron, visualizing the blue fire pouring out from your breath and empowering the symbols on the tool.

Congress

Program the cauldron by performing the following acts: place the cauldron so that it may catch moonlight and then fill it one-sixth of the way with salt, blessing herbs, and alcohol. Light a flame therein and say:

> By the Queen of the Red Flame,
> By the Queen of the Black Flame,
> And by the Queen of the White Flame!

I summon the nine sacred fires!
Be here now in my cauldron's flame
And burn bright with quintessence!

Draw upon the blue fire once again and channel the energy into the cauldron fire. Say:

Blessed cauldron of ancient art,
A gift from the gods they did impart.
Quicken now with the sacred flame
And be blessed with all their names.
By the thrones, I call all nine,
Become one with this cauldron of mine!

Egress

Seal this rite of consecration when the fire burns out by blowing it a kiss and saying:

Awakened now by my desires,
Always to burn with sacred fires.
So must it be.

The Chalice

The chalice is traditionally seen as being sacred to the element of water as well as the female anatomy. It is the breast full of milk and the womb full of the waters of life. In my tradition it represents the regenerative forces of these things as well as being a tool that represents the physical body. Like our skin, the cup holds the blood and life force of the witch. It represents the sacred bond of a coven and community and is sacred to Aradia. It is made of silver or copper and should be blessed at dusk.

Ingress

Place the following sigils on the cup part of the chalice. Visualize and draw upon a white flame, and allow it to circulate through your body for some time. When you feel a sufficient charge, take a deep breath and then blow over your entire chalice, visualizing the white fire pouring out from your breath and empowering the symbols on the tool.

chalice sigil

Congress

Program the chalice by performing the following acts: fill it with water at a stream or river, but do so with the mouth facing the direction the water is flowing; you don't want the water to pour into it but rather to slowly fill as you submerge it. You want the chalice to charge with the energy of this flow of power. Say:

> By the Queen of the White Flame, the power of water I claim.
> Be one with this chalice as you are with the stream,
> Bring thy quintessence into the witch's dream!

Lift the chalice up in the air and then slowly pour the contents back into the running water.

Egress

Seal this rite of consecration by slowly bringing the chalice to eye level and then visualizing the white fire slowly calming and settling into a subtle burn. Kiss the bell of the chalice and say:

> Awakened now by my desire,
> Always to burn with my white fire.
> So must it be.

The Altar Paten

The altar paten is a plate or shallow bowl that is made in the shape of a pentacle or contains within its center a pentacle and is usually made from either wood, metal, or clay. Traditionally, it would be used itself as a tool for consecration; offerings made during ritual are to be placed on the paten. I like to think of it as a charging station on my altar that I can put magical objects such as fetishes, candles, charm bags, and other amulets to soak up energy during workings. Once the paten has been consecrated, it can be used as a powerful tool for manifestation.

The paten has no sigils beyond its pentacle.

Ingress

Visualize and draw upon a blue flame, and allow it to circulate through your body for some time. When you feel a sufficient charge, take a deep breath and then blow over your paten, visualizing the blue flame pouring out from your breath and empowering the symbols on the tool.

Congress

Program and consecrate the paten thusly. Pass the paten over the earth, over a flame, through a doorway, through fresh running water, and through incense smoke. As you do this, chant:

> *By the Queen of the Red Flame,*
> *By the Queen of the Black Flame,*
> *And by the Queen of the White Flame!*
> *By the King of the Red Flame,*
> *By the King of the Black Flame,*
> *And by the King of the White Flame!*
> *By the Numinous One!*
> *By the Numinous One!*
> *By the Numinous One!*

By their power, this be done!
By their power, this be done!
By their power, this be done!

Draw upon the blue fire once again and channel the energy into your paten. Lift it up so it is eye level and visualize the blue fire shooting through it like lightning. Say:

By the witch's power and the triple queen,
By the mystery and the triple king!
I charge this paten to summon the unseen.
By the sign of the art of the spell,
May it marry the worlds from heaven to hell!

Egress

Seal this rite of consecration by visualizing the blue fire slowly calming and settling into a subtle burn. Kiss the tip of the paten on both sides, and then say:

Awakened now by my desire,
Always to burn with my blue fire.
So must it be.

· · · · · · · · ·

There are many ways to weave quintessence. Tools aren't necessary, but they make it easier for us to tap into wells of power in an instant. You are the ultimate tool; you don't need anything other than your will to perform powerful spell and ritual craft. Everything else is just an extension of your power. When you are performing at your best, there is little that can stop you. Sometimes, however, it is harder than others to be at our best, and this is when tools become a boon. The more energy you pour into them *before* you need them, the more powerful they will be when you *do* need them.

Journal Topics

Meditating on the topics presented here in this chapter, answer the following questions in your journal:

1. When you perform magic, how do you reach out and connect with the magical quintessence within your tools and ingredients?

2. What are some ways that you can keep activated quintessence around for quick use?

3. Which of the witch's tools do you have, and how do you work with them? Have you blessed and consecrated them? What is the difference in energy like before and after?

4. Sketch the sigils and symbols you use on your tools and what they mean to you. How do these symbols connect to the witch's dream?

Chapter Nine

Lucid Dreaming and the Witch's Sabbat

She oft and much rode on a pitchfork by night with her paramour, but not far, on account of her duties. At such devilish trysts she met a big man with a grey beard, who sat in a chair like a great prince and was a richly attired.

———

From the "Judgement of the Witch Walpurga Hausmännin," E. Wm. Monter, *European Witchcraft*

Somewhere in time, lost in the fog of memory and myth, lies a realm where witches dance with ghosts and spirits of all kinds. In this place we let go of ourselves and of reality, surrendering to ecstatic oneness and nothingness, daring to look into the darkness of the most hidden places, meanwhile being prepared to make a bargain with the shadowy figures who lurk within them. Here our most sacred rites—rites that bind us as witch kin across tradition and lineage—are performed.

Here we surrender to quintessence as ink surrenders to water, merging life force and essence, losing separateness and dissolving into oneness with the witch power and those who serve as its agents.

In this place, this egregore of preternatural power, we meet with faeries and gods, demons and Nephilim, angels and the spirits of witches who have lived before us and who have never lived at all. Here we slip away from our identities and willfully join the court of the Witch King and Queen. Here, in sabbat, where the holy and the profane become one and the moon eclipses the sun, we witches set our souls free as we dance in bittersweet rapture.

Sabbat is more than a state of mind reached through soul flight or a plane of being tucked away in the witch's tree. Sabbat is the realm of the master spirits of witchcraft, a place that is as much a temple as it is an experience.

Some of you may be reading this and feeling a bit confused, and for a good reason. The term *sabbat* is often used in popular witchcraft or Wicca to describe one of the eight festival days that mark the "pagan calendar." This is something that we know was adopted in the 1950s, and, after a little marketing, became the norm for many pagan traditions. Indeed, the celebration of these eight feast days is one of the few things that can be found as a uniting force throughout most of paganism, just not all.

During the trials of the Inquisition, one of the more viral stories running around was that witches would transform themselves into a beast, or ride on the back of a beast, and fly to the top of a mountain somewhere. There they would meet with witches from all over the region and make deals with the chief of all demons, the Devil himself. In exchange for a few newborn babies, an interdimensional orgy, their souls, and a kiss on the ass, witches were said to receive all sorts of infernal powers to help them do their bidding while on earth. Attendance or even the suspicion of attendance to this soirée was enough to get you killed.

And why wouldn't it? At a place like that, anyone could gain access to powers that not only would put those who didn't have it at a disadvantage, but it would also anchor these forces among the community. This would have been an obvious threat to those with reason to fear such things. It only makes sense to do everything you can to protect what you have, and beyond the motives of the accusers, or what these people often stood to gain if someone were convicted of witchcraft, there was a real fear that the things that go bump in the night were out to get them. We can look back on these times as those of ignorance, but we can't neglect the actual fear those people felt, and I would be remiss if I didn't draw a comparison to our modern war on terrorism.

To the people around during the times of witchcraft persecution in the Western world, witches were the terrorists. They were the ones poisoning lands and killing crops, spoiling fresh milk and bringing illness. They genuinely believed that witches were agents of the devil and that they were out to destroy civilization. No one was safe from suspicion, and while women were the focus of persecution in the Americas and Spain, men were the primary target in Scotland and parts of Germany. Today the evangelical persecution of witches in east Africa is predominantly focused on women and children as young as infants.[7] The response to a belief in such evil and the extents to which people ignored reason (and what science they did or do have) is a direct result of this fear and the political motives of those who know how to use fear. We witches, no matter how far removed time has taken us from this place in history, are still dealing with this sort of fear and fear-mongering in a very real way. It was a tool used to oppress women and keep them subservient, to attack the poor and the undesirable, and to use against your neighbor if they had something you wanted.

7 "Witch Hunt: Africa's Hidden War on Women," *The Independent UK*, accessed July 1, 2017, https://www.independent.co.uk/news/world/africa/witch-hunt-africas-hidden-war-on-women-1642907.html. "Children Are Targets of Nigerian Witch Hunt," *The Guardian UK*, accessed July 1, 2017, https://www.theguardian.com/world/2007/dec/09/tracymcveigh.theobserver.

Most people who died for crimes of witchcraft were not witches, but we carry the weight of their deaths still to this day. Some of us embrace it, some of us ignore it, and some of us tiptoe lightly around the truth that we live in a world that was built on a belief that witchcraft is some sort of spiritual terrorism and that witches are hiding everywhere waiting to attack.

The vast majority of witches out there believe the rites of the witch's sabbat are somehow connected to specific days in a fixed calendar and that they derive from ancient pagan practices that have existed for centuries. The truth is, the modern sabbat—like almost all of contemporary witchcraft and paganism—is a patchwork quilt that has been pieced together by scholars and academics who were themselves removed from these practices. As we reclaimed the word *sabbat,* we divorced ourselves from that magically terrifying place and replaced it with a set of Celtic and Germanic feast days. Yes, words evolve, but that doesn't mean that their origin should be shoved to the side because it makes us uncomfortable or we don't quite understand it.

What does that mean for us? Are we just unwilling spiritual seekers who incidentally became spiritual terrorists? No, and witches as a whole never really were terrorists. Anarchists? Maybe a little bit. The witch power, once live, beckons us to sovereignty, so we don't always like to work with the system that oppresses us. Our sabbat is also not a veritable black market of evil, at least not from our perspective. Like all things misunderstood and lacking the usual Christian tones, the witch's sabbat was demonized and sensationalized to fit a particularly convenient and often patriarchal narrative.

The Witch's Sabbat

While its outward persona may be built on the back of hysteria, the essence of sabbat is both a beautiful and frightening reflection of all the things we forget we were, are, and always will be. The witch's sabbat is a scary place for those who do not know their own strength or beauty, and it is only reachable through the witch's dream. It shows us as we really truly are: the good, the bad, and the ugly of what remains once we are stripped away of ego and the lies we tell ourselves. When we look in this mirror, we see the scars from our past, the augmentation from our spiritual efforts, and the not-altogether-human aspects of our essence. Pardon the phrasing, but here we assume our "ultimate form." This is why it is so scary for most of us; we cannot hide from ourselves anymore or bury our skeletons deep down. Here we see our madness for what it is and wear our motivations like body paint.

Not only do we assume that ultimate form, but we surrender to our ultimate desires and our most basic motivations. Here we are free from the burdens of civility and restraint—here we are beastly demigods embracing everything that means. Here we step into our full power and let it writhe through us in orgasmic bliss. Here is where we obtain the most valuable of all secrets.

To summarize and put it simply, the witch's sabbat is not a day or a set of days, but a plane of being derived from the witch power's connection with the Divine. There, hidden amongst the layers of the witch's tree, we make contact with all those spirits who serve the Witch King and Queen. It is a plane limited only to those who serve as agents in their court and it functions as a sort of temple for many of us, regardless of our persuasion toward or propensity for good or evil, right or wrong.

Traveling to Sabbat

The witch's sabbat can be difficult to comprehend without experiencing it for yourself, so try as I may to describe this wondrous place, words will always fail to do it justice. Traveling to sabbat is not an easy task. This work requires a lot of buildup and self-preparation before you go. To be honest, you will almost never be so vulnerable elsewhere as you are in the witch's sabbat. This usually works out in our favor but can leave the door open for experiences we may not always be ready for. There we are embodiments of our inner selves, and there is nothing to hide behind or protect you other than the good nature of those who rule it. Because of how vulnerable we tend to be during this sort of work, it absolutely requires the use of a protective magical circle.

Sabbatic work is at least 90 percent performed while sleeping or in a deep, deep trance. It requires us to leave our bodies and, like the stories, transform into a beast before flying off to a special destination. The work we have been doing up to this point with the witch's dream has been entirely to prepare you for taking this next step into what we call dreamwork or lucid dreaming.

Dreamwork and the Witch's Sabbat

Lucid dreaming is the mode of operation we use to travel into the witch's sabbat, and while different from astral travel or soul flight, it shares similar fundamental principles with those techniques. The goal, however, isn't necessarily to leave the body and travel to a different dimension, but rather to travel through the inner realms of the mind and the paths of the psyche to get to a different dimension. We are still going to the same places, but we will be getting there differently. Perhaps most importantly, once this skill is developed, it will also give you more power within the planes you visit, making you a formidable force.

You can get to the witch's sabbat through other deep or ecstatic trance methods, but lucid dreaming seems to be the most efficient and pragmatic way of doing so. Is this historically the case? We don't actually know for sure, but lucid dreaming provides the perfect platform for us to experience some of those fantastical elements that were reported during the witch trials, and we do know that witches have been doing magical workings in the dream world ever since witches have been witching. It also invites us, most importantly, to be creators and gods ourselves and to actively engage the subconscious and spiritual. To connect the dots in this way is no far stretch. The witch's sabbat is a very intense place that requires you to be able to experience it in very intense ways. Lucid dreaming provides the necessary environment for this to happen.

Lucid dreaming has a long history of helping people solve some of the most important puzzles of our time, and when applied as an element in witchcraft, it has had a proud history of assisting witches to cultivate and receive some of the most valuable secrets in their trade.

Your witch power is uniquely tuned in to the frequency of the sabbat; you merely need to program the code to take you there. By working with the witch's dream, you have been programming the code all along. The symbols, sigils, and energetic practices that I've shown you are all a part of the work that we do in lucid dreaming. By building your own code and forms of communication with quintessence, you have already opened pathways for this work to manifest.

Dreamworking

When I first tried lucid dreaming, I was wholly unimpressed. It took days for me to have even the slightest experience, and even then I wasn't sure I had anything substantial to claim. After a few more attempts, I gave up and chalked it all up to being New Age nonsense. Eventually, however, I found myself reading the work of Andrew Chumbley and decided to try it again, this time with a more occult focus.

Andrew Chumbley wrote some pretty incredible grimoires, almost all of which have to do with the subject of oneiric praxis and the witch's sabbat, but they are mostly indigestible. I was able to pick up hints from his writings but had to start from scratch when it came to finding a practical approach that yielded results. Occultists can write all of the poetry they want, but none of that is helpful if you can't piece together the operations that one should undergo.

After many failed attempts and lots of trial and error, I stumbled into a successful lucid dream. After experiencing it for myself, I quickly realized that I had been making it way more difficult than it actually was, and it was likely that all the added stress to "make it happen" actually kept it from happening! According to researchers at the University of Northampton, after reviewing the metadata from thirty-four lucid dream studies they performed between 1966 and 2016, roughly 55 percent of the population can lucid dream, and half of those people were frequent lucid dreamers.[8] The same researchers found that it was up to 70 percent more common for lucid dreamers to come from cultures with pastimes related to meditation and video games, which would predispose them to virtual or holographic immersive open worlds. These are two things I am no stranger to, so I figured the odds had to be in my favor.

Once I knew what to look for, I realized I had been lucid dreaming my entire life; I just usually do it at the end of my sleep cycles. It was actually quite a normal phenomenon for me, but my lucid dreaming experiences were different from what I was told they should be. They were different because I am psychic and am plugged continuously into one signal or the other, and some of my most vivid experiences happen in dreams. A constant complaint from my partners has always been that I talk in my sleep—not just a few words here and there but full-on conversations. Sometimes I will remember what was discussed, sometimes I won't, but on more than one occasion I have either come to learn some exceedingly important lesson or I have been helping the spirits of the dead cross over.

Lucid dreams happen when we gain consciousness in our dreams. Once we are conscious, we are capable of taking control of the dream to some extent. Like the witch's dream, the lucid dream is a stage and a laboratory for your magical work, just a much bigger and more powerful one. Spirits can move more freely, as they have fewer barriers to

8   US National Library of Medicine, accessed July 2017, https://www.ncbi.nlm.nih .gov/pubmed/27337287.

contend with, and you have fewer obstacles to get in the way of your will and its manifestation.

There isn't much difference between a dream and a lucid dream on the outside, the most significant being that in a lucid dream you know you are conscious of the act of dreaming and have some degree of control of the dream.

The Witch's Dream and Preparing for the Lucid Dream

As I mentioned previously, all of the work you have been doing in the witch's dream has given you a major head start. The witch's dream is a term I invented to describe the mental and psychic place we, as psychic agents of the craft, can go to and work with so we experience and explore our talents. It is a technique that developed out of a need to control and make sense of my gifts, and it just so happened to be the key to getting the whole lucid dream thing going for me.

For lucid dreaming to work, it requires us to build a set of mental triggers and to prepare the mind by creating an environment where conscious thought is capable of directing the events of the mind once the body has fallen asleep. The work of cultivating the witch's dream provides fertile ground for us to plant the seeds of the lucid dream. In many ways, I have actually grown to view the witch's dream as the waking equivalent of the lucid dream, a lite version of what is possible in the more advanced stages of lucid dreaming. As you develop one, it becomes easier to work with the other, and as you become more influential in the dream world, you also become more influential in the waking world.

Lucid dreams help us to develop gnosis in ways that other techniques can't. So much of our lives are processed during our dreams, and having the ability to be an active participant in them can give you access to parts of your mind that would otherwise be left unexplored. Upon waking, we can then integrate the wisdom obtained by exploring the inner mysteries in this way.

For us to lucid dream, we have to enhance aspects of our practice related to the witch's dream. In addition to the sigils that you have been using to sync yourself into certain aspects of the witch's dream, you will need to install a very important trigger: one that represents the waking world, or real world. It may sound a little odd, but once you start lucid dreaming, it can be easy to get mixed up and end up getting lost, forgetting that you have the power to get back, or worse, the ability to control what it is that you see. Time moves differently in these instances; five minutes when you're awake could feel like months or years in a lucid dream. Having a trigger to check in with to see if you are awake or in a dream can be a significant help in avoiding unnecessary confusion and panic.

In the case of building triggers for dreamwork, we are generally talking about selecting an object we see in everyday life that should be inanimate in nature. I have used many triggers with success; the key is to select a trigger that is ordinary but not likely to pop up in a dream or to involve your other physical senses besides sight. To take it a step further, I also have had much luck working with tools I use in my craft that require me to be mentally and spiritually aligned "in the moment."

For instance, as a card reader, I often have tarot and oracle decks all over the house. What I don't usually have handy is a deck of playing cards. I keep a deck of playing cards next to my bed and in my office. Once or twice a day, I pick up those decks and say "I am awake" while I study and take in all of the unique characteristics of the deck. It is now habitual for me to align myself the minute I pick up a deck of cards—any deck of cards, because I have been reading them for over twenty years. While I might expect tarot cards to pop up in my dreams, I don't expect playing cards to appear, and since I have that automatic response to touching any deck of cards, using the trigger of playing cards has extra mental reinforcement to remind me of being awake and present.

Taste is one of those senses that we often do not experience while dreaming, so I use the taste (and sensation) of cold water as a trigger. I may see a glass of water in my dream, but do I taste it? Do I feel it moving down my throat? Again, each time I wake up and drink a glass of water, especially during the night, I say to myself, "I am awake." Performing the purifying ritual known as Kala[9] is part of my daily practice and requires me to drink fresh water. As a result of the ritual, I am brought into a relaxed, focused state.

After selecting a trigger or set of triggers for yourself, you should spend the next week programming them into your psyche. Each time you see or feel your trigger, reinforce the connection by saying "I am awake" and continuously looking at the details and features of your trigger. Once you have begun to program the trigger, it is unwise to alter it later on or halfway through the process. Finish programming one trigger, and once you can see it and your automatic response is to think "I am awake" rather than having to remind yourself to do so, then you can move on to adding other triggers. We want to get to the point with our triggers that they prompt our awareness of the waking state whether we see them while dreaming or not. Take your time, build your trigger with precision and focus, and then continue to reinforce it throughout your practice.

You will need to keep a dream journal or use your book of shadows or magical journal; it doesn't matter as long as you keep it next to where you sleep and it is easy to get to first thing when you wake up.

You should take your work regarding momentary personal awareness to the next level. Spend extra time paying attention to the details of your surroundings, how things like texture differ from one surface to another, and when you listen to music, try to pick out the different instruments and their parts. Your brain needs to be able to spot multiple details at once when you are lucid dreaming, so start that habit while you are awake.

9 Hunter, *The Witch's Book of Power*, 43.

Lucid Dreaming in Five Easy Steps

It may sound a bit gimmicky, but lucid dreaming really can be done in five easy steps, especially if you have been working with the witch's dream and already have triggers set. Once you get this down, going to the witch's sabbat is just around the corner. If at first you don't succeed, continue to try; even with this being a more relaxed approach, it still may take multiple attempts.

Step One: Spend lots of time in the witch's dream and being aware of the energy that surrounds you. Play music, preferably without words, that makes you feel magical and connected. Cast your spells, tune in to the spirits, and spend time being aligned. The more time you spend in this sort of headspace while you are awake, the easier it will be to slip into it once you are asleep.

Step Two: Two hours before bed, turn off all screens and avoid any unnatural light. If you need light, try to keep it dim or use candles. Turn off the volume on your phone, but keep the alarm functional and give yourself time to relax and sink a little further into your witch's dream. Check in with your spirits, anoint yourself with a psychic type of ritual oil, and meditate or journal while you spend time simply suspended in the witch's dream.

Step Three: Set two alarms, one for four hours before you normally wake up and one for one hour before you normally wake up. Align your souls, and then go to bed.

Step Four: When the first alarm goes off, it will initiate the lucid dreaming process. Allow yourself to wake up for only a few moments and then go right back to sleep and try to keep your eyes closed as much as possible. This time when you go back to bed allow your body to fall back to sleep but keep your mind active. You do this by either focusing on a symbol or sigil, the lines and shapes on the inside of your eyelids, or by remember-

ing the dream you had just woken up from. This will all feel
a bit choppy at first but will eventually smooth into either a
continuation of the previous dream you were having or into a
new dream. You will repeat this process when the second alarm
goes off, each time waking up for only a few moments and then
going back to sleep while holding onto consciousness.

Your goal is to remain conscious when the body falls asleep
and then enter a dream-state. Once in a dream, look around; if
you have control over the way you are viewing your surroundings, you are probably in a lucid dream state. Do a reality check;
do you see your trigger? If not, then you are definitely in a lucid
dream! Have fun, see what comes up to you, and stay calm. If
you get too excited, you will likely wake yourself up. One thing
to mention here is that while doing your reality check, you want
to make sure you are able to see those specific details that you
observed while setting your trigger in the first place. I used the
example of a deck of playing cards as a trigger. Your mind could
easily just show you a deck of playing cards, even one similar to
the one you use as a trigger. As you do your reality check with
your triggers, look for details that are missing. For instance, in
the dream the suits might be different or perhaps the colors are
changed. Regardless of how vivid our lucid dream may be, there
will always be something different in the details that will let you
know whether you are dreaming or not.

Step Five: Wake up and immediately write down what you experienced in your journal. Because this can be difficult and remembering details gets harder the longer you are awake, I do this in
three steps. During the first step, I write down bullet points that
describe the big things about the dream. The second and third
steps are just me going through those bullet points and adding
more details with each pass. By the end of the third pass, I try to
have all of the details I can remember on the page.

Keep doing this, and each time it will get easier and easier. Use your lucid dream experiences as an advanced platform for the work you do in the witch's dream, to solve your long-term problems, and to practice your skills traversing the worlds of the witch's tree. Once you get the hang of it, lucid dreaming is an incredible tool to connect spirit, mind, and the other side.

Flying to the Witch's Sabbat

For this, you will need:

- A healthy pinch each of the following: mugwort, chamomile, wormwood, rue, and lavender
- A small black sachet pouch
- A white pillowcase
- A pillow
- Black thread
- A needle
- The witch's sabbat sigil
- A ritual drum (you can use your hand and your chest if you don't have a drum)
- A stang
- A broom
- The simulacrum of the Witch King
- The simulacrum of the Witch Queen

Being able to successfully lucid dream and perform dreamwork allows you to travel to the witch's sabbat with ease. It is definitely advanced work and isn't for everyone. For some, the images seen within the witch's sabbat are vulgar and intense, while to others they are inviting and subtle. The sabbat contains the memories of many things, many people, and many places, and it is constantly shifting between those memories. As a witch, the map to get there is already inside of you; you just need to find it there inside of your witch power.

You can visit the witch's sabbat at any time or on any day. Because this work is draining and requires both preparation and dedication, we generally reserve it for feast days and full moons. Each visit is special and unique, and it is unlikely that you will always find the same beings when you go each time, save for the sabbat king and queen, so we also tend to cherish the experiences we have there.

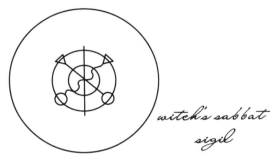

witch's sabbat
sigil

Preparation

You will go about every single process you would if you were going to lucid dream, but we are going to direct the flow of the dream to this special place we call sabbat. To do this, we will need to set some additional triggers. Take a white pillowcase and stitch upon it with black thread the sigil for the witch's sabbat (above). Make a small sachet of mugwort, chamomile, wormwood, rue, and lavender, and place it into the pillowcase along with your regular pillow. Bless and consecrate the pillow with white fire by channeling the flame into the sigil and chanting:

> *By the Queen of the Red Flame,*
> *By the Queen of the Black Flame,*
> *And by the Queen of the White Flame!*
> *By the King of the Red Flame,*
> *By the King of the Black Flame,*
> *And by the King of the White Flame!*

By the Numinous One!
By the Numinous One!
By the Numinous One!
By their power, this be done!
By their power, this be done!
By their power, this be done!

Check and empower all ritual wards and make offerings to any spirits that you work with who have not had an offering recently. It is also customary to make offerings to any dead who have recently passed or who have had recent deathdays (the anniversary of their physical death).

For your trip to sabbat, you will need to lie with your head in the west and your feet in the east, so you will need to orient your bed or create a makeshift bed. At the bottom of your bed place the simulacrum for the Witch Queen and at the top of your bed place the simulacrum for the Witch King. She will guard your body and keep it safe while this working proceeds, and he will lead you to the eternal sabbat. In the north place your stang or staff with the top pointing in the direction of the east. In the south place your broom with the brush pointing toward the west.

Ingress
Ingress must begin several hours before bed and should involve the following steps.

The day of the trip, if not several days before and leading up to it, spend lots of time in the witch's dream and stay aware of the energy that surrounds you. Specifically, reach out to your familiar(s) and spirit allies and engage them frequently throughout the day. Spend time in front of your altar making offerings of drink and incense, lighting the three candles of red, white, and black, and reciting your secret prayers and invocations that you have collected over your tenure as a witch. Play music that draws you in and makes you feel magical and connected to the powers that be, and do your best to avoid being taken out of your atmospheric mindset.

Two hours before the working, turn off all screens and avoid any unnatural light but the ritual fire or candle flame. Turn off your phone and give yourself time to relax and sink a little further into your witch's dream. Check in with your spirits, anoint yourself with sabbat oil, and meditate or journal while you spend time suspended in the witch's dream. Within the witch's dream draw the sigil for the witch's sabbat with white fire, and over the course of your meditation repeatedly come back to this symbol no matter where your mind may take you.

Cleanse and purify your bed and the sabbat pillow as well as the room or area where this will be taking place. Visualize the space flooding with white fire and consecrate the bed with a holy water solution made from blessed spring water and sea salt. Cross the hedge by aligning yourself and visualizing that same white flame emanating from you and casting a circle. Gaze upon the sigil on the sabbat pillow and use it to anchor the energy of the witch's tree. As you summon the witch's tree, allow it to manifest from within the pillow so that when you lay your head upon it, your head will be suspended inside of the base of the witch's tree.

Congress

Invoke the Witch Queen and the Witch King and then take your place upon the bed. From within the pillowcase, remove the herbal sachet. Take a few sniffs and allow the aroma to enter into your nose and awaken your internal senses. Remember the sabbat symbol from earlier in the day and see it come alive in your mind's eye with brilliant white fire. Place the sachet in your lap.

Take up your ritual drum or gently tap your chest, and begin to play a steady, repetitive, and somewhat fast beat (I usually make ⅛ notes at 120 bpm). Continuing to focus on the symbol of the witch's sabbat, allow your mind to sync with the beat, and focus on your breaths.

Open the Gates of Heka[10] by concentrating on the points of stillness and silence at the beginnings and ends of each breath. Drum and build up energy, allowing the energy to flow into those moments of stillness and silence. Do this for some time until the energy between those two moments becomes so large that they merge together, and you experience them as one long, pregnant pause that is about to burst with potential. While still visualizing the symbol of the witch's sabbat in your mind's eye, allow this shift to overtake you completely. Stop drumming, take the sachet one last time and take a good sniff, further drawing your senses into the working, and then place it back into the sabbat pillow. Blow out the candles and allow yourself to slip into darkness.

Lie down, placing your head on the sabbat pillow, and allow the energy to settle into your body. Within a few moments you should feel a stillness take over the space; it is hard to explain, but it's almost as if everything becomes timeless and fixed, and usually my ears will ring. Close your eyes and focus on the darkness, then summon the Witch King by whispering three times:

I summon the man in black, Janicot,
The black goat from the western hill.
Be with me now and take me to sabbat.
I go of free will.

It may take a few moments for him to respond. As a medium, this experience is quite intense and clear. He arrives as a presence within the darkness. It can be startling at first; in the beginning I wanted to snap myself out of it and end the session, but I persisted and faced this presence and was rewarded. Sometimes it is merely a sense in the darkness, but usually, once we perceive him and don't run away, he begins to coalesce from within the darkness as a goat with shaggy fur made

10 Hunter, *The Witch's Book of Spirits*, 47.

of smokeless black fire. As he draws near, you will notice his effect immediately.

This is perhaps the most challenging part of this whole practice. After you sense him, you will need to allow yourself to drift to sleep. If you are creeped out, which happens the first time or two, know that it is perfectly normal and that you are safe. Remember, you summoned your other allies to be with you, and they won't let anything bad happen to you. Way back in the first book of the series we discussed the technique of Darkness Meditation,[11] the practice of submerging yourself in total darkness and then allowing your senses to expand and fill in the details of what your eyes cannot see. As a spiritual practice, its most beneficial qualities are in its ability to train us to be comfortable in the darkness and when we sense another presence in the darkness. I recommend revisiting this practice if you have a difficult time with this part of the trip to sabbat.

As you drift off to sleep, think of yourself as surrendering to this presence in an act of perfect love and perfect trust.

Through the lens of the witch eye, your body will change from a human to that of some beast. For me, this is almost always in the shape of an owl, but each witch that I know has their own personal transformative experience. As your new form takes shape, give yourself entirely to the change and then follow the black goat as he takes you deep into the darkness. Do not hesitate. Do not ask questions. Follow and observe. He will take you to the witch's sabbat in any number of ways. Some report the sensation of flying, some of floating on water, others as a flash of fever visions.

Within time you will find yourself at the witch's sabbat. This special place appears as a candle flame in the darkness at first, but as you draw closer to it, you recognize it as a bonfire sitting atop a tall mountain. When you arrive, you undergo yet another transformation, this time into your true form. Here you can hide from nothing, you have no

11 Hunter, *The Witch's Book of Power*, 248.

secrets, and you are seen as you truly are. All of your flaws and short-comings are displayed alongside all of your perfection and beauty. As you come to the bonfire, you notice that it is the only light source within the darkness and that you are joining an already active event taking place.

All around you spirits from every plane of being stand side by side conversing and eating, but you take no food or drink; instead, you continue to follow the black goat as he makes his way beyond the fire. With a mere shake of his black fire coat, he transforms into the Magister, the man in black, and takes his throne next to the Sabbat Queen.

What you do after this is your business. You can meet with other spirits, speak to the Witch Queen and Witch King directly, or explore the darkness surrounding the fire. Whatever you do, don't stray too far from the light of the fire, as you will find yourself stumbling into an awakened state. I recommend taking a seat next to the fire and seeing who comes to say hello. This has led me to great partnerships in the past. The sabbat dream will end on its own when you wake up.

Egress
Wake up naturally on your own, whenever that happens, be it later that night or in the morning, and savor every moment while your eyes are closed. Immediately write down what you experienced in your journal, turning on a light or lighting a candle to see if needed. Do not speak until you have had a chance to write down everything you witnessed. Align your souls. Release the circle and witch's tree by absorbing their energy as previously instructed. The rite is done. I recommend that afterward, once you have had a chance to wake up, you perform a simple cleansing of yourself and spend time cleaning up your ritual space and contemplating what you experienced in greater depth. What signs or symbols were shown to you? Were there any messages you received that you need to remember now that you are awake?

Not everyone can lucid dream, no, but for those of us who can, it is an incredibly valuable tool in the advanced realms of magic and the occult. What I presented to you here is just the tip of the proverbial sabbat iceberg. The more you perform this technique and are able to develop your own, the more incredible your experiences will become and the more inspiring your witchcraft will be. It is there at sabbat that you will receive deeply important secrets about your work as a witch, and you owe it to yourself to go as deep as you possibly can.

JOURNAL TOPIC

Perform the entry prompts associated with each individual lucid dreaming and sabbat experience. Sketch your experiences and explain what you see.

Conclusion

We are who we choose to be. Nobody is going to come
and save you. You've got to save yourself.

———

Barry Manilow

Witchcraft is an incredibly mental spiritual practice. It requires us not only to hunt down and root out the causes of disempowerment, but to fight back against the source of that disempowerment. For many witches, there are little things that can make a big difference when fighting that good fight. Practices like releasing wicked vows, tapping into egregores, energetic self-orientation, the witch's dream, lucid dreaming, and visiting the witch's sabbat are all incredible steps toward exploring the deeper mysteries associated with our lives as witches. They also help us to get control of the way we see and interact with our past, present, and future.

The first part of this book has been devoted to the witch power as a personal psychic extension within the microcosm of your life. It has been all about using this power and refining our practices so that we can unlock greater mysteries and greater power. In the next several chapters, though, we are going to work with the witch power as a tool to engage the macrocosm of the universe. The work that we do in the second part of the book is directly linked to the work we have done in the first part of the book. As we move forward, I would like to remind you of the power you have to create and sculpt reality, and that you have done this in many lifetimes.

In the following chapters, my hope is that I can take you on an occult journey where by tuning in to a certain set of vibrations and working specific rituals, you will be able to push the limits of what we commonly accept as the craft. Through these we travel down a different road where a new perspective on the previous questions can be gained. By exploring these deep mysteries, we can discover aspects of ourselves and our talents that can and will change our lives forever. Even though some of these practices come from my own tradition, I have done my very best to make them as accessible as possible here.

Part Two

Exploring the Guardians of Creation

A labyrinth is a symbolic journey . . . but it is a map we can really walk on, blurring the difference between map and world.

———

Rebecca Solnit, *Wanderlust: A History of Walking*

With this last part of the book, we will work with all that we have to take our gnosis and our witch power beyond our limitations and make contact with our maker. These are mysteries usually revealed to those who undergo the study of the priesthood, who choose to live fully within their power and forge their own bond with the universe. We will explore the concepts of light and darkness and of living as an embodiment of all nature, transfixed in the presence of the Grigori and God Herself.

The Grigori are often under-explored in contemporary witchcraft, but they are the most chief among spirits aside from the creator and her two halves. They are each the spiritual personifications of the primordial forces that together comprise the universe. They are sovereign spirits of the fundamental components of creation, and in our mythology they were among the first powers to come from the Void as God Herself sprang into being. Sometimes referred to as Watchers/Watchtowers, Governors, Beings of the Outer Darkness, Guardians, Fountains, Grand Fathers/Mothers, Gates/Gateways, Shining Ones, Elder Gods, or Primordial Deities, the Grigori are powerful spirits that predate the "gods of mankind."

In some traditions the archangels are worked with as Grigori, in others they are seen as Nephilim. Almost universally, these spirits are seen as angelic in nature because they are beings of order that came forth from the void or that repel the forces of the void (chaos). In my tradition we often refer to them as the Pillars or Wells of Creation, and we work with them both cautiously and respectfully.

Ritually, the Grigori are often invoked as agents who watch over our workings either to bear witness or to protect the proceedings from outside involvement, depending on tradition. As allies, however, they are capable of much more than that. The Grigori can act as psychic wells of power that can be channeled and woven into our magic. Our main focus, however, is their ability to help us meet and develop a relationship with the Star Goddess, initiating endless communion with the numinous spirit of creation and the universe as we know it.

To do all of this, however, we first must make contact and develop a relationship with these powers. In chapter 10 we will explore the mysteries of the Pyramid of Light and the Labyrinth of Darkness. Here we will make contact with the beings we refer to as the "Terrestrial" Grigori, those whose influence is earth, air, fire, water, and spirit. As an advanced practitioner, you are going to be approaching this work with years of study and understanding when it comes to these forces, as they no longer represent mystery to you. This will make short work of our introduction and exploration and will allow the Pyramid of Dianus to be a place of familiarity and strength when discovering the mysteries of the darkness. In this chapter you will also receive the opening ritual for entering the Labyrinth of Diana and be able to take the first steps toward discovering the unknown.

Chapters 11 and on will be dedicated to the Pyramid of Darkness, also known as the Labyrinth of Diana. Here we will meet the Grigori of space, time, matter, energy, and quintessence. To better understand these spirits, we will need to investigate the facts behind the forces they govern and expand our knowledge of how they are interconnected. This will take a bit more time and effort; however, once we have done this, we have made our way through the Labyrinth of Diana and will find ourselves face to face with God Herself.

Unlike some of the other work we have done, reaching these spirits requires little but maturity, commitment, genuine curiosity, and a few supplies. Namely, you will need a journal or sketch book to record your experiences, something to write or draw with, your favorite incense, a black pillar candle, white chalk, and access to fresh water.

The pyramid and the labyrinth will unfold within your witch's dream and are intrinsically tied to the lonely road. Each of the gates exists within your dream and can only be summoned once you have worked with the corresponding Grigori. There is no rushing this stuff; only practice and observation can yield results. Again, the point isn't to duplicate my experience, but rather to use my experience to inspire your own. The rituals will observe the same protocols we discussed earlier and will help us to cultivate and stabilize the energies of the Grigori.

Chapter Ten

A Pyramid of Light and a Labyrinth of Darkness

The only person who can solve the labyrinth of yourself is you.

———

Jeremy Denk

As I have expressed within my other books, Diana, the Goddess of Witches, fulfills many roles for us: she teaches us, guides us, empowers us, protects us, and through her work she helps us to understand ourselves and our magic. She has been called by many names and known by many faces, any one of which could have reached out to you and ignited the spark of witch power that was smoldering in the coals.

She is the goddess of darkness, mystery, and power, and it is through her that the authentic nature of the soul is revealed. Within her labyrinth are six gates, five watched over by the Cosmic Grigori, the last by Diana herself. Meet the Grigori, perform their rites, and initiate into their mysteries. Only then will the sixth and final gate be revealed, the one that leads to the void where God Herself can be found.

Mapping the Labyrinth

The Labyrinth of Diana may reveal itself through the witch's dream, but it can still be mapped—though not just any map will do, of course. Our map is going to have to be three-dimensional in design and four- to five-dimensional in concept. The gods of witches aren't of nature, they *are* nature, all of nature. They are primordial forces whose opposition provided causation for all that there is and ever will be. Our gods are genderless forces that ask us to give ourselves wholly to the expression of divinity. We recognize that these forces exist in new forms all over and that part of our job is to identify those forces and bring them into harmony.

In most of paganism, a primary spiritual focus derives from a similar notion: bringing the male and female halves of our species together so that life may be created and the cycle of life can continue. But this is perhaps the most basic expression of the mysteries. As genderless forces, the gods can be either or all, and the creation of life did not happen when they were brought together as biological sexual partners. It happened when the forces that comprise the universe became unified. Sex is a simple way of looking at it, but sex and gender are two very different things. Sexually, these two energies came together, but the act resulted in a total union, not climax and impregnation.

When we describe the creator spirit as being a coin with two halves, this is what we are talking about. If the coin were to be divided in half, it would lose total value. If Diana or Lucifer were to not exist, then nothing would exist. These are not interchangeable forces but rather the initiating forces behind all that we know. Their expression comes in many forms, and pieces of them can be found in all aspects of nature: birth and death, geometry and illusion, the calculable and the incalculable.

To make this a bit easier, if the creator of all things had a brain like ours, Diana and Dianus would be the left and right halves of the brain. Both are needed for consciousness and both inform and create reality. In this way, we can also see them as forces that are continually developing, learning, and experiencing for the first time but that are also vital to the function of the body. In our case, the body is creation, aka the universe and everything within it. To map the labyrinth we will need to keep in mind that we are the product of forces being in harmonic opposition to one another.

The Tetrahedron and the Merkaba

To help get a visual idea before we dive in, imagine there is a triangular pyramid before you made of light that is roughly five feet tall and wide. There are four faces total, four points or vertices, and six edges. This shape is called a tetrahedron and has been known since the time of antiquity as being one of the fundamental three-dimensional shapes in the universe. For our purposes here, this form is referred to as the Pyramid of Dianus and symbolizes everything that falls under his domain as the body of light-force in the universe.

pyramid of
dianus

See another tetrahedron before you, but this time upside down and made of darkness; this is the Pyramid of Diana. It is identical in shape and size but of the exact opposite material.

Now, let's take it a step further and fuse the two together to form what we call a star tetrahedron, or merkaba. At each point of the merkaba, as well as in the exact middle, rest the Grigori and the gates of power we seek.

The Medicine of the Grigori

When we work with any spirit for empowerment of any kind, we are working with what is often referred to in the shamanic community as the "medicine" of that spirit. Spirits that we work with religiously or for long periods of time (three months or longer) often make this sort of psychic and spiritual adjustment to our individual home frequency (your natural, unencumbered psychic resonance). The more we work with that spirit, the more we encounter its medicine, and the longer we work with that medicine, the closer and more in resonance we become with that spirit. To receive that medicine, we have to allow the connection with the spirit to be symbiotic—to fairly take and fairly give with this spirit, and to make room for the many ways their medicine might manifest in your life.

The Cosmic Grigori are not unlike other spirits in that they do have medicine to share; to receive it, however, we must allow ourselves to be moved by their message. Each introduction is meant to inspire and to encourage your gnosis, to reinforce what you potentially are already feeling and thinking, and to evoke the witch power in your soul through exposure to their medicine. They are without question angelic spirits of the highest order and do not lightly engage mortals. Our witch power is uniquely suited to engage and interact with them. But that doesn't mean they are our friends; it means that they know we can see them, too.

Approach each of the Grigori as their own school and come prepared for a new class each meeting. Once you have visited them, continue to do so and ask questions of them. Work with these spirits to better understand your power and your potential, and always seek guidance from your own spirit guides and familiars when processing the information you are given during your sessions. Write down what you can remember of your sessions, sketch out the spirits as you see them, and keep track of your experiences with them as a scientist would. Most importantly, however, when all is finished, ask yourself the following questions, and do not act on the information given to you until you can answer them.

1. **Is this information relative to my current lifetime and current situation? If not, how is this information valuable to me? What information do I need to clarify in a follow-up session with this spirit?** We need to find out if this is useful to you now, if it is something that can be explored at a later time, or if it is random information that doesn't have a particular purpose. Sometimes we will collect information or be told something by a spirit that isn't actually of any use. For instance, you might discover at

the temple of time that you were a shoemaker in a past life. That might be useful to know if you were suffering from a shoe addiction, but otherwise it is white noise. In my experience, nine times out of ten the information is valuable and applicable to my current situation, but this isn't always the case. As a powerful witch who is interacting with primordial cosmic forces, it is essential to separate the valuable information from the rest.

2. **How does this information apply practically? How does this information apply spiritually?** Not all information is going to have a real-world application, and not all information is going to apply to your spiritual paradigm. In my experience, people tend to get caught up in experiences and knowledge that aren't applicable, despite their interest or energetic investment. You might find while visiting the Grigori of Space that you feel at home in another galaxy, perhaps even that a piece of your soul once lived there. That information isn't exactly applicable in real life, but it might be spiritually. Likewise, visiting the molecular structure of an apple while traveling with the Grigori of Matter isn't likely to help you with your day job. Record as much information as possible, but always be sure to look for practical or spiritual applications for it outside of your interactions with the Grigori.

3. It has also been my experience that because of the nature of the information you will receive while visiting the Grigori, every message is in some way a reflection of you: your past, future, desires, fears, secrets, and inner truths. I have taken to asking myself one fundamental question: **What does this information mean about me?** Sometimes you won't find the answer quickly, but it is nice to know how this information is reflective of both your conscious and subconscious efforts.

The Medicine of Earth

We work with the Grigori of Earth to better understand stability, substance, structure, and growth. Earth teaches us to be strong and firm and encourages us to persevere and overcome obstacles through growth, balance, and the development of deep roots.

The Medicine of Air

We work with the Grigori of Air to better understand communication, knowledge, thought, and clarity. Air teaches us to listen before we speak and to speak with purpose. It also teaches us to be creative and to grow by harmonizing with the vibrations of our home frequency instead of the frequency of others.

The Medicine of Fire

We work with the Grigori of Fire to better understand passion, determination, creation/destruction, and the mysteries of the internal flame (metabolism). Fire teaches us to destroy the bonds of the old so that something new can be forged in their place and to overcome obstacles through action and discipline.

The Medicine of Water

We work with the Grigori of Water to better understand emotion, the subconscious, the physical senses, and cleanliness. Water teaches us that healing comes through purification and renewal and to find peace in surrender. The medicine of water is also closely linked to psychic abilities and prophecy.

The Medicine of Spirit

We work with the Grigori of Spirit to better understand our gifts, life purpose, and our connection to the Divine. Spirit is associated with personality and consciousness, teaching us that the mind and soul are not too separate from one another and what is good for one is often good for the other. The medicine of spirit is also related to gnosis and the witch eye.

The Medicine of Space

We work with the Grigori of Space to better understand limitation, emptiness, expansiveness, and connection. Space teaches us to be vast and endless, and not unlike everyone's favorite blue box, it teaches us that we are much bigger on the inside than we appear to be on the outside. Space is everywhere; around and inside of everything, and as a force within nature, it connects all things together.

The Medicine of Time

We work with the Grigori of Time to better understand our soul's history and its promise. Traveling to previous lives to find the root of a problem that vexes you in this life, discovering the power that was stripped away from you in an earlier incarnation and restoring it in this life, even rediscovering spirit allies from another existence are all immensely powerful experiences for us as witches who seek to live in our truth.

The Medicine of Matter

We work with the Grigori of Matter to better understand how chaos becomes order, how from nothingness comes everything, and of the cycles of creation. Exploring the natural progression from randomness to structure allows us to better understand how we manifest and bring magic from the other planes to our own.

The Medicine of Energy

We work with the Grigori of Energy to better understand the forces that move creation, are the result of creation, and that continue to shape creation. In doing so, we better understand how our own power relates to the universe as well as how it may have influence within it.

The Medicine of Quintessence

We work with the Grigori of Quintessence to better understand magic and the ways it permeates the universe around us. Magic is not physical, spiritual, mental, or psychic, but rather a combination of all of the above. Communing with the Grigori of Quintessence helps us to connect with the hidden veins of magic that exist all around us and to tap into and harmonize with them. Furthermore, as beings of magic, exploring quintessence also allows us to expand our personal definitions of magic and our potential-related abilities.

The Medicine of the Light God

After working with the Terrestrial Grigori, we will work with the spirit of Dianus to declare ourselves ready to enter the Pyramid of Diana. All that is known, seen, and understood lies under the domain of Dianus. Among many things, he is an embodiment of science, knowledge, alchemy, and confirmed gnosis. The Terrestrial Grigori, those related to earth, air, fire, water, and spirit, combine as the separate parts that equal his whole. In our creation story, Dianus sacrifices his body so that it may become the bones and flesh of the universe, the spark that ignites the big bang and ultimately brings on the actualization of God Herself and the birth of all that is. As the universe expands, the Grigori are brought into existence and become the spiritual embodiments of the fundamental forces of that universe. Those primary forces that make "life as we know it" are of his domain; those that represent mystery and the unknown are of hers. The medicine Dianus has to offer relates to sacrifice and the potential of discipline and action.

The Medicine of the Dark Goddess

Lastly, once we have worked through the rites pertaining to the Grigori, we will hopefully be admitted access to Diana herself. She is the guardian of the ultimate mysteries and the keeper of secrets, and it is by her that we may gain entry to the edges of creation so that we may know God Herself, the creator and force of all things. The medicine that Diana has to offer relates to the freedom and authority of the soul, its sovereign right to exist and thrive, its path toward greatness, and the unbinding of its essence.

The Medicine of the Void

It is said that the void can bring madness or prophecy to those who gaze upon it, but no one walks away the same person. For me, the experience was not exactly what I had thought it would be at first, but it quickly evolved into some of the most life-changing work I have ever done. My priorities changed; my needs, my drives, my motivations and desires all went up in the air, and I realized that I was taking so many things for granted. Suddenly I stopped inviting drama and chaos into my life, I started to hold myself and those around me accountable for our actions; I stopped feeling sorry for myself, and I began to see the world in an entirely new way. The thing was, I didn't know I was doing any of those things until I met God (or the spiritual consciousness of the universe, if you like). It wasn't that God made me feel petty or shameful, but that she made me feel precious and coveted. I learned of my real value—of all of our value—and it made me feel like I had been wasting so much time on things that just didn't matter in the end. The medicine of the void is to experience universal ecstasy, to gaze upon the outer reaches of everything and look back at it all in stunning clarity, and to redefine what it means to be a conscious part of it all.

This is the work of the priesthood, of those who wish not only to connect to the higher powers but to channel and embody them as living temples of God Herself.

The Rituals

As I mentioned earlier, the rituals we will perform to meet and engage with these spirits will follow the protocols we have discussed in this book. Also, you will need a handful of other techniques under your belt, which I have discussed in depth in my previous books, such as soul alignment and mediumship. Where these aspects of the work come up, I try my best to guide you through the process regardless of your individual skill level. It would be a good idea to reference these techniques before engaging in these rituals.

The labyrinth is easy to get lost in as it is uniquely staged within the witch's dream. It is a mental puzzle whose pieces can be put together only through careful thought and consideration. You will notice that the preparatory aspects of the work are there to prime your mind, to open the way for the initial introduction to the spiritual force behind these fundamental aspects of existence. The ingress of each working will place us in contact with the conscious aspects of these forces and invite them into our own lives. When we hold congress with these spirits, we can ask them questions and seek out hidden knowledge about ourselves and our purpose. During this phase of our workings, we will fuse our life force with their own and initiate into their individual mysteries. Finally, the egress portion of each working allows us to separate from these spirits while bringing the wisdom gained during congress back with us, so we can add it to our gnosis and continue with the journey. Once connected to these spiritual forces, you will never be disconnected. It is like hearing a sound that has been there the whole time: once you know it is there, you will always hear it.

The Opening Ritual

Preparation
It will be important for you to do three nights of purification before starting the journey. Each consecutive night you should take a bath or shower, dry yourself with a clean white towel, and invest fifteen minutes in meditation and reflection, and then another ten minutes at least to writing in your journal or sketching your thoughts. During this time, it will be essential to free your mind of excess burdens and free the spirit of unneeded or harmful energies. Be sure to visit the witch's dream to communicate with your allies regularly over these three days, and spend as much time as possible in an aligned state. You will also want to cleanse your home and ritual area during this period.

Ingress

On the final night, lay the compass and summon the witch's tree in the space where you will be performing the working. Look around you: memorize this place and reconstruct every detail in your mind. Feel the energy of the compass touch and imbue everything with power, feel the guardians who watch over us and spirits move around its edges, and feel your awareness extend in all directions. At the center place your altar, and upon that altar place a black candle.

Light the candle. Place your right hand over your heart and your left hand over that to touch the right side of your chest and recite the following prayer invocation to the Star Goddess. As you finish, gently bow in reverence and solidarity.

THE STAR GODDESS PRAYER

Holy Mother, in you we live, move, and have our being.
From you all things emerged, and unto you all things return.

SUMMONING THE PYRAMID OF DIANUS

Next, we will want to summon the first tetrahedron, known as the Pyramid of Dianus. Focus on the candle flame and notice how its tip comes to a point. Envision a small pyramid emerging from that point and then growing so large that it stands tall enough to fill the space. Take a deep breath and feel grounded. Draw the sigil for Gia in the air with yellow fire and recite the following invocation to the Guardians of the Elements:

Spirits of the Pyramid, ancestors of bone!
Come and bring form! Come and bring life!
By the power of Gia, great Guardian of the Earth,
I bid you rise from the caverns below and be here now.

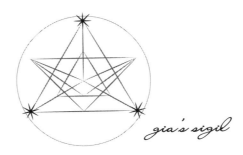

gia's sigil

Feel a presence move from the edges of the compass to join you and see the bottom left corner of the pyramid glowing brightly in response, signaling the arrival of the first guardian. In the witch's dream, reach out and sense the presence of Gia, allowing it to coalesce and take shape around a pair of dark brown eyes. Take a few deep breaths and gaze deeply into the eyes of Gia, and see that a line of raw power connects you both. As you notice it, let it fill you with the energy of earth. Find yourself feeling grounded and your energy stabilized.

See the pyramid turn clockwise 60 degrees, so that the point that was to the bottom right is now to the bottom left. Take a deep breath and feel focused. Draw the sigil for Wind-Walker in the air with yellow fire and say:

> *Spirits of the Pyramid, ancestors of breath!*
> *Come and bring inspiration! Come and bring life!*
> *By the power of Wind-Walker, great Guardian of Air,*
> *I bid you come from the deep meadow and be here now!*

wind-walker's sigil

Feel a presence move from the edges of the compass to join you, and see the bottom left corner of the pyramid glow brightly as before, signaling the arrival of the second guardian. Reach out in the witch's dream and sense the presence of Wind-Walker, the Grigori of Air, and allow this spirit to take a form around a pair of brilliant light blue eyes before you. Take a few deep breaths, gaze deeply into these sapphire eyes, and notice that a line of power connects you. As you notice this, allow Wind-Walker to fill you with the power of air, and find yourself feeling clear-headed and focused on the moment.

Take a deep breath and see the pyramid again turn clockwise 60 degrees. Take a deep breath and feel passionate. Draw the sigil for Fire-Dancer in the air with yellow fire and say:

Spirits of the Pyramid, ancestors of desire!
Come and bring creation! Come and bring life!
By the power of Fire-Dancer, great Guardian of the Flame,
I bid you come from the desert sands and be here now!

fire-dancer's sigil

Now envision that the pyramid begins to rotate clockwise on its own. Take another deep breath and recite the charge. As before, feel a presence move from the edges of the compass to join you and notice that the top of the pyramid is glowing in response to the arrival of the third guardian.

Reaching out through the witch's dream, find yourself staring at a pair of red eyes off in the distance, and notice that the shape of Fire-Dancer takes form around them. Gaze deeply into their fiery eyes and feel a sense of warmth move through you. Take a few deep breaths and notice a cord of power connecting you, and allow it to fill you with the power of fire. Soon you will feel excited and possess a sense of anticipation.

Take a deep breath and feel your own depth. Draw the sigil for Ophion in the air with yellow fire and say:

Spirits of the Pyramid, ancestors of blood!
Come and bring purity! Come and bring life!
By the power of Ophion, great Guardian of Water,
I bid you rise from the darkest depths and be here now!

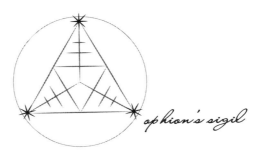

ophion's sigil

Just as before, reach out through the witch's dream and sense the presence of Ophion, the great Grigori of Water. Find yourself staring into a pair of black eyes, and allow the Grigori to take shape around them as you gaze. Take a few deep breaths and notice that there is a line of energy that connects you and this spirit. Allow Ophion to fill you with the powers of water and feel your blood tingle for just a moment. As the energy settles, notice that you feel cleansed and purified.

With the pyramid continuing to spin clockwise, bring your attention to its exact center and recite the invocation of the final elemental guardian as you draw the sigil for the Fata in the air before you in yellow fire:

Spirits of the Pyramid, Guardians of Destiny!
Come and weave the threads! Come and bring life!
By the power of the Fata, great Guardians of Fate,
I bid you fall from the heavens and be here now!

fata's sigil

Feel a presence move from the edges of the compass to join you, heralding the arrival of the final Terrestrial Grigori. Reach out in the witch's dream and sense the presence of the Fata, the three sisters of fate who together are the Grigori of Spirit, and allow them to take form around six white eyes before you. See them spinning a thread of power that connects to you, and take a few deep breaths of power as the Fata fill you with the power of spirit. After a few moments, you feel a sense of spiritual purpose and intention.

As you finish, feel a presence move from the edges of the compass to join you, and see the entire pyramid light up as if turning on a light bulb. Take three grounding breaths and then seal the pyramid with the following invocation to Dianus:

Father of the witches, come, be here now, complete the sum.
By four points and sacred center, I call Dianus to here enter.
I summon the elements fivefold, by your might this power hold.
What is of light shall this contain;
What is of darkness shall not remain.

Feel the powers of the Terrestrial Grigori join in unison as they move around and through you. Notice that you can sense a new but familiar presence there with you in the witch's dream: the power of Dianus, radiating from the still-spinning pyramid of light. Say:

I am earth, air, fire, water, and spirit. I am wise, and I am cunning;
I am bold, and I am strong! I embark upon this journey
Knowing that what lies beyond is darkness and mystery.
I take this responsibility and shoulder its burden
As I walk upon the lonely road seeking Diana, Queen of Witches all!
Dianus, bear witness and be my guide;
Stay with me and be the light at my side.

Visualize the Terrestrial Grigori all returning back to the boundaries of the compass, but notice that the spinning pyramid of light still remains, along with the sense of Dianus emanating from it.

Summoning the Pyramid of Diana

Approach the black candle once again and lift your palms upward in the air over your head as you recite the "Invocation of the Cosmic Grigori," below. While doing this visualize the darkness that surrounds you caving in and condensing into the shape of an upside-down tetrahedron. See before you an upside-down black pyramid hovering just above the pyramid of light. We will go through point by point in the following chapters; for now just focus on the darkness condensing into a perfect pyramid and then seeing that pyramid expand to mirror the size of the other.

Invocation of the Cosmic Grigori

Next, feeling the confidence and strength found by invoking the Pyramid of Dianus, visualize the second pyramid and say:

I part the worlds with my desire and burn all blocks with sacred fire.
I call the spirits of the witch's tree, I call these spirits to set me free.
I call to Oronos, the Grigori of Space.
Infinite Keeper of the Endless, Winged Serpent of Emptiness,
Come now from the starry labyrinth and open the sacred gates,
Be here now and in your fullest, for destiny awaits!
I call to Aeon, the Grigori of Time.
Boundless Keeper of the Great Ages, Winged Serpent of Eternity,
Come now from the starry labyrinth and open the sacred gates,
Be here now and in your fullest, for destiny awaits!
I call to Proto, the Grigori of Matter.
Immeasurable Keeper of all Dimension, Winged Serpent of Mass,
Come now from the starry labyrinth and open the sacred gates,
Be here now and in your fullest, for destiny awaits!
I call to Zoann, the Grigori of Energy.
Untamable Keeper of Perpetual Force, Winged Serpent of Power,
Come now from the starry labyrinth and open the sacred gates,
Be here now and in your fullest, for destiny awaits!
I call to Quetra, the Grigori of Quintessence.
Unconquerable Keeper of Providence, Winged Serpent of Gnosis,
Come now from the starry labyrinth and open the sacred gates,
Be here now and in your fullest, for destiny awaits!
By the Grigori of Creation, the Guardians of God Herself,
I summon the Pyramid of Diana so I may know myself!

Take a few deep breaths, allowing the energy to settle, and then visualize that this pyramid slowly descends to interlock with the first pyramid and start spinning like a top, counter-clockwise, in the opposite direction of the first pyramid. Extend your awareness outward in all directions and notice that there are new spirits, new guardians who walk its perimeter. These are the Cosmic Grigori. Like the light from a distant star, they now can be seen in the darkness and can be called upon to plot our course. Do nothing; only observe their presence as they join the other Grigori at the edges.

Congress

Focus on the sensation of feeling the opposing energies move through and around you. As you have been instructed before, observe the space around you, recording as much sense memory as possible. How does it feel to be standing in the center of these two pyramids? What does the space around you look like when there is that much energy present? Now close your eyes and continue to breathe slow and deep.

Within your mind create an exact replica of what you see and feel while present here. Extend your consciousness so that it fills the Pyramid of Dianus, and breathe into it. Now do the same with the other pyramid, and fill both tetrahedrons with your awareness. Breathe slow and deep, sensing both of these spinning pyramids—two energies, two forces, each in balance, each pulling and repelling the other.

Take a deep breath, and as you exhale vocally tone the vowel "O" and slowly visualize these two forces condensing into your energy body. Feel this energy swirl around you and within you, and open yourself up to receiving it. Take a deep breath once more and add this memory to duplicate in your mind. Remember to focus on the sensation of this experience as well as the visual aspect of it. Notice that your energy body now as a result of your work has taken on, or has begun to take on, the shape of the merkaba—that from within you pulses the vibration of Diana and Dianus, and that you are somehow changed.

The mental duplicate of the space that you have created must now be installed as an active part of your witch's dream. This will allow you to visit it in the flash of a thought or a subtle shift in consciousness.

It will keep you forever in tune with the pyramids and maintain your connection with the gods as a preset on your own dial. This is the last point where you can stop before you can no longer get off the ride. Once we move forward, you will be unable to close your connection to the labyrinth without completing it. To finish now, thank the spirits by making an offering of incense, and ask your familiar spirit or spirit guides to disconnect and block your psychic energy from this work until you are ready to move forward. You haven't gone too far or upset anyone; you just got to peek at what lies here. Once this is done, it cannot be undone; some part of you will forever be in the labyrinth until you complete the work and commune with the void. This is, in many ways, a baptism by darkness so that you can truly appreciate the light. Speaking of light: the Pyramid of Light, however, will always be with you, and you will still be able to revisit it where you left off. So, if you do need to take a break from the work, return there as an excellent place to start.

To fuse this with the witch's dream and officially take the first step into the Labyrinth of Diana, you need to sit before the black candle. Visualize that the candle has gone out in the mental duplicate in your mind; that space is now filled with darkness, and only the feeling of energy remains.

To Summon the Labyrinth

Close your eyes and focus on the spinning pyramids of the merkaba. Know that it represents the living world, all that we know and will ever know. It represents knowledge, life, existence. In our lore, when the darkness finally realized that the light was within, Diana embraced Dianus, as the pyramids now embrace each other. When this happened, Dianus, the primordial force that we worship as the King of Witches, sacrificed his whole in union with Diana and divided himself into the stars that fill the known universe. This embrace was the big bang, the birth of everything. From nothing, darkness came, and from the darkness, light. When they chose unity, they transformed into God Herself and became locked together for the life of the cosmos. They are separate but equal, yet somehow together they are more than the sum of their parts, an impossible paradox consisting of endless possibilities.

With creation came the powers that rule it: the guardians of creation. Those related to earth, air, fire, water, and spirit are known as the Terrestrial Grigori, or the Guardians of Dianus, and have been with you since you became a witch. These are the elemental powers that you have known, seen, and felt since you cast your first circle. They are tuned to your witch senses and have been feeding your witch power this whole time. You are familiar with these elements and the spiritual consciousness of the guardians that watch over them. That work has been done, and that is why they so easily joined you when they were called. But there are other forces at play that also fill and shape the universe as a whole—the ones unknown to you, the ones who still remain a mystery and that in many ways represent mystery. As you move forward, always keep that confidence and strength you gained by working with the Pyramid of Dianus, and allow it to empower you as you explore the unknown.

The pyramid of darkness that spins counterclockwise through and around you has stationed within it the Cosmic Grigori, or the Guardians of Diana. Recite the following incantation and summon the doorway that will act as the psychic passage between these two pyramids, allowing you to move from a place of knowing to a place of mystery.

Gate Invocation to the Labyrinth of Diana

*I have studied the mysteries of my teachers and have read the books
    of those who have come before me, but still I seek to know myself.*

*Still I wander on the lonely road, looking for answers to questions I
    know not to ask.*

*Still I wander on the lonely road, looking for true direction and to be
    given a sacred task.*

*Still I wander on the lonely road, looking for purpose in a world
    that would take my light.*

*Still I wander on the lonely road, looking for freedom from fear that
    would take my sight.*

I call out to primordial providence that Janus may hear my call.

Open a door to end my suffering, an entry through the wall.

Let darkness behold light's brilliance, may that which resists fall.

For in the labyrinth I seek Diana, so I may know the all.

*labyrinth's
sigil*

As you do this, draw the sigil to the labyrinth in the air before you in yellow fire. Once it is complete, see it fade away, and in its place, a doorway of the same yellow fire appears. This doorway leads you to the Labyrinth of Diana.

You will revisit this place often and will be able to reach this door easily the next time you need to. For now, our work here is done.

Egress

If you did not proceed with the summoning of the labyrinth, use this opportunity to shift gears and do other work or release the witch's tree, if desired. Be sure to perform the Star Goddess prayer on page 294 before finally finishing your working, blowing out the black candle at the end. This will be the same exit we will use once the Labyrinth of Diana has been completed.

If you did summon the labyrinth, return your focus to the space that sits in darkness in your mind, that perfect duplicate of the ritual area. See that the doorway you summoned resides in this space in your mind as well, illuminating the immediate area surrounding it. Notice that in your mental replica, the black candle continues to remain unlit.

Take three deep breaths. On the final exhale vocally tone the vowel *Ah*, and visualize the compass and the witch's tree, along with the spirits and guardians who walk the edges, transferring from the space around you to the duplicate in your mind. Stand before the black candle, bow in reverence to its symbolism, and then extinguish the flame.

As the candle flame goes out, immediately visualize the black candle that sits on the altar in your mind lighting up, transferring the final essence of the working into your mind and cementing it in your witch's dream. You are finished for now. The opening ritual is complete.

Take a few minutes to journal about your experience, and then sketch out as many details about the space that now resides inside of your witch's dream. Re-create what you see in your mind and express it creatively. This will be an essential method as we move through the rest of the working.

The labyrinth will continuously remain open to you at this point, which means that the vibration of the labyrinth will continuously stay in your energy field. Over the weeks to come, you will experience weird things happening in life, out-of-the-ordinary things that get your attention and make you think. You will likely find that your psychic senses increase and that your spell work gets a bit more efficient. This will be the case until the end of the labyrinth, when these heightened abilities settle into something more. While you do this work, be sure to align your souls daily, perform cleansings at least once a week, and document everything you experience related to the labyrinth.

Essentially, we just installed a channeling device into your witch's dream. This means that the guardian spirits you encounter can appear in the space you created in your mind at any time. Be sure to visit this place periodically when you are not actively working the labyrinth to see if one of them might be waiting for you or has perhaps left a message for you.

While this work does take time and lots of contemplation, taking a break now and then is entirely healthy. Just be sure to keep yourself moving forward on the journey.

Journal about your experiences. Sketch out a scene from the witch's dream and do your best to record details that will help you sense the energies of the Grigori with ease. Feel free to work with any of the Terrestrial Grigori if you feel inspired and go to them when you need their medicine, especially as we move forward into mystery.

Chapter Eleven

Oronos and the Well of Space

*In all our searching, the only thing we've found that
makes the emptiness bearable is each other.*

———

Carl Sagan

Space, the final frontier—or, in our case, the first of a handful of
frontiers we will be exploring in the labyrinth.

The ruling philosophical thought says that we live in two states of
being: the phenomenal and the numinal. Phenomenality extends the
concept that everything is limited to the conditions of space, time, and
causation. This hints that everything in the phenomenal is quantita-
tive and composed of some measurable substance. We think of space
as being the thing that an object takes up, as that extra room on the
airplane (or lack thereof), and we think of things like length, width,
depth, and height. Space, however, is a bit more complicated than that.

Yes, space is that thing that gets filled up with stuff, and dimensional properties make for great descriptors, but space is also within stuff and around stuff, and there is not one piece of time, matter, or energy that isn't affected by space.

We also think of the cosmos, or outer space—of planets and galaxies and nebulas. But between you and those places is space, and lots of it. The term *outer space* refers to all of the space that exists outside of Earth's ecosystem. Within the ecosystem, we experience space in an acute form compared to the vastness that extends beyond it. For comparison, the continental United States from coast to coast is roughly 2,600 miles (4,185 km), the distance between the United Nations' headquarters in New York to the Eiffel Tower in Paris, France, is roughly 3,626 miles (5,256 km), and the distance from my office to the kitchen is roughly 70 feet (21 m). However, from the planet's surface to our moon is 238,900 miles (384,472 km), the distance from our moon to our sun is roughly 94.5 million miles (152 million km), and from the sun to Pluto is 39.5 astronomical units (AU). Each AU is approximately forty times the distance between our planet and the sun, which means that Pluto is roughly 3.6 billion miles (5.9 billion km) from the sun. It would take me about four days to drive across the country, but it would take me over six thousand years of constant travel in a car at average highway speeds to drive between the sun and Pluto. Our solar system alone is roughly four light years in diameter and would take somewhere around 38 billion years to drive tip to tip.

To put that into perspective, there are an estimated 200 billion solar systems in our galaxy alone, and currently it is estimated that there are over 100 billion galaxies in the observable universe. The math is too frightening to break into, so just sit for a moment and think about all of that space.

Space exists inside of things as well. There is space between the cells in our body. There is space between every atom. There is even space between protons and neutrons. Space isn't just a thing that can be filled; space is something that fills and even can suspend. At some point space becomes a bit too hard to fathom, doesn't it? Not only is it everywhere, even inside of us and the stuff we are made of, but entire galaxies are randomly floating within it. Everything resides within space; space is the vessel for all of creation.

Numinosity and Space

Imagine space for a moment and then take away all of the stuff. Empty space—nothing exists within it, no matter or time or light or darkness or anything for the rules of physics to apply themselves to. Just an endless expanse of emptiness and nothingness. We call this the void, and it is the origin of everything. It is theorized that the universe as we know it is surrounded at its edges by the void, and that the singularity that sparked the big bang somehow formed within the void.

To truly appreciate space and the void, and to bring this back to the spiritual, we need to switch gears from the phenomenal to the numinous. The numinous cannot be explained by the laws of the phenomenal; it is a divine presence, a quality that can be only felt and observed.

A numinous view of space yields different results than those we found formerly. After contemplating how big the universe is, how much stuff it contains, and what it is like without all of the stuff, you might have been hit with a sense of awe. I know I was and still am. That sense of being struck by the unimaginable is what running into the numinous is all about. Ask yourself: What is divine about space?

For me, it is space's ability to be everywhere, in everything, literally all at once. Space can extend beyond creation and be within creation simultaneously, even though it is a component of creation. If there were ever a natural force that was deserving of spiritual adoration, space would be the apparent front-runner.

Space has no gravity, nor can it affect an environment within its confines. It merely exists as an endless state of emptiness. What fills it and what it fills are both the infinitesimal and the infinite.

Preparation: The Feeling of Space

STEP ONE

Go to the doorway in your mind and recite the invocation of Oronos while you draw their sigil in yellow fire.

I call to Oronos, the Grigori of Space,
Infinite Keeper of the Endless, Winged Serpent of Emptiness,
Come now from the starry labyrinth and open the sacred gates,
Be here now and in your fullest, for destiny awaits!

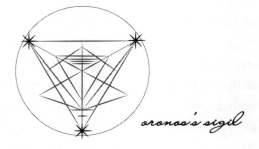

oronos's sigil

See the sigil fade into the doorway, and then focus on your breath. Allow yourself to breathe naturally but follow the flow of air in and out while doing so. Take a step into the gate. As you do this, relax your body and your mind by releasing physical and mental stress or discomfort with each exhale. Simply allow yourself to acknowledge these points of stress and then let them pour out of you.

As things come up that feel unmovable, remember that even the densest of materials contain space within. Find space within the moments of stillness and silence between your breaths, and then use that to connect to the space within your blocks. Once you find that space within, move through your blocks and find the space that exists on the other side of them. As you continue to breathe, repeat this process until you find yourself on the other side of all present distraction. Remember: acknowledge, let go, and move beyond.

STEP TWO

Breathe even deeper now, and eventually you will stumble upon a moment free of distraction, accompanied by a sense of weightlessness. You have stepped through the gate for the first time. Just as you have been following the flow of your breath in and out, follow this sense of weightlessness as it expands like ink in water. Release yourself into this emptiness. Allow yourself to let go of any one plane or dimension or form of measurement. Become borderless in all directions.

STEP THREE

After some time suspended like this, reach out for the doorway and see it appear beside you. Take a step back through it and allow emptiness to remain behind you. As this happens, take three deep breaths and feel yourself slowly slip back into the confines of your own body. Take a few moments to reflect. When you feel prepared, open your eyes and journal about your experience.

Things to follow up on:

1. Besides emptiness, what other emotions or feelings did you perceive with this exercise?

2. If there was a shape or symbol beside the sigil of Oronos presented in this book that might represent your experience, what might it be?

3. Draw what it was like becoming space.

Shifting Through Space (Remote Viewing)

We can use our budding connection to space to remote view. Repeat steps one and two of the previous exercise.

Conjure from within yourself the desire to see a friend (pick someone you can follow up with to see if they noticed you) and picture their eyes. As you focus on the image of their eyes, continue to breathe deeply and then push through the empty canvas of space around you so that person and their surroundings become clear.

When you are finished, return to a state of floating darkness and then perform step three of the previous exercise.

Things to follow up on:

1. What did it feel like to visit someone in this way?

2. Ask the person you visited if they sensed your presence.

3. Visit at least three other people and record your experiences.

4. If there was a shape or symbol that might represent your experience that could be used in the witch's dream, what might it be? Draw this symbol and explain what it means to you.

Other Preparations

Perform those exercises a few times and get a feel for the sensation of space. It is a lot to imagine and a lot to appreciate. In addition to visiting the labyrinth, it would behoove you to do some research about space and the science behind it. Part of what we need to do at this time is to really tune in to the essence of this guardian, and one of the best ways to do that is to wrap your rational mind around the science behind the spiritual force. If you get overwhelmed or confused, take a break and then ask your guides to help you through it. As an act of devotion, give no less than seven hours of study to the concept of space. When you learn something new, visit the doorway in your mind to reinforce the connection, and when you have those moments of deep interest and curiosity, lend that energy to the doorway as well. As you interact and learn more from Oronos and the others, find time to bring their lessons into your life. Meditate, reflect, and apply the wisdom gained while doing so to your work within the witch's dream. For example, we discussed how space surrounds everything and is everywhere all at once. This means that by working with the spiritual forces of space, our magic can be anywhere we need it to be at any place. Incorporating space as a component in spell work can be an inspiring insight that could yield dramatic results if applied properly. Let what you discover through research inspire your soul to feel and sense the spiritual qualities of what it is that you learn. This doesn't mean I'm encouraging anyone to create or invest in fake science to validate their spiritual claims; rather, that as spiritual people we look at the scientific and factual with awe. Science can give us part of the equation, an essential part of the equation, but it is up to us to solve it.

Once you have devoted time to study and are in a place of deeper understanding, you will be ready to meet Oronos.

Oronos

Oronos appears in many forms, most frequently for me in a transparent humanoid body that will sometimes be filled with stars and nebulas, but other times with just emptiness. Sexless and lacking much of a form, this energy feels ageless but ancient.

We like to talk a lot about "sacred space" in witchcraft and occultism; think of Oronos as the sacredness of space. Oronos is older than the other Grigori and teaches us that the microcosm mirrors the macrocosm. The space within is the space that surrounds and encompasses us. They also bring with them wisdom pertaining to the sovereign nature of your soul and its potential. Time, matter, and energy are each subject to space, as each theoretically could not exist outside of it. Space is essentially the emptiness that fills the universe, but what fills it are time, matter, energy, and quintessence. What exists outside of space is beyond our current level of understanding, but we imagine that even if atmospherically the universe we exist within does have its boundaries, other universes exist separate from it. As far as we are to understand for the foreseeable future, space is the stage on which everything is set. Oronos, being the Grigori of Space, is our spiritual host to the party.

Because the microcosm does mirror the macrocosm, we can think of our souls as the space within. Like the universe that space fills, they are seemingly limitless and full of every potential, capable of perceiving and even manifesting throughout time as matter and energy. The primal soul, which I equate to the physical body, is a product of matter and space. The ego is a product of time and space. The higher soul is a product of energy and space. What binds these agents is quintessence. So as space is the stage for all of creation, so too is your soul and all of its parts—what you find within, you are sure to find in the space that surrounds you. Oronos doesn't only rule over the space that you fill, but also the space that you contain.

Oronos teaches us that by making the space within ourselves sacred, we make the space that surrounds us sacred as well. Essentially, the more we build and construct our gnosis, which is an exploration of our spirit, the more we build our understanding of the world that surrounds us. As the bud of gnosis blooms, so too does our connection to our environment. As we expand our definition of one, we expand our definition of the other. They are intrinsically tied together. It is through Oronos and space that "as above, so below; as within, so without" is made capable, and it is through our connection to them that we deepen our intuitive understanding of that process.

Congress: The Rite of Oronos

Have your journal or sketch pad handy. Perform the rites of preparation and ingress from the opening ritual. While standing before the black candle, reach out with your senses and connect this ritual space with the one in your head. Visualize the doorway of yellow fire manifesting on our plane, and then recite the invocation of Oronos (page 236).

This time as the sigil fades away, a door appears in its place. You notice the sigil of Oronos prominently displayed on the front and intuitively know to open the door. Reach out with your aligned state and push through the door. Once open, allow yourself to step into the chamber waiting beyond.

When you move forward, you find yourself floating as you have so many times before. Say the name Oronos three times and find yourself somehow standing on a firm, translucent platform. Emptiness surrounds you in all directions; you have no sense of up or down, north or south, only a sense of stillness where you stand. Say their name three more times.

From the edge of the platform a figure emerges, one just as empty as its surroundings. As it draws closer, you perceive the figure of a human but notice no defining features, and you instantly know this to be the Grigori you seek. Reach out with your consciousness and embrace this spirit as Diana embraced Dianus, fusing together, if only for an instant, to create something new and then returning to your original form.

Ask Oronos the following questions and record their unique response and the information you take from that in your journal. Take time to ask these questions as well as any others you might have for them and then to record your answers. Draw a sketch of how Oronos appears to you and any other experiences that you feel are worth recording in this way.

1. Who am I?

2. Is there anyone or anything in all of creation that is like me?

3. How do I use and consume the energies of space? Is this proportionate to others?

4. How does space affect my spell and ritual work? How does knowing this help me?

5. Do I have a sacred connection somewhere else in space that I currently do not know of?

6. What, if anything, can space teach me about the origin of my soul?

7. What, if anything, can space help me discover about my life purpose that I do not know?

8. What mysteries can space reveal to me?

9. How does my experience with you bring me closer to knowing myself?

10. How does my experience with you bring me closer to revealing the mysteries of Diana?

11. How can I better work with the mysteries of space to impact my life?

12. What should I know that I haven't asked about?

Egress

You may not get to every question on your first visit. Oronos will let you know when they are finished with you by showing you a well in the center of this place. This well is what we refer to as the Well of Space and can be used to spiritually access anyplace, anywhere. On another journey you might gaze upon its surface to find omens or discover new places, but for now it is our only exit. Its arrival signifies that Oronos is getting ready to leave the building. Climb into this well and just as your entire body has entered it fully, find yourself crawling out of another well, this one the shape and size of a doorway. Take a deep breath and find yourself back in the space of your witch's dream. Complete the ritual by performing the rite of egress as explained in the opening ritual. Continue to visit Oronos and to document your experiences over your following journey. You should feel their presence join you now when summoning the Pyramid of Diana.

Chapter Twelve

Aeon and the Dawn of Time

Who controls the past controls the future.
Who controls the present controls the past.

———

George Orwell

Time flashes by us in an instant, and before we know it, we run out of it. What we experience as time during our lifetime isn't even a blink in space-time; it's barely a grain of sand in its hourglass. Since the big bang, time has been a constant companion to creation, a continuum that expands as our universe expands, unfolding into the fourth dimension and bearing witness to all that has been made manifest and every process it took to bring it to fruition.

Time is a force within the universe that carries us and all that we are made of forward on a current that cannot be stopped, only observed.

Matter, which we will continue to discuss in the following chapters, has a life cycle, and anything composed of matter is subject to that cycle. Time is like a rushing river, and matter is like the stones that get caught up in its torrent and tumbled along the way. Eventually, those stones will erode and become sediment, which will turn back into stone, which will ultimately go through a similar erosion process again and again until all the original components in that first stone have undergone so many cycles that their energy is all used up. During the entire lifespan of the stone and all the stones it became a part of later, that river continued to flow, never skipping a beat.

On our plane we measure time based on our rotation around the sun. There are 365 rotations around the sun for every one Earth year. Each rotation is divided into twenty-four distinct but equal units of time called hours. Each hour consists of sixty smaller units of time called minutes, and so on. Our entire system is based on the cycle of our planet as it hurtles through space. If our planet were to stop moving through space, however, and instead simply remain suspended, time as we know it would stop. We also know that time is subject to things like gravity. The farther away we move from a body of mass with a gravitational field, the slower time passes. This we know thanks to Albert Einstein's theory of general relativity.

As philosophers tackle the dilemma of time, they notice that it is eerily connected to space. The term *space-time* refers to a three-dimensional universe (space) that is merged with time as part of a four-dimensional continuum. Imagine that you are seeing the big bang on television. If space-time did not exist, the expansion of the universe would not happen because space and time would have to increase simultaneously. It would be like looking at the big bang on pause. Everything that happens does so because time provides causation. This, of course, is assuming that time is linear.

There are two prevailing theories regarding the arrangement of events in time, known as A-series and B-series. First proposed by Scottish philosopher John McTaggart, A-series events happen along a continuum where there is a definite past that leads to a present and that present leads to a future. Time is progressing forward along this line and is continually transforming as a result. B-series theorists (B-theorists) take a much different approach. They surmise that what we observe as the past, present, and future are actually events that are happening simultaneously to one another.

This is where things can get complicated; B-theory suggests that instead of time traveling along a line that progresses from the past to the present and the present to the future, everything that could be categorized as happening *is* happening—all at once. This means that according to B-theory, time is unchangeable and the idea of free will goes right out of the window. These events aren't separate from one another but equal; the only progression or change is in observation.

Numinosity and Time

So which theory is the most accepted? Modern theorists have agreed that both theories have their flaws and have moved beyond the terms; however, to understand the new way of thinking, these two theories still must be followed. Currently, we believe that time is objective, something that comes up with both theories but rewrites the rules a bit when taken into consideration. In this, we must understand that time is made real by its observation.

Presentism, the new A-theory, suggests that time is basically linear but that the past and future are not real in the same way the present is because they cannot be observed in the present. Unlike traditional A-theory, the future simply hasn't happened yet, so the line of time in that direction has not been drawn. The past exists because we can trace a series of events backward to their origin (through space), but the future is not in any way real, merely a theoretical possibility. Think of it as if you had a vehicle that instead of moving you through space moved you through time; the vehicle could only ever drive back because there is no paved road to the future, only the one currently being paved and the path that leads from the past to it.

Eternalism has evolved from B-theory, on the other hand, to suggest that all states of time are equally real in the way that all locations in space are real. This leads to the idea of a four-dimensional universe that has a fixed measurable amount of both space and time that are unilaterally agreeable to one another. Essentially the idea according to eternalism is that not only is time not linear, but the concept of the past happening before the present and the future happening after it are both illusions of the human mind needing to project order.

To the presentist, time is something that happens as the result of things moving through space. To the eternalist, time is something that exists in a fixed state alongside space.

Both modes of thinking could be right, or there could be another explanation altogether that we just haven't stumbled upon yet. Either way, for the time being, both theories allude to one dynamically important aspect of time that we can't overlook: observation. For time to be real, it must be observable. This doesn't mean we have to be present during every moment, but it does mean that we have to be able to trace the order of events back to the point of causation. It also means that what we do now will act as a point of causation for future events. Whether these events are simultaneously happening or not is irrelevant in the observable universe. When it comes to time, what is real is what can be observed; the rest is waiting to become.

A numinous view of time shows us that it genuinely *is* relative to the observer, and that because of this it moves according to our will.

Preparation: A Sense of Time and Wisdom

STEP ONE

Align and center yourself, and then go to the doorway in your mind and recite the invocation of Aeon while you draw their sigil in yellow fire.

I call to Aeon, the Grigori of Time,
Boundless Keeper of the Great Ages, Winged Serpent of Eternity.
Come now from the starry labyrinth and open the sacred gates,
Be here now and in your fullest, for destiny awaits!

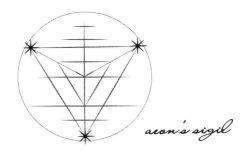

aeon's sigil

See the sigil fade into the doorway, then focus on your breath and follow the flow of air in and out. As you do this, relax your body and your mind by releasing physical and mental stress or discomfort with each exhale. Simply allow yourself to acknowledge these points of tension and then let them pour out of you.

As things come up during this exercise that feel unstoppable, remember that what we observe becomes real, and that in this moment investing attention into these distractions will only make them more real for you. Focus on perceiving a time when these issues will no longer be so intense and vivid, and then move forward to embrace the sensation of your distractions coming to an end. Take a step into the doorway.

STEP TWO

Take a deep breath and reach backward in your mind to the first time you can remember feeling uncertain about life. As you emerge on the other side of the doorway, step into this memory. For me, this was the night that my father left for work and didn't come back home. I was almost four. Something told me then that things would be different forever as I gave him a kiss on the cheek and watched him leave.

Like me, you have a moment of uncertainty that made you incredibly aware of time. Maybe it seemed to slow down for you, or perhaps time felt stuck altogether. Follow your gut and go back to this place in time.

Observe this memory subjectively, study it, but do not become a player in it. Focus on this younger version of yourself. At present, you know how the story works out for the more youthful you, but in that previous moment the world was a very different place and your awareness was at a very different level. If you were to quantify time as memory (what you have observed), the distance between that younger version of you and the present version of you is wisdom. You are at the center of both of these versions, looking out upon the world with two varying degrees of wisdom

Step Three

After taking a few more moments to observe this place in time, take a deep breath, reach out for the doorway with your senses, and then see it appear beside you. Take a step back through the doorway and allow all psychic and spiritual ties to that time to release from you and remain there. As you emerge again in the prepared space within your witch's dream, take three deep breaths and feel yourself slowly slip back into the confines of your own body. Take a few moments to observe the sensation, and when you feel ready, open your eyes and journal about your experience.

· · · · · · · · ·

Things to follow up on:

1. Compare the distance in time as measured by years and wisdom. How many years ago did the experience you visited happen? How much wisdom has been gained since? If this was a painful memory to visit, write about how the present version of you would have intervened if you could physically manifest there.

2. If there were a shape or symbol other than the sigil of Aeon that could represent your experience, what might that be? Sketch it.

3. As you review the experience, sketch any details that you noticed when you visited that weren't there or that you don't remember being there when it initially happened.

Stepping Into the Future

Gaze into a full-length mirror for a few minutes before performing the first step of the previous exercise. Instead of stepping into the doorway, however, see that as the sigil disappears, your reflection takes its place. Look into your own eyes and envision what those eyes will look like in five years. What wrinkles will you have then? What depth have the colors gained? Step through the doorway.

As you emerge on the other side, notice that you are coming out of the door you just entered and have come back to the hidden place within your witch's dream. As you look around, notice that the space has changed and now reflects five years of your growth. Take a deep breath and then allow yourself to momentarily leave the space of the witch's dream and enter your life at this future moment. Look around you and take notice of as many details as possible.

After taking a good look around, return to the witch's dream and find yourself standing before the doorway. See your reflection in the doorway once again, this time remembering the eyes of the present-day you, and step through. Emerge back in the present-day witch's dream and then take three deep breaths, feeling yourself slowly slipping back into the confines of your own body. Take a few moments to observe this sensation, and when you feel ready, open your eyes and journal about your experience.

Other Preparations

Perform these exercises on your own a few times and map out a sense of time that is fluid in observance. Keep visiting the labyrinth and spending time tuning in to the essence of what Aeon is really all about. As we did when preparing to meet Aeon, spend seven hours learning about the science of time, and keep your journal nearby so you can record insights.

This would be an excellent time to start visiting the space within the witch's dream that you have carved out for this work before you go to sleep at night. Spend five minutes exploring and looking around there before you lie down. Pay close attention to your dreams, engage your dreamworking skills, and record your findings.

Once you have devoted time to study and are in a place of deeper understanding, you will be ready to meet Aeon.

Aeon

Aeon can appear as any form they choose. Most frequently I see them as a humanoid figure made of light and eternal fire. They are light that casts itself upon the darkness like shadow. Timeless in the way only time can be, Aeon is an ever-present force that sees all.

Aeon teaches us that what we focus on we make real. What we have manifested is only made real through causation in the past, and what we seek to manifest in the future can only be done so through an action in the present. Time may be relative to the other forces of space, matter, energy, and quintessence, but each of those things are also dependent on time and subject to its reign. In this, Aeon is both the observer as well as the progression from past to future.

As the microcosm mirrors the macrocosm, we see that time exists both outside as well as within ourselves. As observers, we contain a record of time as memory. Memories are recordings of events, but what is captured is not just information, but time itself. We also record time differently depending on the memory and know that no two people's memories are the same. This means that no two people have the same timeline in the way that no two people walk the same lonely road.

Congress: The Rite of Aeon

Have your journal and/or sketch pad handy. Perform the rites of preparation and ingress from the opening ritual. While standing before the black candle, reach out with your senses and connect this ritual space with the one in your head. Visualize the doorway of yellow fire manifesting on our plane, and then recite the invocation of Aeon.

As you stand at the doorway and the sigil for Aeon fades, a new door appears in its place. Not unlike the other, this one burns with yellow fire, but it does so with a different consistency. These flames seem to move slower, and as you bring yourself closer to the door, they move faster. On the door, as if carved into the yellow fire, you see the sigil of Aeon appear and know to walk through it.

As you emerge from the doorway on the other side, you enter into a familiar emptiness. A platform like glass is beneath you, translucent yet somehow visible to you. The door behind you vanishes, and in its place you see a brilliant yellow sun emerge over the east, noticing that as its beams of light touch the vastness, they create the shape of a person. Their arms, legs, and body stretch out from the sun and fill your immediate position with light, and you know this to be Aeon, the Grigori of Time. Reach out with your consciousness and embrace this spirit as Diana embraced Dianus and fuse your essence together with their own, creating something new for just a moment before returning to your original form.

Ask Aeon the following questions and record their unique responses in your journal. Take all the time (no pun intended) you need to ask these questions, as well as any others that you might have. Draw a sketch of Aeon as they appear to you.

1. Who am I?

2. Is there anyone or anything in all of time that is like me?

3. My time is limited; in what ways do I waste or misuse it?

4. How does time affect my spell and ritual work? How does knowing this help me?

5. Do I have a sacred connection somewhere else in time that I currently do not know of?

6. What, if anything, can time teach me about the nature of my soul?

7. What, if anything, can time help me discover about my life purpose that I do not know?

8. What mysteries can time reveal to me that I do not already know?

9. How does my experience with you bring me closer to knowing myself?

10. How does my experience with you bring me closer to revealing the mysteries of Diana?

11. How can I better work with the mysteries of time to impact my life?

12. What should I know that I haven't asked about?

Egress

As with Oronos, you may not get to all of your questions on the first visit. That is okay; keep coming back and working on exploring the mysteries that are being revealed to you. You will notice that, like the sun, Aeon will move from their place of origin over your head and eventually set. When the light goes out completely, the darkness will consume you, and you will find yourself stepping back into the space within the witch's dream. Complete the ritual by performing the rite of egress as explained in the opening ritual. Continue to visit Aeon and to document your experiences over your following journey. You should feel both Oronos and Aeon join you now when summoning the Pyramid of Diana.

Chapter Thirteen

Proto and the Heart
of the Matter

*Nothing is accidental in the universe—this is one
of my Laws of Physics—except the entire universe
itself, which is Pure Accident, pure divinity.*

———

Joyce Carol Oates

The *Encyclopedia Britannica* defines *matter* as "material substance that constitutes the observable universe and, together with energy, forms the basis of all objective phenomena." Essentially, matter is one of two components that make up and fill space and time. It is the stuff that everything is made of: you, me, the chair you're sitting in, the candles you carve, the trees that blow in the wind, and this book all have this one thing in common. We only exist because matter exists.

Matter comes in all shapes and sizes, but we believe that for the most part there is a finite amount of it that keeps getting used over and over again to make different things.[12]

Our understanding is that all of the matter in the universe was once condensed into one individual particle called the "point of singularity." The big bang is the result of the point of singularity exploding, releasing the matter and energy that were being held tightly together. Essentially, our entire universe is made up of space expanding to meet the flow of matter and energy that came from this singularity. Matter may very well be the reason that our universe exists in three observable dimensions (excluding time as the fourth).

Now, here is where things get really interesting. In the early 1970s a group of physicists created what we call the standard model, which identifies the fundamental components of matter and how they react. All matter is made up of particles, and those particles can be categorized as one of two basic varieties called quarks and leptons. Each of these groupings consists of different types of small particles, which group together to form the larger particles that we know as protons, electrons, and neutrons. Each of these particles is capable of carrying a charge of energy; protons have a positive charge, electrons have a negative charge, and neutrons are carrying a neutral charge. These particles are attracted to one another, and through the process of fusion, various charge pairings lead to the creation of the periodic elements.

These elements then continue to be fused with other elements and raw particles, eventually making everything we see today. This process happens inside of every star, which are natural fusion chambers that are constantly cannibalizing their own mass to create new elements.

12 Matter can be created from energy. Photons have been observed converting into an electron-proton pair. This is not something easy to duplicate, and the science behind it goes a little more into physics than I can reasonably share with you here. This is something that you should research on your own, however, as it is really quite inspiring to a magician!

Eventually, a star will begin the process of fusing particles together to make iron, and that will be the last thing it builds before it dies.[13]

Numinosity and Matter

As a spiritual force, matter is the fundamental building block of the universe. It not only creates the world we live in, but it also creates life and provides for the universe inside of ourselves to exist. We live in the material world, a world of matter and causation, and it is through this world that we ourselves take form. As witches, we tend to spend a lot of time and energy trying to escape the trappings of the material world. We see it as a land of want, pain, and greed rather than the natural providence of the soul that it is and can be.

The microcosm always mirrors the macrocosm. Because the universe is both material and energetic (spiritual), so too are we. A craft that is focused solely on one or the other cannot be a full craft. A worldview that only contains a perspective of the material but rejects the spiritual cannot be balanced or realistic. A worldview that solely focuses on the spiritual and denies the material cannot be balanced or realistic either. The way we define these things for ourselves categorizes the way we invest in them. As we seek to better know ourselves and the universe as magicians and metaphysicians, we cannot overlook the value of the material. This doesn't mean being a materialist; this means taking full appreciation of what the physical world has to offer.

There are four fundamental forces that come about in the universe because of matter: gravity, electromagnetic, the weak force, and the strong force. Each force has its own type of force-carrying particle known as a boson, which allows it to distribute energy, but only the bosons of the final three have actually been detected. Gravity still remains a fundamental force, just one with some mathematical

---

13 As a side note, I believe this is why iron is so good at breaking spells and why it is classically known for warding against faeries, demons, and other undesirable spiritual energies.

frustration within the standard model. The study of gravity gave way to the discovery of a special kind of matter known as dark matter.

Scientists and astronomers have discovered galaxies in our universe that are spinning so fast, the force generated by them should be significant enough for them to separate and collapse. For some reason, however, they seem to have unknown mass helping them produce enough gravity that they remain intact. This unknown mass was named dark matter because it remains an almost unobservable phenomenon. Normal matter emits and absorbs light, which means it interacts via electromagnetic force. Dark matter, on the other hand, doesn't absorb or emit light, meaning that it does not carry a charge. It only interacts with regular (or "light") matter via weak and gravitational forces, and it is otherwise undetectable by current observation techniques, though scientists are close, and its existence is a mathematical likelihood.

According to the scientists at CERN (Conseil Européen pour la Recherche Nucléaire), light-matter only accounts for 5 percent of the contents of the universe.[14] Dark matter also seems to outweigh light matter six to one, so it is theorized that roughly 27 percent of the universe is composed of dark matter. This leads to the notion that there are hidden worlds and dimensions, likely even one or several parallel worlds to our own. Matter isn't just what we can see and feel on our plane, but what exists on other planes as well.

Preparation: Going Deep

STEP ONE

Align and center yourself, then go to the doorway in your mind. Recite the following invocation to Proto and draw their sigil in yellow fire.

---

14 From CERN's educational website, https://home.cern/about/physics /dark-matter, accessed January 2018.

I call to Proto, the Grigori of Matter.
Immeasurable Keeper of all Dimension, Winged Serpent of Mass,
Come now from the starry labyrinth and open the sacred gates!
Be here now and in your fullest, for destiny awaits!

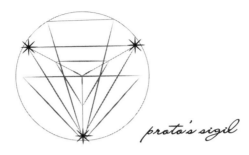

proto's sigil

See the sigil fade into the doorway and focus on your breath, as
you have before: follow the air as it flows in and out of your chest.
When you feel ready, step into the doorway. As you continue to
breathe, notice the weight of your body more so than normal, and as
you emerge from the doorway into a familiar empty space, this weight
suddenly feels independent of you. Now it is something that can be
observed instead of felt.

Step Two

Examine the heaviness of your body as you would a painting.
Where do you feel the most density in your muscle system? Where do
you notice the most tension and discomfort? Now, visualize this part
of your body only. Re-create it in your mind.

Take a deep breath, and fill this area of your body with your consciousness. As you exhale, take a moment to observe the sensation.
With the next breath, pour your consciousness into the muscle that
feels the tensest. Rest for a few moments, and then as you take another
breath allow your consciousness to follow even deeper and become
aware of the tissues that create that muscle. Again, rest momentarily and observe. Next, take another deep breath and pour your

consciousness into the cells that make up that tissue. Become aware of the millions of cells that together make up the tissues that make up your muscles. As your mind follows, allow the tension you felt in this place to relax. Spend a few moments taking that all in.

Now go even deeper: choose one cell and pour yourself into it. Remember to take time and enjoy the view. With the next breath, allow yourself to pour into one of the carbon molecules that link with hydrogen to create that cell. Observe the sensation of going from cell to molecule. Finally, go one more step deeper and pour your mind into one of the atomic carbon particles. Continue to breathe slow and deep, and take it all in. This is existence on the elemental level.

Step Three

When you feel ready, slowly work your way back through the molecular, cellular, tissue, and muscular systems we visited. As you find yourself back in the muscular system, see if the tension you felt there has changed at all. Take another deep breath, pour yourself from that muscle back into the empty space, and then step through the doorway. Once you emerge back in the prepared space within your witch's dream, take three deep breaths and feel yourself slowly slip back into the confines of your own body. Take a few moments to observe the sensation, and when you feel prepared, open your eyes and journal about your experience.

· · · · · · · · · ·

Things to follow up on:
1. Besides tension and heaviness, write about the other emotions or feelings that you perceive with this exercise.

2. If there was a shape or symbol beside the sigil of Proto presented here that might represent your experience, what might it be? Sketch it.

3. Draw what it was like becoming a carbon atom.

Materia Magica

Perform step one of the previous exercise but do not enter the doorway; instead, sit down beside it. In the waking world, you will want to be sitting with your sketch supplies. Visualize something that you want to manifest in your life, something material. This should be something that should be realistic in circumstance but just a bit out of possible reach at the moment. Draw the outline of it. As you do this, continue to pay attention to what is happening in your witch's dream. Listen for messages coming from the other side of the door, look for things to appear near the doorway, etc. Write notes about what you see.

STEP TWO

Over the next several minutes, fill in the details of your drawing. As you do this, remain tuned in to the witch's dream and visualize this thing forming for you inside of that space. See the atoms coming together to make the molecules, see those molecules coming together to create elements, see those becoming the components of what you are drawing, see those being put together, etc. Be as detail-oriented as possible and act as if your drawing was somehow 3D printing in your witch's dream.

STEP THREE

When you are finished, focus on this object in your mind, then kiss your fingers and place them on the drawing as if blessing it. While you do this, visualize the object transferring from your witch's dream onto the paper, and say "So mote it be!" Leave the space as outlined in the opening ritual and keep your sketches for later.

Things to follow up on:

1. Visit this picture at least once a week, and visualize the process of its becoming again. Bless it at the end as described. Continue to do this until this thing manifests for you.

2. Try this with a few other things and record your results. Mix it up and apply this technique to other spell work; do you notice a difference in effectiveness? If so, write about why you think that is.

Other Preparations

Perform these workings, devote time and energy to research, and get to know the concepts behind matter. Give no less than seven hours to reading, watching documentaries, listening to podcasts, whatever it is that you need to do to expand your understanding of matter. As we continue to develop our gnosis and open our minds with each new insight, we are bridging the worlds of the spiritual and material. Use those moments of inspiration to help you develop questions, ask those questions of your spirit guides and allies, and engage your new awareness spiritually as much as possible. Once you have done this, it will be time to meet Proto.

Proto

As you might imagine, Proto takes on whatever shape they feel like, and while partial to geometric shapes, they have no consistent form. No more than once have they ever shown me the same figure, but the uncanny feeling of heaviness is always present when they are.

Proto is the spiritual essence of matter and the guardian of its power. They are continually changing and always moving, never staying in one place or form for too long. As a result, they teach us that nothing remains the same forever, and that everything that emerges from the elements will eventually return to them. Everything is connected via this cycle because we are all subject to the laws of decay.

Proto also teaches us of endless variety and the potent power of possibility. We have been limited in our exposure to the infinitum of ways matter takes shape in our universe. Not only haven't we entirely explored our planet, but what we know of our universe is limited to telescopes, satellites, and a bunch of theories. Imagine how minerals form under different gravity and pressure; that quartz point you love so much might look very different on another planet. On Earth life is carbon based, but on another planet life could be based on another element like silica. Imagine what aliens from a place like that would look like. The possibilities are staggering—this is, of course, before we take dark matter into consideration. Proto is a spirit that can teach us many things about manifestation.

With Proto come the properties of matter and lessons about gravity, force, and energy. We must study the way we impact the space around us and be aware of our own forcefulness and gravity. It is easy to get caught up in the gravity of another person's mass. It is easy to get caught up in the gravity of a situation. It is not, however, easy to remain in your own orbit. When we lend our force to another gravitational body, we lose the ability to direct ourselves. Proto teaches us how to take on the extra mass necessary to keep our world together without it ripping apart.

Congress: The Rite of Proto

Have your journal and/or sketch pad handy. Perform the rites of preparation and ingress from the opening ritual. While standing before the black candle, reach out with your senses and connect this ritual space with the one in your head. Visualize the doorway of yellow fire manifesting on our plane, then recite the invocation of Proto.

This time as the sigil fades away, a door appears in its place. You notice the sigil of Proto prominently displayed on the front and intuitively know to open the door. Reach out with your aligned state and push through the door. Once open, allow yourself to step into the chamber waiting beyond.

When you move forward, you find yourself floating, as you have so many times before. Say the name Proto three times and find yourself somehow standing on a firm, translucent platform. Emptiness surrounds you in all directions, and you have no sense of up or down, east or west; only a sense of stillness where you stand, of invisible gravity pulling you down. Say their name three more times.

With a flash of light, a strange geometric crystalline figure emerges with twenty facets. You no longer feel the gravity pulling you down; you now feel weightless and find yourself drifting toward this strange form. You notice that as you breathe and draw nearer to this figure, it is much larger than you had initially thought and just keeps getting bigger and bigger. With no sense of dimensional depth, you find that this shape now fills the emptiness entirely.

As you find yourself consumed by this force, you acknowledge it as Proto, the Grigori of Matter, and release yourself, merging with it for only an instant before returning back to your original form. Soon you find yourself slowing down and reaching a smaller version of the twenty-sided crystal that seems to beat like a heart. The rhythm you notice, however, is not unlike a human heartbeat, only somehow more profound.

Ask Proto the following questions and record the unique responses given in your journal. Take time to ask these questions as well as any others you might have for them and then record your answers. Remember it might take a few visits to get all the answers you seek. Draw a sketch of how Proto appears to you and any other experiences that you feel are valuable enough to record in this way.

1. Who am I?

2. How did I come to be made in this shape?

3. How does my use of materials in life benefit or harm me?

4. How does matter affect my spell and ritual work? How does knowing this help me?

5. Do I have a sacred connection to a certain mineral or periodic element that I currently do not know of?

6. What, if anything, can matter teach me about the origin of my soul?

7. What, if anything, can matter help me discover about my life purpose that I do not know?

8. What mysteries can matter reveal to me?

9. How does my experience with you bring me closer to knowing myself?

10. How does my experience with you bring me closer to revealing the mysteries of Diana?

11. How can I better work with the mysteries of matter to impact my life?

12. What should I know that I haven't asked about?

Egress

When you are ready to leave, step up to the beating crystal and place your hands on it. If Proto is at any time ready for you to go, the beat from the crystal will get louder, signaling for you to get up and touch the crystal. As your hands touch it, notice that it stops beating and you are suddenly standing once again on the translucent platform with the doorway to your witch's dream waiting before you. Complete the ritual by performing the rite of egress as explained in the opening ritual. Continue to visit Proto and to document your experiences over your next journey. You should feel their presence join you now when summoning the Pyramid of Diana.

Chapter Fourteen

Zoann and the Spheres of Energy

The energy of the mind is the essence of life.

———

Aristotle

Energy is the other thing that fills the universe up alongside matter. It comes in several different types within the known universe, and we are sure that there are still other forms of energy we have left to discover. For the most part, energy comes in two different forms: heat and work. Because energy can be neither created nor destroyed, according to the first law of thermodynamics, energy is understood to be something that only can be transferred or released through heat.

The type of energy that can be transferred, such as kinetic, potential, chemical, nuclear, etc., all fall under the "work" category of energy. As the name might suggest, this is energy that can be put to work, and it exists in a state of thermodynamic equilibrium—or, in other words, it exists in a fixed system and cannot be altered without another fixed system also being altered.

Heat energy is energy that is being exhausted instead of transferred and is the final step before energy dies. Thermal energy cannot be as easily converted as work energies, which means that most of that energy will remain radiant until it can travel no further. The sun releases massive amounts of energy while it is busy fusing hydrogen into helium, like light and heat energy. Earth is stationed at just the right place in our solar system for that energy to warm our planet without completely baking it. This, in turn, keeps water liquid (around most of the planet), crops growing, and provides much of the essential components for life on earth.

However, none of this would be possible without our planet's ability to emit its own energy, creating a protective shield called a magnetic field. On Earth the magnetic field is created by the molten metal in the outer layer of the planet's core rotating as it spins in orbit around the sun. Without this field, our atmosphere would have burned off, and Earth would look a lot more like Mars than the luscious blue sphere we have today. Earth absorbs about 70 percent of the energy it comes in contact with from the sun. The other 30 percent is reflected back into space.[15]

Numinosity and Energy

As I mentioned in the last chapter, matter and energy have a strange connection: they can be converted into one another. You might remember $E=mc^2$, the famous equation from Albert Einstein's theory of special relativity, which states that matter as mass (m), when multiplied by the speed of light squared (c^2), equals the amount of energy (E) found equivalent to a particle's mass. This strongly suggests that

15 From NASA's website, https://earthobservatory.nasa.gov/Features /EnergyBalance/page4.php, accessed January 2018.

matter is energy, just a highly condensed and specialized form of it. It also suggests that a lot of what we believe in metaphysics regarding vibration and resonance is likely true.

When you pick up a crystal and can feel energy coming from it, what is it that you are actually feeling? The belief in many circles is that we are psychically sensing the potential energy found in the stone. Because we are doing this via the sixth sense, we also are able to pick up other aspects of that potential energy that are spiritual in nature and would otherwise go undetected. If this is something that can be done with a crystal, then it is something that can be done with any form of matter.

Channeling energy is a bit trickier to explain, as fundamentally you are acting as a receiver and amplifier. What type of energy are we actually channeling? That is a good question. We can sense the energy we are channeling in the same way we can sense the potential energy within a stone, but moving through our own energetic field. We are always altered by the energy we channel, so we know that if only for a moment we are conductive for that energy. We also know that if we were not literally conducive to this energy, we are at least spiritually, as the movement of force within the closed system of the energy body can be observed. In other words, because we can feel something happening, we know that in some way, no matter how small, there is a transfer of energy occurring.

In the first part of the book, we discussed ritual tools and how to actually turn them into beacons of power. When we cast spells, perform rituals, and connect with spirits from the other side, we are working with the unique energies of our tools so that they may be the channels for the power we seek. When we combine these channels of power together and weave them in an act of magic, we are tapping into the potential energies that flow through them to bring about the force necessary to manifest our outcome.

Preparation: Spheres of Energy

STEP ONE

Align and center yourself, then go to the doorway in your witch's dream and recite the invocation of Zoann, the Grigori of Energy. As you do this, draw their sigil in yellow fire.

I call to Zoann, the Grigori of Energy,
Untamable Keeper of Perpetual Force, Winged Serpent of Power,
Come now from the starry labyrinth and open the sacred gates!
Be here now and in your fullest, for destiny awaits!

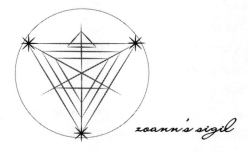

zoann's sigil

See this sigil fade into the doorway and bring your focus to the familiar emptiness that is revealed on the other side. Do not enter the doorway.

STEP TWO

Create a ball of yellow fire and then toss it into the doorway, seeing it disappear in the darkness the farther along it travels from you. Take a deep breath, and as you exhale, see the ball come back to you as if being tossed by someone on the other end. As you catch this ball, you notice that the fire burns brighter and is a bit larger. Toss the ball of yellow fire back through the doorway and watch it as it comes back, again catching it and noticing that it has grown larger and brighter.

Continue to do this until the ball of yellow fire can no longer pass through the door. Hold this sphere in your hands and feel the difference from when you first began this exercise to now. Take three deep breaths and condense this sphere into a small ball of energy the size of a marble. Remember to focus on the sensation of the energy as it moves and condenses; nothing is lost, only changed. Take this tiny ball of energy and place it on the altar.

Repeat this exercise and amass a collection of these tiny spheres. When you go to perform a spell, take one of these spheres of condensed yellow fire and use it to fuel your working as additional energy.

STEP THREE
When you are finished, visualize the door emerging from the outline of the doorway and take a few moments to ground the remaining energy. Take a few moments to observe the sensation and to think about your experience, then journal about it.

· · · · · · · · ·

Things to follow up on:

1. Perform magic using the spheres to assist in adding energy to your working and record the results.

2. Working with the list provided in chapter 1, continue to do this exercise but instead work with other flames besides yellow.

3. If there were a shape or symbol other than the sigil of Zoann that could represent your experience, what might that be? Sketch it.

4. Use the spheres outside of your spell work. When you wake up in the morning, envision adding them to your coffee, the food you eat, and other things that you consume. Record any difference in overall energy levels, focus, and mood.

Conductivity

We are conductors, and the energy we charge ourselves with attracts the frequencies we will inevitably end up conducting. Every time we meet someone new or old, we are transferring energy that was transferred to us. This can keep us in a closed loop if we are not aware of what we may or may not be attracting. We know that people exchange energy because with every new encounter we are left a little changed. The other truth to this is that you can tell how someone feels about you after they meet you in response to the energy they just received from you. This is expressed through body language, mannerisms, speech patterns and tone.

Even if we aren't aware of it, something rubs off each time we make a connection. If you were to record the different people and energies you interact with on a daily basis, you would likely find that your original frequency has been adjusted as a result of its conductivity throughout the day. It is like putting on a new pair of white sneakers every morning and then walking to the office. Unless you are extremely careful, you will likely show up at work with shoes that are no longer white. For the most part, the natural flow of energy through our body filters and cleans most of the impurities, but we still run into things that cause a more prominent stain on those shoes than we could have expected, and immediately taking care of it isn't always an option. So what do we do? We adjust our frequency to compensate for whatever it is that we stepped in, and we move on. Meanwhile, we are continually running into new people and ultimately tracking whatever it is we picked up through their systems. The cycle repeats and—well, you get the picture.

We can make an adjustment to our vibration when we need to, however, and mostly we can choose the impact we are going to have on other people. Sometimes two people just repel each other, and there is little you can do to stop that, but for the most part, if you can remain conscious of how the energy that you are bumping into is affecting your personal vibration, then you can be a more effective filter for the overall system of energy in your life. If you remember, back in *The Witch's Book of Power* we talked about soul alignment and its use in finding our home frequency. By performing rituals and workings that help you reset or remember this frequency, you can actually take control over the flow of energy and what type of energy you are conducting.

The idea essentially is that if you want to attract money, then every time you meet someone or have a moment of presence with another person, you should become conscious of what energy you are sending out to them via your frequency. If you don't feel good about it, do something to adjust it, like paying them a compliment or holding the door open. When you are finished adjusting the vibration between you, send them a pulse of prosperity. Think of something they might want or need and visualize them getting it. That is all you have to do. If you do this enough, you will essentially rewrite your own charge to draw in the energy of prosperity.

When you consciously shift the vibration and send them a pulse of energy, send them the tiny sphere of condensed blue fire. As it transfers from you to them, see them receive something they really want. Even if you don't know what it is, envision their face lighting up like on Christmas morning.

Spheres of Manifestation

Think of an energy you want to manifest in your life, and then create a sigil for it or use a symbol that you particularly associate with it. Perform the Spheres of Energy exercise but instead of tossing a ball of yellow fire, toss in a ball of blue fire that has been infused with the symbol of your desired manifestation. Build this ball in the way you have before, tossing it back and forth as it grows in intensity, and then condense it into a marble-sized sphere of energy. Do this several times. Complete the ritual as instructed.

Things to follow up on:

1. Trace the effect your energy has on others and on yourself. Do you notice a shift in their life or in yours?

2. This is an exercise I do to quickly manifest things in my life when I need them. After applying this technique, do you feel that you are more in tune with the energy of what you are trying to manifest? Do you feel any closer to manifesting it?

3. Draw or sketch the symbol you used, and explain what it meant.

Other Preparations

Just as with the others, spend time learning the science behind the phenomena. The topic of energy is vast and fascinating and way too complex to explain here, so devote seven hours to discovering more about the energy in our universe. Again, look at the science as a point of inspiration, and when something new comes up that you don't understand, reach into the witch's dream and ask. Take your journal, spend time sitting beside the doorway, listen for messages and write them down. Once you have done this and feel ready, it will be time to meet Zoann.

Zoann

Zoann takes the shape of a fluid metal sphere that is not unlike ferrofluid. The liquid metal stretches out to make waves and peaks that ripple across the surface. With each ripple of fluid, the air around Zoann moves and quakes in response.

Zoann is the spiritual consciousness of energy and force. They are perhaps the easiest of the cosmic Grigori to contact and work with, as they are the most mutable. Zoann teaches us that everything is energy, and that the universe we live in is filled with various forms of it. Each of these variations contains within themselves a piece of Zoann, a link to the spiritual force of energy, and in this all things are connected back to this Grigori.

Zoann also teaches us that we are conductors for the energies found within the universe. As conscious beings, this places the burden of responsibility on our shoulders as to what we do with the energy we come in contact with. As witches, this reinforces our fundamental theories regarding the importance of spiritual and psychic cleanliness.

Congress: The Rite of Zoann

Have your journal and / or sketch pad handy. Perform the rites of preparation and ingress from the opening ritual. While standing before the black candle, reach out with your senses and connect this ritual space with the one in your witch's dream. Visualize the doorway of yellow fire manifesting on our plane, then recite the invocation of Zoann.

As the sigil fades, visualize a door resembling liquid fire takes its place with the sigil for Zoann prominently etched into it. Take a deep breath, reach out with your witch power, and push through this door. As it opens, step into the all-too-familiar dark empty room that awaits you on the other side.

As you emerge in the dark room, you instantly feel a buzzing in the air around you. The emptiness seems to be filled with this ecstatic tension, and you instinctively know to follow the flow of this energy through the darkness. As you do so, call out the name Zoann three times. Each time you say it, feel the air growing thicker and thicker with this strange buzzing sensation, but immediately after you say it the third time, the buzzing stops as if you popped a balloon.

Before you, the darkness appears to move as if somehow stirring, vaguely capturing the outline of a giant wave before it catches you and pulls you under with an invisible force. Surrendering, you find yourself merging with the invisible force for just a moment, becoming something new, before returning to your original form. Take a deep breath.

The awareness that this is Zoann, Grigori of Energy, washes over you as you allow the wave of force to take you deeper into the darkness.

Notice now that before you a sphere of light appears in the distance. As you get closer, you see that this is a multicolored ball of intense energy waiting for you to arrive, and you feel a sense of hurriedness. When you arrive, you notice in clearer detail that the multicolored light is emanating from a black sphere and that waves of color wash over it, affecting the space around it.

Ask Zoann the following questions and record their responses in your journal. Take time to ask these questions, as well as any others you might have for them, and then record your answers. Remember it might take a few visits to get all the answers you seek. Draw a sketch of how Zoann appears to you and any other experiences that you feel are valuable enough to record in this way.

1. Who am I?
2. What energies came together for me to exist?
3. How does my use of energy in life benefit or harm me? How does it affect others?
4. How does energy affect my spell and ritual work? How does knowing this help me?
5. What types of energy should I be bringing into my life to help me better have influence over my life?
6. What, if anything, can energy teach me about the origin of my soul?
7. What, if anything, can energy help me discover about my life purpose that I do not know?
8. What mysteries can energy reveal to me?
9. How does my experience with you bring me closer to knowing myself?

10. How does my experience with you bring me closer to revealing the mysteries of Diana?

11. How can I better work with the mysteries of energy to impact my life?

12. What should I know that I haven't asked about?

Egress

When you are finished, step closer to the black ball emanating light and place your hands on it. If at any time Zoann is finished before you are, this light will grow until it eventually encompasses you. As you touch the sphere of pure energy, it ripples in response, and in an instant you find yourself once again standing on the translucent platform. Before you lies the doorway to the witch's dream. Complete the ritual by performing the rite of egress as explained in the opening ritual. Continue to visit Zoann and to document your experiences over your next journey. You should feel their presence, as well as the other three, join you now when summoning the Pyramid of Diana.

Chapter Fifteen

The Quintessential Ingredient

> The Quintessence of Magick is not to be found by the combination
> of externals, but solely by the direct realization of its innate
> source. [...] it is not found by uniting the "elements" in their
> temporarily manifest forms. For beyond the Outer, beyond
> the dualistic and substantive manifestations of element and
> element, the Quintessence is already attained. Its unity
> is constant as the primordial and intrinsic nature of the
> Sorcerous Being; its attainment is this very realization.

Andrew Chumbley, *The Azoetia*, Sethos Edition

No amount of science or logical thinking will allow me to lay the
groundwork for understanding quintessence. Still, pardon me
as I try. As we have moved through the Labyrinth of Diana, we have
explored the powers that the Grigori preside over as both scientific
inspiration and numinous phenomena. Some things still defy those

laws—energies that shape reality that cannot be accounted for. Logic cannot explain them away; these things are either acts of god-force or some "higher power." Regardless, they remain outside the realm of observed natural phenomena.

Quintessence is the force that presides over the miraculous, the events leading to the explosion of the singularity, life somehow springing forth from primordial broth, or even someone suddenly recovering from a terminal illness. There is an influence that somehow connects the forces of our world with those of other planes of reality. We can all feel it in the beat of every drum or in between the moments of ecstasy when we are both ourselves and something else at the end of every successful spell. There is a power that still remains unidentifiable but somehow discoverable all around us.

Quintessence is the origin and matrix that connects all things in the continuum of space-time. It is the thread that has been spun by the fates, the great pattern that all things are woven into, the tapestry mapped by the gods. Despite being able to sense and feel it all around us, it is in many ways the Holy Grail of occultism. Alchemists, ceremonialists, cultists, kabbalists, witches, and sorcerers have each attempted to discover a way of distilling the essence of all things, to tap into the ultimate regenerative force in the cosmos. But like gnosis, it is something that must be experienced to believe.

Quintessence means "fifth essence" and is the final piece of creation. Space, time, matter, and energy—the first four essences—are the vital ingredients that make up the universe. Each of these forces, however, originates from quintessence and is made real through it. Quintessence is also the force that sculpts, builds, designs, intervenes, propagates, and destroys by manipulating these forces. It is both chaotic and orderly, always moving forward, always seeking to better know its limitations and then find a way around them, ever expanding and becoming. It is zero-point energy (Z energy) and the life force that pulses through all of creation.

The only two points that correspond between both the Pyramid of Dianus and the Pyramid of Diana are spirit and quintessence. The spirit of something is the metaphysical embodiment of its consciousness; spirit is an element that speaks to the intelligence that resides within the natural world. Its favor can be gained; it can be summoned and, most importantly, manipulated. Spirit has a mutable quality. Quintessence, however, is not mutable, and unlike spirit it is impervious to change because it is the force of change. For lack of a better example, spirit is like your internet service provider, but quintessence is like the internet itself.

Quetra

Quetra is the consciousness of quintessence, the will of creation. As the Grigori of Quintessence, they are the one mind, the collective consciousness that connects us each to the one pervading force that was before any other thing in creation. Quintessence *is* the substance that all things emerge from, and it is ultimately what all things will return to. As Grigori, Quetra stands at the threshold of creation and oversees the ultimate of processes that allow for the manifestation and destruction of the universe—the genuinely vital operations required for the maintenance of universal equilibrium.

Quetra cannot be explained. Like quintessence, they must be experienced. To do this, we have to tap into the spiritual influence of the other four Grigori by way of their individual initiations. Since the beginning of your journey through the Labyrinth of Diana you have been working with these forces, and at this point you should be well aware of these spirits, their roles, and how they interact with each other to bring about the universe we live in. To gain access to Quetra, we will need to visit each of the other Grigori, and with their guidance we will use the wisdom we have accumulated throughout our journey to find our way to the final doorway in the labyrinth.

The Rites of Quetra, or the
Initiations of the Cosmic Grigori

These rites can be done individually or as one passage, as they are written here. Technically, the entire point of this journey has been about building a personal relationship with the powers that be. As we perform these rites and initiate into the mysteries of each Grigori, we will be imbuing ourselves with the medicine that each of them brought to our gnosis. We each got different answers to the questions we asked throughout, and we all received a different piece of a much larger puzzle. The pieces need not fit together collectively, but when they do, a new depth to what is true about the universe can be found. Those existential truths, the ones that really matter in the end—such as why you are here and what you are meant to be as part of it all—will always remain invisible to those who exist outside of ourselves. Only we can see them, and only we can do the work necessary to discover them.

Ingress

Perform the rites of ingress and congress from the opening ritual and find yourself at the doorway made from the empowered yellow flame. Draw the sigil of Quetra with yellow fire and watch it be absorbed by the doorframe. Just as countless times before, when the sigil fades, the doorway opens, revealing a familiar empty space on the other side. You step through the doorway and are met with another familiar sense, that of weightlessness.

quetra's sigil

Instinctively you call out to Oronos, the Grigori of Space, and say their name three times. As you say their name the final time, you find yourself standing on a translucent platform face to face with the Grigori of Space. Take a deep breath, then recite the following incantation:

Oronos of Space, Infinite Keeper of the Endless,
I seek to know the all.
Give me the blessings of your providence
So Quetra will hear my call!

Take another deep breath, and as you exhale, open yourself up to Oronos and show them that the microcosm mirrors the macrocosm. The space within you is just as vast and endless as the space that fills the universe. What is above is below. Take another deep breath and bring yourself back together. In response, see Oronos draw their sigil on your forehead with the same yellow fire you used, and as they complete this, see their essence being absorbed into the symbol.

For a moment, this symbol vibrates rapidly, as if burning, but you feel no pain. You take a deep breath and acknowledge that you now bear the mark of Oronos above your brow and have been initiated into the mysteries of Space. You feel different, stronger somehow, as if given a sense of purpose that is slowly being revealed. As the energy finally settles, the symbol of Oronos fades away.

· · · · · · · · ·

Draw now in the darkness before you the sigil of Aeon in yellow fire. As you do this, summon your might and call out to Aeon three times. On the third invocation, you find that the darkness suddenly fills with the light of a brilliant eternal flame, signaling the arrival of the Grigori you seek. As you take a breath, Aeon moves to meet you face to face, waiting for you to state your purpose.

Say:

Aeon of Time, Boundless Keeper of the Great Ages,
I seek to know the all.
Give me the blessings of your providence
So Quetra will hear my call!

Take another deep breath, and as you exhale, open yourself up to Aeon and show them that the microcosm mirrors the macrocosm. Housed within you are memories, pockets of time that have been stored. This comes from your ability to perceive the present and ultimately gives you the ability as the observer to move time at your will. As within, so without. Take a deep breath and pull your energy back together. See that in response Aeon draws their sigil on your forehead with yellow fire, and as they do so, their essence is absorbed into the symbol.

Take a moment to feel the energy settle into your body. As you breathe, acknowledge any changes you feel within and that you now bear the mark of Aeon upon your brow and have been initiated into the mysteries of Time. Like after your encounter with Oronos, you feel as though you have been changed somehow. Take a deep breath and allow the remaining energy to fully absorb; as this happens, notice the sigil on your forehead disappearing.

· · · · · · · · ·

Draw now the sigil of Proto in yellow fire. As you do this, summon your strength and call out to Proto three times. As you finish the third and final invocation, find yourself standing before the twenty-sided crystalline figure you know to be Proto, the Grigori of Matter. As you breathe, notice that the distance between the two of you rapidly decreases, and that by the time you exhale, your face is staring at your own reflection, which is being projected back to you from one of Proto's facets. You interpret this as them waiting for you to state your purpose. Say:

Proto of Matter, Immeasurable Keeper of all Dimensions,
I seek to know the all.
Give me the blessings of your providence
So Quetra will hear my call!

Take a deep breath and open yourself up as you have before, this time revealing to the guardian that you understand the connection between matter and self. Show Proto that the microcosm mirrors the macrocosm, that you too are made of matter and that you know where that matter comes from. Share with them the many ways you have expressed yourself throughout your lifetime and the endless diversity of your spirit. As below, so above. Take a deep breath and pull your energy back together. See that, in response, Proto draws their sigil on your forehead with yellow fire, just like the others before them. As they complete the sigil, watch as their essence is absorbed into the symbol.

Allow yourself to absorb all of the energy, and spend a few moments contemplating the sigil on your brow and your initiation into the mysteries of Matter. After the energy has settled, notice that the symbol on your forehead no longer tingles and all that remains is the memory of being touched by Proto

· · · · · · · · ·

Draw before you the sigil of Zoann with yellow fire. As your intent pours from your mind, call out to the Grigori of Energy three times, each invocation a little louder than the one before it. On the final call, find yourself staring into a black ball that radiates multicolored light in all directions. This light is not uncomfortable for your eyes, and as you look at the strange moving surface of the sphere, know that Zoann is waiting for you to announce your final proclamation. Say:

Zoann of Energy, Untamable Keeper of Perpetual Force,
I seek to know the all.
Give me the blessings of your providence
So Quetra will hear my call!

Without hesitation you find yourself opening up to reveal the intricate systems of energy within and how they are connected to the people, spirits, places, and forces of nature present all around you. As you do this, Zoann sees that the microcosm mirrors the macrocosm and that what is without also lies within. In response, just like the other, you feel a force reach out and draw a sigil in yellow fire on your forehead. As they do this, their essence pours into the sigil. You know this to be the symbol of Zoann. You absorb this into your system and witness the remaining particles of the Grigori entering your body.

Take a few deep breaths and let the energy settle entirely into your body. As you do this, become aware that you have been initiated into the mysteries of Energy and now bear the mark of Zoann. As the sigil fades, draw your attention to the sensation of the four Grigori within.

Congress

Draw before you the sigil of Quetra in the air with yellow fire. Watch as it hovers in the darkness and then reach inside of yourself, call forth the essence of the Grigori waiting within, and place your hand over the sigil. Say the names of the first four Grigori together three times and watch as their power pulses from within you. See it move outward through your hands, empowering the sigil. Take another deep breath and invoke Quetra by now saying her name three times.

Suddenly you find that the forces around you begin to collapse, and the darkness begins to fold upon itself. Within a matter of just a few breaths, you watch as the empty space around you condenses into a black crystal. Find yourself back in that particular place within your witch's dream and feel a noticeable shift in the vibration of the space from when you had just previously been there. Something isn't quite right. The doorway is missing.

Your attention immediately shifts to the black crystal, and you sense a hidden presence emanating from within. Reaching out with your senses, you touch the crystal; in response, a strange light begins to spill forth. Unlike anything you have ever seen before, a being emerges now from this light and slowly moves to face you. As you take a breath, you understand that it is time to do as you have done with the other Grigori and open yourself up to receive a blessing.

You feel your witch power reach out and embrace Quetra, something that first you aren't sure if you should be worried about or not, but you soon realize it feels quite natural. As you touch the Grigori of Quintessence, you learn that the microcosm mirrors the macrocosm and that you are filled with quintessence. Take a deep breath and bring all of the pieces of yourself back together again. In response to this, Quetra reaches out to you and touches your third eye.

The spot tingles at first, and you instinctively know that once again you have been initiated into a new set of mysteries. As the sensation fades, Quetra's presence also fades, the figure they took returning to the black crystal and the light that once emanated from it now just a memory. You look for a way out but notice again that the door is not there any longer, but the crystal is still there. You reach out to touch the crystal and find yourself being absorbed into it as if it possessed some immense gravity from deep within.

Suddenly you find yourself on the other side of this force, standing in the familiar empty space on a transparent platform. As you look before you, a doorway of yellow fire awaits, and you happily walk through it, entering the true witch's dream on the other side.

As you emerge into the familiar place in your mind, the doorway dissolves and the floating particles are absorbed into your body. You know that the journey through the Labyrinth of Diana has led you back to where you started. You are different now: wiser, more sensitive, and capable of tracing the patterns of quintessence that unfurl all around you. You can feel the subtle elemental forces of space, time, matter, and energy thrumming within.

With your new senses, reach out to the space in the witch's dream and feel that it too has changed. You know that what is within the witch's dream must also be outside of it, and so you take three deep breaths and return to your physical body. There at your altar, which is poised at the center of the compass where the witch's tree stands tall in all directions, reach out with your new senses and understand that even this space has changed as a result of your work. You are somehow more connected to the compass and can feel the energy pulsing from the tree, but not just the tree, pulsing from *you*. As you look around, you see that the great merkaba with its two spinning pyramids of light and dark now radiates outward from the center of the witch's tree.

Egress

Take all the time you need, but our work here is done for now. When you feel you are ready, go ahead and perform egress as described in the opening ceremony on page 231 (had you not summoned the labyrinth, outlined in the first paragraph of that section).

As you have done with the other parts of this journey, journal about your experience and sketch the things you saw while traveling. Be sure to capture the image of Quetra as they appeared to you and record any feelings, emotions, urges, and all sensory-related detail about your experience with them.

You are likely feeling a little fried after all this work; I know I was (I am tired even writing about it), but there is still more work for us to do. At this point, I think it is essential to take some time off to collect your thoughts and assimilate the information and energy that you received while in the labyrinth. Now that you are out, the most important thing is to make sure that what you gained can be brought into your gnosis. While you may continue along the lonely road, you are now more equipped than ever to fulfill your responsibilities as a witch.

· · · · · · · · ·

Things to follow up on:
1. The space within your witch's dream is still active and should be visited whenever possible. The candle still burns in this

sacred space and anchors the Pyramid of Diana to you. Before moving on with this work, continue to incorporate this place with your dreamwork. Together with your guides and familiar, summon the doorway once again, this time from inside of yourself, and travel with your companions at night when you sleep. Allow this technique to reveal new insights.

2. It would be an excellent idea to perform some cleansing work now. You just got an upgrade and will need to purge and purify your system so that you can get rid of the old and make way for the new. Over the course of five nights, perform a cleansing ritual of your choosing to help your energy body assimilate your new upgrade.

3. Spend time away from being lost in the labyrinth and enjoy the mundane aspects of life. Remember, those are formed of quintessence too.

Chapter Sixteen

The Closing Ritual

*I promise you that the same stuff galaxies are made of, you are.
The same energy that swings planets around stars makes electrons
dance in your heart. It is in you, outside you, you are it. It is
beautiful. Trust in this. And you and your life will be grand.*

—

Kamal Ravikant, *Live Your Truth*

There is one last ritual to perform, the one that finishes our work
with the labyrinth and gives us access to the void. If all this has
taught us anything, it is that the microcosm mirrors the macrocosm.
We house within ourselves the same universe that we live in. We both
know this to be true and yet find it paradoxical. As we seek to gain one
last bit of gnosis together from the labyrinth, we must proceed with
the understanding that we are made of the same stuff that even the
Grigori are—that the only thing separating us is vibration, and even
that can be mutable under the influence of quintessence.

You have likely made an educated guess by now. The labyrinth gave us the ability to fill in the missing pieces required to activate the Pyramid of Diana. If the elemental forces within the Pyramid of Diana and the Pyramid of Dianus make up the universe, they also make up you. As occupiers of space, observers of time, beings of matter, conductors of energy, and shapers of quintessence, the powers of earth, air, fire, water, and spirit move through us. As witches, we have always had the witch power to help us see and feel this, but now after all this work we truly know it.

What we will seek to do next is something that we are told by the ruling paradigm we cannot do without the help of a priest or religion: reach God. Throughout this entire book we have been persuing little conversations with her, tuning in to her frequency and building gnosis from what is revealed as a result. Now we must go even further and assemble all the pieces that we now have access to. To speak to God Herself, we need to unite the forces of light and dark within ourselves. We must allow their powers to fuse together so that we can create quintessential equilibrium. We must merge the two pyramids and become the Merkaba of Creation.

By becoming the Merkaba of Creation, the powers within ourselves find balance with those outside. We achieve harmony and become the point of origin for all things. There is nothing that separates us from the animals or the wind, nothing that ranks our importance or categorizes our value. The individual becomes the singular all. Only then can we conceive of creator.

Closing Ritual:
Activating the Merkaba of Creation

If you have followed along with the text and have completed each of the other rituals, then you are already prepared for this working. In many ways it is a very natural experience to do this; the energies want to connect. The most challenging part, aside from what I explain here, is that you are on your own. Now more than ever you must rely on your gnosis, your instincts, your witch power. Now more than ever you will be required to figure out what comes next on your own. This final act of ascension puts the responsibility of answers squarely on your shoulders.

Ingress
Lay the compass, summon the witch's tree, and then open your senses once more and remember that this space has been empowered as a result of your work. Take a deep breath and summon both the Pyramid of Diana and the Pyramid of Dianus. See the two merge into one, and as they do so, see yourself merge with them as well. Continue to breathe slow and deep, and allow this process to happen naturally.

Congress
As you merge with the two pyramids, find yourself looking out from the point of fusion where the two meet. There, from the center, you can feel the powers of all ten Grigori moving through you as well as the distinct frequencies of Diana and Dianus that they too comprise. You can feel the energies of light and dark pulling each other apart and then mending one another. You can feel light become darkness and darkness become light, energy becoming matter and matter becoming energy. You can feel space expand and gravity pull. You see all of time in an instant.

The pyramid of light, spinning clockwise around and through you and fed by your gnosis, brightens as you settle into this awareness. From within the pyramid of darkness that rotates through and around you counterclockwise, you feel waves of energy washing over you. Both pyramids now begin to move faster, pulling you in all directions. Recite the following incantation:

Of light and darkness I am bound, of peace and chaos I am found.
Of the Grigori am I made, and through their power shall I fade.
I am that which can be found within, that which has always been.
I am that which can be found about, that which cures all doubt.
I am the Holy One that does descend, the serpent rising to meet its end.
I am the mind that is the all, I am the spirit that hears the call.

Take a deep breath and feel the power within yourself reach equilibrium with the power that surrounds you. Feel that instead of tension between the light and dark, you have reached a place of union where these energies rise and fall within you in a rhythmic pulse. Be aware of both halves, but also be aware of the sensation that comes from the whole. Breathe slow and deep and reach out through your witch's dream to find the presence that rises from deep within this union. Follow the pulse of power with your breath, and allow it to guide you as you open yourself up to the presence of God Herself and recite the Star Goddess Prayer:

Holy Mother, in you we live, move, and have our being.
From you all things emerged, and unto you all things return!

See that within the unity of creation a great winged serpent arises from the all, writhing as if it had been plucked from the earth and is separating itself from the emptiness of the void. Watch as the unity becomes this serpent, as its body twists so that its mouth can grasp its tail. Finally, watch as this serpent folds itself into the familiar shape of an ouroboros.

What you do now and what questions you ask are choices that are entirely up to you. I would suggest allowing them to show themselves in whatever form they choose to and asking at least one question: "Who am I?"

As I mentioned, these rituals will leave you forever changed, and that is made real with what happens next.

Egress

Getting to this place is difficult. There has been a lot of work that we needed to do and many lessons we needed to learn. Leaving this place, however, is impossible; you can never leave. You now know things that you can never un-know and have built gnosis that can never be deconstructed. You have acknowledged the Grigori and received their blessing. You are now the priest, the guide, the mentor, the embodiment of their power. You now know God Herself. Leaving that behind simply is not a possibility. It has been written in time and will continue to manifest in every present until the end of time.

You can, however, return to a sense of self and allow what you have learned on this journey to actually change your life. How you do that and what you do as a result of that are, again, entirely up to you. To get back to your place of origin, take five deep breaths and shift your focus from the void and the serpent to the point at the center of the ouroboros where the head and tail now meet. As you change perspective, notice that you lose sight of the void and the serpent but become aware of the flow of endlessness that moves through you, eventually meeting the river of endlessness that flows through all things. Take three deep breaths, becoming aware once again of your individuality, and allow this energy to become part of you as you say:

As without so within, with my breath I draw you in.
As without so within, with my breath I draw you in.
As without so within, with my breath I draw you in.

Open your eyes and find now that from where you stand, the Merkaba of Creation emanates from you and that from this merkaba the witch's tree and the compass extend. Realize that you are now the apex and vertex of time and space, you are now the center and the circumference; you are sacred. Take a deep breath, and as you exhale, lift your hands up in exultation to the glory of creation and say "So must it be."

Completion

We are God. There, I said it. That is, in many ways, the entire point of the work related to the Labyrinth of Diana. Sure, it can be heavy to think outside of the box and to expand our definition of both what the universe is and how it works. But to truly appreciate and engage it, we have to learn more about it. You've done that and are now ready to keep challenging yourself and make informed decisions about how you exert your own power over the world.

Keep your journal, keep the sketches you made, keep everything! These are excellent reminders of what you have learned and still likely have a lot of information to reveal. The work is never done; we only ever shift perspective and discover new things to learn. These notes will help you to do that the next time life becomes challenging. You have the power; never be afraid to use it.

Conclusion

*The truth doesn't always set you free. Sometimes it saddles you with
a burden you can never escape. So choose very carefully where you
decide to start digging and what dragons you choose to slay. Prepare
to be taken places you never wanted to go. Gnosis isn't always a
flower—sometimes it's a sword. Maybe more often than not.*

———

Chris Knowles, *The Secret Sun*

When I began writing this series, I made it my goal to explore
the witch power in ways that it had not been done before. In
doing so, I hoped that those of us who had been around for a while
and were looking for a new way of seeing our power and its potential could actually find some renewed value in exploring witchcraft
through a different perspective. At the end of the third and final book
in this series, I hadn't expected to feel so changed myself.

The witch power is something that I found immense value in developing. It has been there to guide me through the bad times and has
helped me find my way to the good. It is a part of the craft that rarely
gets the attention it deserves, even though it is always there, always

reaching out, searching for answers. With each book we have peeled back its layers and have eventually found ourselves at the end of our road together, staring off into the distance and wondering what comes next.

With this last book, we wrapped up our study of the witch power (for now) and engaged some of the most complicated topics in modern occultism. We explored the concept of egregores and broke the chains from our pasts that would have otherwise kept us grounded and unaware. We broke wicked vows and remapped our energy bodies. We took back the missing pieces of ourselves as we treaded the mill and sought out ecstatic union in the witch's dream. We visited the witch's sabbat and met the Witch Queen and King there, only to meet them again in the Merkaba of Creation. This series started with the study of the witch power as a part of every witch and now concludes with the examination of how everything is connected to the witch power, even God Herself. We now come full circle and find that what we have been looking for truly has been within us the whole time.

Regardless of your background, all of the mysteries that we have explored here can be performed outside the confines of a tradition. These energies do not belong to anyone; if anything, we belong to them. In the end, what matters most won't be the collection of books and herbs you have amassed or the ritual tools and secret oil recipes you've collected. In the end, the only thing that matters is gnosis because gnosis is the only currency for the soul.

In closing, I will leave you with this: the universe is chaotic and contains all of the good and the bad, but it is not itself either. It has no morals or ethics and holds not the ability to be judge or jury; it simply exists. We are all subject to the laws of this universe and are each at the mercy of the same forces. After my own conversations with God, I have grown increasingly aware of the fragility of life and of the powers that protect it. We must be kind to one another. We must live as examples of the change we seek. We must use our powers to help our fellows as well as ourselves. Not everyone has the witch power, and I have no judgment on how those who do use it, but as agents of that power, I believe it is imperative that we use it in a way that makes the world a better place for everyone.

Go in light and darkness. Go in peace.

Sigils for the Witch's Dream

1. Guidance from Dianus

2. Anti-Glamour to See Truth

3. Raise General Awareness

4. Bring Prophetic Vision

5. Connect to Past-Life Allies

6. Attract Ancestors

7. Attract Familiar Spirit

8. Attract High-Vibrational Allies

9. To Channel Power

10. To Raise Power

11. To Find New Direction

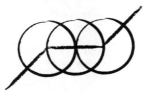

12. Warding from Evil

13. Bring Balance to All Worlds

Bibliography and Recommended Reading

Anaar. *The White Wand: Toward a Feri Aesthetic.* Self-published, 2005.

Anderson, Victor. *Etheric Anatomy.* OR: Acorn Guild Press, 2004.

Andrews, Ted. *The Intercession of Spirits: Working with Animals, Angels & Ancestors.* TN: Dragon Hawk, 2008.

Auerbach, Loyd. *Psychic Dreaming: Dreamworking, Reincarnation, Out-of-Body Experiences & Clairvoyance.* MN: Llewellyn, 2018.

Bogan, Chas. *The Secret Keys of Conjure: Unlocking the Mysteries of American Folk Magic.* MN: Llewellyn, 2018.

Briggs, Katharine. *An Encyclopedia of Fairies, Hobgoblins, Brownies, Bogies, and Other Supernatural Creatures.* NY: Pantheon Books, 1976.

Bruce, Robert. *The Practical Psychic Self-Defense Handbook: A Survival Guide.* VA: Hampton Roads, 2011.

Buckland, Raymond. *The Spirit Book: The Encyclopedia of Clairvoyance, Channeling, and Spirit Communication.* MI: Visible Ink Press, 2005.

Cheung, Theresa. *The Element Encyclopedia of the Psychic World.* NY: Barnes & Noble, 2006.

Chumbley, Andrew. *Azoëtia: A Grimoire of the Sabath Craft (Sethos Edition).* UK: Xoanon, 2002.

———. *Mysticism: Initiation and Dream.* CA: Three Hands Press, 2012.

———. *Opuscula Magica Vol 1.* CA: Three Hands Press, 2011.

———. *Qutub: The Point.* UK: Xoanon, 1995.

D'Este, Sorita, and David Rankine. *Hekate Liminal Rites: A Study of the Rituals, Magic and Symbols of the Torch-Bearing Triple Goddess of the Crossroads.* UK: Avalonia Publishing, 2009.

DuQuette, Lon Milo. *My Life with the Spirits: The Adventures of a Modern Magician.* MA: Red Wheel/Weiser, 1999.

Farrar, Janet, and Gavin Bone. *Lifting the Veil: A Witches' Guide to Trance-Prophecy, Drawing Down the Moon, and Ecstatic Ritual.* OR: Acorn Guild Press, 2016.

Farrar, Stewart, and Robert Matheisen, Chas Clifton, and Robert Chartowich. *Aradia, or the Gospel of the Witches by Charles G. Leland with Additional Material.* WA: Phoenix, 1998.

Filan, Kenaz, and Raven Kaldera. *Drawing Down the Spirits: The Traditions and Techniques of Spirit Possession.* VT: Destiny Books, 2009.

Gary, Gemma. *The Black Toad: West Country Witchcraft and Magic.* London, UK: Troy Books, 2012.

Godwin, Malcolm. *Angels: An Endangered Species.* NY: Simon and Schuster, 1990.

Grimassi, Raven. *Italian Witchcraft: The Old Religion of Southern Europe.* MN: Llewellyn, 1995.

Harner, Michael. *The Way of the Shaman.* CA: Harper San Francisco, 1980.

Heaven, Ross, and Simon Buxton. *Darkness Visible: Awakening the Spiritual Light through Darkness Meditation.* VT: Inner Traditions, 2005.

Howard, Michael. *The Book of Fallen Angels*. UK, Capall Bann, 2004.

———. *Children of Cain: A Study of Modern Traditional Witches*. UK: Xoanon, 2011.

Howard, Michael, and Nigel Jackson. *The Pillars of Tubal Cane*. UK: Capall Bann, 2000.

Hunter, Devin. *The Witch's Book of Power*. MN: Llewellyn, 2016.

———. *The Witch's Book of Spirits*. MN: Llewellyn, 2017.

Huson, Paul. *Mastering Witchcraft*. NY: Perigee, 1970.

Jackson, Nigel. *Masks of Misrule* UK: Capall Bann, 1996.

———. *Call of the Horned Piper*. UK: Capall Bann, 1994.

Kaplan-Williams, Strephon. *Dreamworking: A Comprehensive Guide to Working with Dreams*. US: Journey Press, 1991.

Konstantinos. *Summoning Spirits: The Art of Magical Evocation*. MN: Llewellyn, 1996.

Kuzmeskus, Elaine. *The Art of Mediumship: Psychic Investigation, Clairvoyance, and Channeling*. UK: Schiffer, 2012.

Kynes, Sandra. *Llewellyn's Complete Book of Correspondences: A Comprehensive & Cross-referenced Resource for Pagans & Wiccans*. MN: Llewellyn, 2013.

Leitch, Aaron. *Secrets of the Magickal Grimoires: The Classical Texts of Magick Deciphered*. MN: Llewellyn, 2005.

Leland, Charles G. *Etruscan Roman Remains*. WA: Phoenix Publishing, 1999.

———. *Gypsy Sorcery and Fortune Telling*. NY: Citadel Press, 1962.

Liddell, Scott, Jones, and McKenzie. *A Greek-English Lexicon*. UK: Oxford University Press, 1819.

Miller, Jason. *Protection and Reversal Magick (Beyond 101)*. NJ: The Career Press/New Page, 2006.

———. *The Sorcerer's Secrets: Strategies to Practical Magic*. NJ: The Career Press/New Page, 2009.

Pearson, Nigel. *Treading the Mill: Practical Craft Working In Modern Traditional Witchcraft*. UK: Capall Bann, 2007.

Sowton, Christopher. *Dreamworking: How to Listen to the Inner Guidance of Your Dreams*. MN: Llewellyn, 2017.

Index

GET MORE AT LLEWELLYN.COM

Visit us online to browse hundreds of our books and decks, plus sign up to receive our e-newsletters and exclusive online offers.

- **Free tarot readings • Spell-a-Day • Moon phases**
- **Recipes, spells, and tips • Blogs • Encyclopedia**
- **Author interviews, articles, and upcoming events**

GET SOCIAL WITH LLEWELLYN

Find us on  @LlewellynBooks

www.Facebook.com/LlewellynBooks

GET BOOKS AT LLEWELLYN

LLEWELLYN ORDERING INFORMATION

 Order online: Visit our website at www.llewellyn.com to select your books and place an order on our secure server.

 Order by phone:
- Call toll free within the US at 1-877-NEW-WRLD (1-877-639-9753)
- We accept VISA, MasterCard, American Express, and Discover.
- Canadian customers must use credit cards.

 Order by mail:
Send the full price of your order (MN residents add 6.875% sales tax) in US funds plus postage and handling to: Llewellyn Worldwide, 2143 Wooddale Drive, Woodbury, MN 55125-2989

POSTAGE AND HANDLING

STANDARD (US):
(Please allow 12 business days)
$30.00 and under, add $6.00.
$30.01 and over, FREE SHIPPING.

INTERNATIONAL ORDERS,
INCLUDING CANADA:
$16.00 for one book, plus $3.00 for each additional book.

Visit us online for more shipping options. Prices subject to change.

FREE CATALOG!

To order, call
1-877-
NEW-WRLD
ext. 8236
or visit our
website

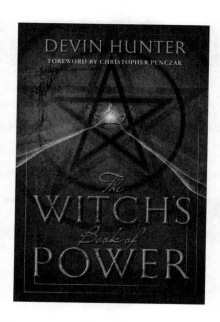

The Witch's Book of Power

Devin Hunter

Witchcraft isn't always about the search for enlightenment; sometimes it's about power and the path to obtaining it. *The Witch's Book of Power* shares the secrets to unlocking the witch power within you, offering specific techniques for working with personal, cosmic, and ally energies to realize your full magical potential.

Professional witch and psychic Devin Hunter has helped thousands of people discover their power and gain influence, and in this book he skillfully explores the concepts behind creating magic that can change your life. *The Witch's Book of Power* is the perfect resource for witches who intuitively feel that more power is available but seems to be just beyond reach.

978-0-7387-4819-1
6 x 9 • 360 pp.

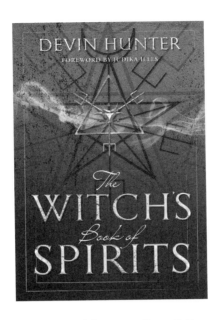

The Witch's Book of Spirits

Devin Hunter

Profound spiritual insights and powers await beyond the material world. In *The Witch's Book of Spirits*, Devin Hunter invites you to perform rituals and magic with spirit guides, familiars, angels, the deceased, faeries, and demons. Develop and enhance your relationships to your allies in spirit through soul flight, mediumship, and conjuration. Explore the inner workings of the Witch's Tree as well as the planes and peoples who dwell in its many layers. Expand the scope of your magic with the 33 Spirits, a system transmitted to the author by a special priesthood of spirits, his familiar, Malach, and the goddess Hecate. Working with spirits is the cornerstone of the witch's art. This book shows you how to stay in control as you increase your witch power and deepen your connection to forces seen and unseen.

978-0-7387-5194-8

6 x 9 • 336 pp.

To Write to the Author

If you wish to contact the author or would like more information about this book, please write to the author in care of Llewellyn Worldwide and we will forward your request. Both the author and the publisher appreciate hearing from you and learning of your enjoyment of this book and how it has helped you. Llewellyn Worldwide cannot guarantee that every letter written to the author can be answered, but all will be forwarded. Please write to:

Devin Hunter
℅ Llewellyn Worldwide
2143 Wooddale Drive
Woodbury, MN 55125-2989

Please enclose a self-addressed stamped envelope for reply
or $1.00 to cover costs. If outside the USA, enclose
an international postal reply coupon.

Many of Llewellyn's authors have websites with additional information and resources. For more information, please visit our website:

LLEWELLYN.COM